HEALTHY BUILDINGS

Healthy Buildings

How Indoor Spaces Can Make
You Sick—or Keep You Well

JOSEPH G. ALLEN

JOHN D. MACOMBER

 Harvard University Press

Cambridge, Massachusetts
London, England
2022

First Harvard University Press hardcover edition published as *Healthy
Buildings: How Indoor Spaces Drive Performance and Productivity*, 2020.

Cataloging-in-Publication Data available from the Library of Congress
ISBN: 978-0-674-27836-3 (alk. paper)
Library of Congress Control Number: 2022933284

Contents

Preface to the 2022 Edition

Healthy Buildings as the Foundation of a Health-First Era

The global crisis created by Covid-19 has ushered in a new, "health-first" era. The world was brought to a standstill by a virus that spreads almost exclusively indoors, revealing a simple but long-ignored truth: your building can make you sick. Or it can keep you well. No one will forget this anytime soon.

Going forward, couples shopping for apartments, retirees booking cruises, parents looking at schools, businesses thinking about new locations, and investors or insurance companies looking for safe assets will be sizing up buildings in terms of their health impacts. The safety of these indoor spaces will play a key role in their calculus. Who will want to spend time in a building that isn't healthy? Who will want to be an owner of one?

The terrorist attacks of 9 / 11 gave the world twenty years of "security-first"—two decades in which seemingly every decision, dollar spent, and public campaign was informed by safety considerations. One after another, new security protocols crept into our daily lives. The Covid parallel is clear. The new, equally fundamental shift to a health-first mindset is so profound that, in this updated edition of *Healthy Buildings*, we've added a new chapter spelling out how buildings can be the first line of defense against infectious diseases. Our original research and guidance was at the forefront of the fight against the pandemic. We helped put protocols into place that kept tens of millions of people safe across every sector of the economy, from offices and schools to retail shops, shelters, manufacturing facilities, theaters, and restaurants. Not long after the very first reports out of Wuhan, we were working hard to broadcast the importance of this, but unfortunately, the world took a long time to fully hear the message.

In this revised edition, we explain and distill the basics of respiratory virus transmission to make it clear what exactly we are trying to defend against, which sets up why buildings matter so much for our response. Then we offer a simple roadmap for how to pragmatically and effectively secure individual buildings and a wider portfolio of properties. The lessons for protecting people and business are not just about Covid-19. They apply to *all* airborne infectious diseases, from seasonal influenza to whatever virus your colleagues may be carrying back from their latest trip. We outline how to mitigate the enormous costs to businesses and society of contagious diseases without derailing operations or breaking the bank. And, yes, these strategies will offer broad resilience in the face of future pandemics—because we know the question is not *if* there will be another one, but *when*. It doesn't have to be an existential threat to your organization if you're prepared and know what to do.

When we first set out to write this book, our goal was to make a compelling case to homeowners, CEOs, people handling large real estate portfolios, and everyone in between, that it was worth investing in the health of their buildings. The book came out in April 2020 and that argument was forcefully proven as news came out over the following months of indoor superspreader events in underventilated buildings—the very kinds of risks we were warning about.

Coming out of Covid, Healthy Buildings are no longer "nice to have." They are the new minimum. And people everywhere are getting a lot savvier about what this means. In fighting this virus, institutions have developed a new acceptance—even *expectation*—of health protections and reporting in their life. Portable health-sensing technology is getting cheaper and more ubiquitous. This includes wearable devices like FitBits and Apple Watches, but also real-time air quality sensors from startup vendors like Awair and Airthings, and long-established players like Carrier. Devices that once cost several thousand dollars and required an advanced degree to operate now are priced at just a few hundred, and are as easy to use as flipping a switch and reading the results on your phone. That means as you enter a store, office, gym, or plane, you can immediately get an answer to the question: *Is it safe in here?*

What's more, all of this public health data is becoming, well, public. People increasingly can—and do—share what they're finding on a real-time basis, shaming businesses by posting high carbon dioxide measurements, airborne particle levels, and even volatile organic compound (VOC) readings on social media. And it's not just individuals who care. Several countries have created laws that require businesses not only to *measure* indoor carbon dioxide concentrations—a proxy for ventilation—but also to *display* this information prominently. These expectations of screening, sensing, and sharing will not be reversed.

Access to crucial Health Performance Indicators (HPIs), a concept we introduce in Chapter 11, dramatically changes a number of key aspects of the evaluation of indoor spaces in the commercial world, and influences the entire value chain from manufacturer to designer to developer to owner, tenant, and investor. How so? First, it gives any potential renter, hotel guest, or office tenant better information to distinguish between properties on the basis of measurable air quality. Second, it flips negotiating power into the hands of individuals who can take their own measurements, rather than relying on proprietary information generated for the landlord by a private indoor-air-quality expert. Third, investors now have another way to value property, factoring in its health potential.

In *Healthy Buildings*, we combine our two disciplines, health science and business science, to make a compelling case that an investment in a Healthy Building is an investment in people—and *that* is an investment in your organization's future. We first thought of calling this book "The Healthy Building Dividend," because we wanted to emphasize that small investments in Healthy Buildings yield highly attractive returns to the bottom line. This is not hand-wavy, wishful thinking. We offer hard empirical evidence.

But Healthy Buildings are about still more than people and profit. They are also about planet and purpose.

Covid-19 was not the only challenge organizations were confronting as our book was first released. Technology had already been driving a "work from anywhere" shift, and this accelerated during the pandemic, as *Fortune* 500 companies redefined the boundaries of where, how, and when work can be done. At the same time, a social justice movement focused on disparities and equity became a centerpiece of many organizations and their boardrooms, and many, too, responded to the "slow-roll" crisis we are rapidly running out of time to address: climate change. The focus on firms' environmental, social, and governance (ESG) performance is here to stay, and we show how buildings have a key role to play in it.

Together, these forces are reshaping how we think about our offices, our homes, and our schools, and Healthy Buildings are at the center of them, whether executives know it yet or not.

The world has changed in dramatic ways since we first released *Healthy Buildings,* as countless schools closed their doors, patients flooded hospitals, and workers around the world were sent home. Covid-19 upended science (and architecture) in many ways and rendered some prior research less valid. But in the case of our work, the opposite happened: what made sense for buildings with respect to cognition and health before Covid-19 became even more important in the face of this airborne pathogen. The argument for Healthy Buildings is even more sound, more relevant, and more compelling. The indoor spaces we all share are an important focal point for high-level response to disasters and crises. They are also key, as you will see, to the resilience, productivity, prosperity, and long-term health of the people who use them.

The great news is that we know what needs to be done. In the chapters ahead, we will show the way forward and arm you with all the evidence you'll need to advocate for better buildings. From both a business and a health perspective, the case is airtight—and it starts with better air quality. Going forward, Healthy Buildings should be the norm, not the exception. We hope, once you've read this book, that you'll agree that this is one of the greatest health, business, and career opportunities of our generation. Welcome to the Healthy Buildings movement.

Preface

Why This Book?

Finding shelter is one of the most primal human needs, right alongside food and water. But we are long past the time when shelter was a place to return to after a day of foraging—when it meant a roof over our heads and not much more. In that long-gone era, we spent all of our time outdoors. Today, our "shelters" are the places where we live, work, learn, play, rest, and recuperate. Over several millennia, humans have evolved from an outdoor species into an indoor one.

Yet despite the fact that buildings are now central to our lives and livelihoods, the quality of the air we breathe inside them is generally an afterthought. Have you ever seen a news story about outdoor air pollution? Yes, of course. Every day. Have you ever read a story about indoor air pollution? Rarely, if ever. But how often do you read a story about indoor air pollution? Rarely, if ever (at least, not until Covid-19 hit and the world started to appreciate, perhaps for the first time, that indoor spaces were key to the spread of infectious disease). Much more time is spent worrying about outdoor pollution, yet it's the indoor environment that has the greatest impact on our health.

Most buildings today have been designed to perform specific functions. Their "health worthiness" is defined by a variety of building codes: there are standards for sanitation, electrical wiring, fireproofing, lighting and ventilation, access, and many other things. A quick glance at the history of urban form suggests that aesthetics, comfort, and grandeur are important to us as well.

At some level we all know that indoor environments influence how we feel and perform because every one of us has experienced a poor-performing indoor space, be it a stuffy conference room or a friend's house that makes you sneeze as soon as you walk in the door. There are office buildings that give you an immediate and visceral reaction—"*This* is a place I want to work," or "Get me out of here." What has been elusive is piecing it all together.

We have good news to share: there are easy ways to make a building "healthy." Even better, Healthy Building strategies are good business strategies. Because it turns out that the true cost of operating our buildings is not energy, waste, and water (the drivers of the "green" building movement); it's the impact on people inside. When we make our buildings healthy, we make the people in those buildings healthier and more productive, and that translates into a healthier bottom line.

This convergence of health science, building science, and business science is revealing what is perhaps the greatest untapped business and health opportunity of our time.

As the green building movement transitions to the Healthy Building movement, savvy business leaders can capitalize on this once-in-a-lifetime opportunity by tapping into the science underpinning these three previously siloed disciplines. As you will soon see, it turns out that Healthy Building strategies are a win-win value proposition for all stakeholders: business leaders, workers, investors and developers, and the public.

For business leaders: You know better than anyone that you are in a global competition for talent. What you may not recognize is that you can use your building to attract and retain the best and the brightest. And then, once your organization has invested so much in attracting talent, you can manage your building to optimize the performance of that talent. This book reveals the secret to capturing the value locked up in your building's most important and expensive asset: the people you hire. *Are you using your building as a Human Resources tool?*

For workers: Prospective employees ask questions about the nature of their responsibilities, their boss, their salary, and how much vacation time they will get. Now it's time to ask questions about the one thing that will have the biggest impact on your health and performance: the place where you will be working. What are your building managers doing to optimize your indoor environment? Are they tracking indicators of environmental quality and taking corrective action when something is "off"? Are they simply meeting minimum performance requirements, or are they adopting strategies that promote your well-being? *Are you interviewing your building?*

For investors and developers: The green building movement is giving way to the Healthy Building movement, and for good reason. The green building movement was largely built chasing monetary savings from energy savings. By one estimate, over $7 trillion in real estate institutional capital tracks the performance of green buildings. Yet this investment was driven by chasing 1 percent of the cost to operate our buildings—energy, waste, and water. But we don't build buildings to save energy; we build them for people. *Is your investment future-proofed for the coming Healthy Buildings movement?*

For all of us on this planet: Buildings affect our health through their intimate relationships with our energy system and the changing climate. Global energy production is dominated by fossil fuel use, and buildings consume 40 percent of that energy. In some places, like New York City, it's close to 80 percent. Energy-saving features in buildings therefore come with a health co-benefits in the forms of reduced emissions of air pollution and greenhouse gases. *Does your building come with a public health benefit?*

In this book we bring together 40 years of health science, building science, and business science to explain why buildings matter so much for our health and wealth. The three disciplines have been historically treated as separate, but they are in fact inextricably linked. We provide the hard, scientific evidence to make the business case for Healthy Buildings, while showing in practical terms how buildings can be used to create this win-win value proposition for owners, occupants, developers, and society. In this book we will show you how you can unlock this value proposition by providing answers to questions that the market is asking:

What is a Healthy Building, anyway?
How do Healthy Building strategies affect the performance of my company?
What is driving this movement?
How will smart buildings intersect with Healthy Buildings?
How do we create and capture value by mapping investments to benefits?
Can we scale this globally?

These are just a few of the questions we will tackle as we show you how to unlock the potential of your buildings to create economic value and improve human health and performance.

HEALTHY BUILDINGS

PART I

The Case for Healthy Buildings

CHAPTER ONE

Who Are We and Why Should You Care?

The first wealth is health.

—RALPH WALDO EMERSON

John's Awakening

I was born to build. Before I could talk, I had trucks and bulldozers in a cornmeal mini-sandbox in the kitchen. I regaled my infant sister by stacking up cantilevered block structures from floor to ceiling. How much width can we get off a single block base? How few units to reach the ceiling?

This aptitude for building is in my DNA, one could say. In 1904 my great-grandfather left a big national construction firm to establish the George B. H. Macomber Company. He built the first structural steel building in Boston (it's now called 79 Milk Street) and the Weld Boathouse at Harvard before there was a bridge across the Charles River.

The firm passed from father to son in 1927, and then my own father bought the family business in 1959. One of his early projects, the hexagonal "waffle" slab floors at the Yale Art Museum, showcased his ability to think in three dimensions across time. He had to imagine how the finished concrete would look, where the reinforcing steel would go, and (upside down and backward) how the plywood should end up so that he could effectively strip it from the underside without ripping it apart.

My siblings and I bought the family business in 1990 and picked up where Dad left off. I designed formwork for cast-in-place buildings, where stairs might alternate above and below a continuous sidewall made of the same monolithic concrete pour. No easy feat, but the logic of the puzzle appealed to me, just as it had to my father.

My father and I were both natural physical-world problem solvers, and the projects we worked on included high-rise apartment buildings, data centers, and total mechanical rehabilitation of operating hospitals or museums where the walls themselves were part of the collection. I was the chairman and principal stockholder of the George B. H. Macomber Company for about 15 years, working alongside my siblings. We built landmarks all over New England for clients including MIT, Fidelity, State Street, Mass General Hospital, Children's Hospital, the Isabella Stewart Gardner Museum, and the Institute of Contemporary Art. We also built dozens of office structures, apartments, and stores for commercial real estate developers.

By 2006, the construction business had become exceptionally competitive, adversarial, and low margin in Boston. I wanted to be a builder, not a full-time litigator and collector of accounts receivable. So my siblings and I sold the business, after four generations and 102 years, and I embarked on a second career as a teacher.

When I first came to Harvard Business School (HBS), I taught two courses. One was Real Property, which is essentially Real Estate 101: how to finance, buy, and flip an office building. It's taught in the Finance unit at HBS and has an investor-focused orientation. My other course was Real Estate Development, Design, and Construction, jointly listed with Harvard Design School, which got more into the "bricks and sticks" aspect of the industry. I found them both rewarding, of course, but there is not a lot of new academic work going into the purchasing of ceiling tile or the refinancing of an apartment building.

Then two things happened. First, HBS started offering executive education in real estate in India. I was the program chair and I made many trips to India to teach but, more importantly, to do research and write. The subjects of my HBS case studies ranged from water franchising in Gujarat in the Northwest to the redevelopment of informal housing in Mumbai, to low-income housing development in Kolkata in the East, and infrastructure finance nationwide.

It was quite clear that building promoters in India could not rely on the state to provide reliable infrastructure like electricity, consistent clean water, steady sanitation services . . . or even roads. What's more, the tools I grew up with—cash flow, concrete, hardhats, and structural visualization—applied just as much to horizontal infrastructure as to my personal experience in vertical buildings. (Most commercial real estate and institutional construction is classified by the US Commerce Department as "light general building"—even skyscrapers and museums—and it is mostly vertical. The other category is heavy construction and civil works like roads, power lines, pipelines, and airports, which are largely horizontal; power plants and refineries also are in this "heavy construction" category.)

Beyond environmental issues, it was clear that the government could not provide housing for everyone; but in certain configurations, the private sector could. My HBS case study "Dharavi: Developing Asia's Largest Slum" is now used in dozens of schools and was featured in the *Wall Street Journal* and other outlets. It looks at how public-private partnerships can be used to improve housing for low- and middle-income groups.[1]

At the same time, I became more and more involved with the Harvard University Center for the Environment and with the HBS Business and Environment Initiative. I'm not qualified to discuss policy issues like how much atmospheric carbon dioxide might lead to how much global warming, and I don't have the background to discuss COP 22[2] and the implementation of the Paris accords. So how could I help move the needle?

It turns out that what I am highly qualified to think about is money and construction: notably, how to get trillions of dollars of private capital off the sideline to make high-impact investments in water, sanitation, roads, power, and mass transit that will impact the lives of hundreds of millions of people. Public health is obviously directly connected to society's success in answering this call.

My research today focuses on cities and buildings. There are several reasons for this: First, cities generate most of the world's gross domestic product. Second, cities also generate most of the world's greenhouse gases. Third, cities tend to be the political units that can act. Mayors and city councilors are often closer to their voters, are held more accountable, and can do a lot by thoughtful use of city contracts, zoning, codes, and more. And finally, cities are the right size for private investors: they get how to invest in a road or bridge or power plant or cell tower network at a city scale in a way that's near impossible to implement at a federal level in a country any larger than Singapore, Israel, or Panama.

Cities are, of course, all about the people who live and work in them. But the hard assets create the framework for these people to thrive. So I look at the design, finance, and delivery of hard assets, including energy and transportation, water and sanitation, and information and communications technology infrastructure. At the center of cities, of course, are buildings.

This led me to two frustrating paradoxes.

The first is the "infrastructure paradox." One hears a lot about the "infrastructure paradox" in meetings of infrastructure investors, multilaterals like the World Bank, and academics. Here's what it is. According to Deutsche Bank, there are more than $50 trillion dollars of financial assets invested in the fixed-income portion of the global financial system (from wealthy individuals, pension funds, insurance companies, endowments, and sovereign investment funds)—all seeking yield and currently earning only about 3 percent returns (the current US Treasury bond yields).[3] At the same time, there are hundreds if not thousands of seemingly worthy, cash-flow-positive, society-benefiting projects in the infrastructure space. How can we match up the capital and the need to make these projects "bankable"? My HBS course Sustainable Cities and Resilient Infrastructure explores the opportunities, mechanisms, and controls for this. A lot of it has to do with the perception and allocation of risk.

The second paradox is even more vexing. Call it the "healthy real estate investing paradox." As a society, we are wasting money on bad buildings . . . and we are wasting lives in bad buildings. To be blunt, the air in our buildings makes us sick and saps our productivity.

This paradox is not about uncertainties at the project level—defaults, accidents, or cash flow problems. It's about who needs to take what action to make the right long-term engineering investments. Who needs to make what choice to make the right operating decisions? Who benefits in the long run from health—and can investors capture some of that benefit?

Until recently, the benefits of Healthy Buildings have been so abstract that it's been hard to make an investment case for them. Even now, the incentives for lenders, landlords, tenant companies, and employees have not been aligned. But new quantitative research shows in an objective and reproducible way that our cognitive abilities, health, productivity, and well-being are directly impacted by decisions in the engineering, operations, and running of our buildings.

This is an exciting new way to look at the business models underlying the physical structures where we all spend our time. It's a way to map tangible health interventions onto our financial models. But before I could make progress, I felt I needed to know more about the science of a Healthy Building. That's why I sought out Joe.

Joe's Awakening

Like John, I followed in my parents' footsteps. Kind of.

My dad was a homicide detective in New York, and a good one—winner of Detective of the Year in the mid-1980s. When he retired after 20 years on the force, he started a private investigation company. He did the field-work and my mom kept the books. So my late childhood and early adult-hood were spent being a private investigator. Although I never had a Ferrari like Magnum, PI, I spent my days running across the five boroughs of New York doing surveillance, undercover stings, forensic investigations, and skip tracing. ("Skip tracing" is the industry term for the practice of tracking people down to find out where they live, work, and generally spend their time and money. The term comes from the practice of trying to trace the whereabouts of someone who has skipped town.) My PI background is a not-so-secret secret. But be forewarned: if this compels you to Google "Joe Allen private investigator Boston," you will stumble onto a scandal. That Joe Allen is not me! No relation.

I did this private investigation work through college and after, and when our best client signed my dad up to be their head of security, my brother and I took over the business. I loved it. But I always knew I was a scientist at heart. So while I was a PI, I started applying to graduate schools in environmental science. And, to hedge my bet on the science career, I also applied to the FBI.

I was darn close to heading to Quantico to become a Special Agent, too. They liked my application and invited me to take a multihour written exam, which I passed. I then submitted a 50-page dossier about everyone I ever knew and interacted with (they contacted many of them, if not all). After that I was selected to advance to the next round and was flown to

Philadelphia for an all-day grilling by a roundtable of FBI Special Agents. This was followed by another exam, this one involving combing through lengthy documents and piecing together a cogent argument on financial fraud. I passed that, too.

My last two tests before heading off to become a Special Agent were going to be easy—a polygraph test and then a fitness test. I'd been training for months for the fitness test and was ready, so the polygraph was the last real hurdle.

I failed it. Before you go thinking I was the first incarnation of Robert Hanssen hiding some secret life of crime, I was really the victim of an unskilled examiner. In a polygraph exam, you're hooked up to the machine, and after the formal set of questions, the examiner comes around the table and engages in small talk. You're still hooked up to the machine, obviously, but the ploy is to get you to think the test is over. Then, the examiner continues the conversation. Well, my examiner started in on a series of laughably preposterous scenarios designed to make me feel at ease about opening up about some nefarious secrets I might be hiding.

"Hey Joe, I have a friend who's got a friend who's a dentist, and that guy gets him prescription drugs on the side. It's really not a big deal, so you can just tell me and I'll keep it confidential. Is that what you're doing?"

Me: "Um, no," trying to keep from laughing out loud.

"Hey Joe, I have a friend who is on an antigovernment internet forum under a pseudonym. It's no big deal, we're all entitled to our opinions, right, so why don't you tell me and we'll get back to the exam. Is that what you're doing?"

And on and on. We covered sex, drugs, rock and roll, communism, and everything in between. Each topic followed the same pattern: "Hey Joe, my friend is doing _____. It's no big deal. Is that what you're doing?"

Naturally, I formally appealed after I learned I had failed. My FBI handler agreed with the appeal. As a result, the FBI literally flew in their top interrogator from Iraq to retest me. (Didn't he have better things to do?) The guy they brought in was right out of central casting—a six-foot-six-inch-tall hulking mass of a man with a mean scowl. He came in wearing his ass-kicker boots, ready to beat the hell out of me mentally (while trying to physically intimidate me).

We did the same tests, but this guy was skilled. None of the silly scenario stuff. His approach was to be as intimidating as possible. But I stayed calm, even when he got up and stood two inches from my nose and yelled at me. He kept saying, "I know what you're doing, so cut the bullshit!" And all I could think was, "I don't know what you're talking about, but weirdly I'm finding this fun!"

I stayed cool. I figured this was part of the test—seeing how I would respond to intense intimidation. After it was all over, I was certain I had passed, even as he continued his tirade while leading me out of the examination room, screaming at me in front of hundreds of other Special Agents and nearly hitting me in the back as he slammed the main door on me. I thought this slamming of the door was the big finale of the test, so I remained very calm and collected, thinking, "Nice try, but you can't rattle me." I half-expected the door to reopen with him standing there smiling, telling me I'd won, kind of like Willy Wonka at the end of the *Charlie and the Chocolate Factory* movie.

Well, the door didn't reopen. They failed me again. This time they failed me for performing "countermeasures." Which, of course, is ludicrous. I have no idea what a polygraph countermeasure would be. I didn't know then and don't know today. I did learn one thing that day, though—I came away with a healthy dose of skepticism about the misapplication of "science."

The crazy thing was, the same day I took and failed the polygraph for the second time was the first day of classes for my graduate program in public health. I guarantee I'm the only public health student ever to fail an FBI polygraph in the morning and start graduate school a few hours later. I sometimes wonder if I would've gone to that first class if the FBI had passed me earlier that day . . .

I think I would have been a pretty good FBI Special Agent, but I'm really glad that guy screwed up in failing me on that polygraph test. It led me to my true calling and passion. Oddly enough, it was still in the field of forensic investigations.

It was during one of my first forensic investigations of a "sick building" that I first saw the power and potential of this burgeoning Healthy Buildings movement. This was no ordinary case of sick building syndrome; it wasn't a stuffy cubicle farm where people sometimes report symptoms like headaches, eye irritation, dizziness, or allergic reactions. I don't mean to diminish those types of sick buildings in any way, but this was a hospital and the lives of four people were in jeopardy.

It was Grady Hospital in Atlanta in 2009. Four patients on the same two floors had developed Legionnaires' disease within the same month: a classic disease outbreak scenario.

Before we go any further with how the Grady Hospital outbreak unfolded, let me give you some quick background on Legionnaires' disease, a disease that to this day continues to impact many thousands of Americans every year, in and around buildings. Legionnaires' disease is pretty common—7,500 cases are reported each year, but this is a gross underestimate of the actual number of cases. Legionnaires' disease is underdiagnosed and underreported. It's also a deadly disease—1 in 10 people who get it die.[4]

Legionnaires' disease was first "discovered" after the infamous outbreak at the convention of the American Legion at the Bellevue-Stratford Hotel in 1976. Over the course of a few days, 2,000 people became sick with a severe, life-threating type of pneumonia. Twenty-nine of those people died.

The scariest part? No one knew the cause. The other 10,000 people who attended the convention were, rightfully, in a panic about their own health. This was front-page-of-*Newsweek*-type stuff. (In the age before the rise of internet news, making the cover of *Newsweek* was a big deal.)

The disease was dubbed "Legionnaires' disease" because of the location of this outbreak—at the American Legion meeting, where members call themselves Legionnaires. After several months of investigation, the US Centers for Disease Control and Prevention identified the cause of the outbreak: a bacterium in the building air-conditioning system that they named—you guessed it—*Legionella*.

Legionella are naturally occurring waterborne bacteria that can cause a pneumonia-like illness. Out in the natural world, where they are everywhere, their numbers stay small. But given an environment where water stagnates and where temperatures stay lukewarm, they proliferate. That makes a few places in a building a nice home for *Legionella*. They like to live, and grow, inside the biofilm in water pipes, inside cooling towers on the roof of a building, or, in the case of that infamous American Legion outbreak, in the condensate drains of air conditioners.

Within a building (a hospital, for example), *Legionella* are also commonly found in "dead legs" of a building's plumbing system. Dead legs are sections of the plumbing system areas where an old line was cut off, say, during a renovation in which a water fountain was removed. Sometimes, for reasons of efficiency, cost, laziness, or shortsightedness, rather than cutting the water line all the way back to its joint in the plumbing system, the building owner just caps the pipe where the fountain used to be and patches up the wall. Thus, a dead leg is created.

The dead leg of the system is that extension of pipe that is no longer part of the normal circulating water flow, so the water stagnates and stays lukewarm. These are the perfect conditions for *Legionella* to grow. And importantly, they grow in an area where they can't be easily "attacked" by residual disinfectant in the building's water supply (traditionally chlorine), and therefore they act as a source that continually feeds bacteria into the main line of the water system.

But simply having *Legionella* in water doesn't mean you'll get sick from it. The way we can get Legionnaires' disease is by breathing in the bacteria. So the mere presence of *Legionella* in a building doesn't mean there's a problem; the bacteria must also be aerosolized, or released into the air in tiny droplets. In the case of the American Legion outbreak, the bacteria were aerosolized and distributed around the convention through the air-conditioning system.

Since that time, we have done a much better job of controlling *Legionella* in our cooling systems. (For the most part, anyway. Outbreaks still frequently occur, like the outbreak in Disneyland in 2017 that impacted 22 people, or the outbreak in Portugal in 2014 that sickened 336 and killed 10.) And in most commercial buildings, there really aren't many opportunities indoors to aerosolize the water in any meaningful way, other than through spray from the sink or postflush spray from the toilet. (Yes, you read that right.) Hospitals, on the other hand, have a lot of opportunities for aerosolizing water that other types of buildings don't always have—showers. (Hotels fall into this category, too, and there have been many high-profile outbreaks in hotels.)

Now that you're armed with the basics of *Legionella*, let's go back to Grady Hospital in Atlanta. When we sampled the water in the plumbing lines, sure enough, we found *Legionella* in the water on the two floors experiencing the outbreak.

To be fair, what happened at Grady Hospital wasn't, and isn't, all that unusual. *Legionella* in buildings, including hospitals, is common. In fact, it has been found in up to 90 percent of US hospitals, according to some surveys.[5] And having cases of Legionnaires' disease isn't all that unusual either; remember, there are thousands of cases per year in the United States. What was unusual about Grady Hospital was that four cases occurred on the same two floors, in the same month. This was an outbreak.

The leadership team at Grady Hospital immediately recognized the severity of the problem. After trying a few techniques that failed to fully eradicate *Legionella* from the pipes on those two floors—like shocking the water system with high levels of disinfectant—they hired the environmental consulting firm Environmental Health & Engineering to take the lead. This was the company I worked for right after getting my graduate degrees in public health.

Our charge was to stop the outbreak. Pretty straightforward goal, but pretty complicated in practice. (Of course, that's why they hired us. As I said to my team anytime we came across a tough project and there were complaints about how hard or complex a particular project was, if it were easy, they wouldn't have called.) So there I was, newly minted "Dr." Joe Allen, with my fancy new degree, on a plane with the owner of the consulting company, heading to Atlanta, Georgia, to help stop this outbreak.

The biggest problem, put to me by my astute wife as I packed my bags for the trip, was this: "What the hell do you know about Legionnaires' disease?" Solid question. She was right, of course. I had graduated from a school of public health, but my dissertation was focused on toxic flame-retardant chemicals found in products in your home and office. I had all of 30 minutes of formal lectures on Legionnaires' disease in my graduate coursework as part of an Introduction to Environmental Health seminar. Now I was headed to work on an outbreak in a hospital where lives were at stake. Was this gross negligence?

No, it wasn't. I may not have had formal training on *Legionella*, true, but I did have real expertise in my field, exposure and risk assessment science. You may ask, "What does that even mean?" It means I was trained to evaluate sources of exposures to chemicals and biological hazards; understand how these toxics migrate through our air, water, and dust in buildings; and figure out how they get into our body, what happens once they are in our body, and how to mitigate the source of exposure. This, it turns out, is precisely the skill set that comes in handy for investigating Legionnaires' disease—or any other sick building problem.

So I told my wife, "I got this. I'm just applying these exposure and risk science tools to a new problem—bacteria in water." I was saying this to myself as much as to my wife. "I got this," I said in my head, to build my own confidence. And I had to be right, because the stakes were high.

But that was actually true then, and it's still true today. I've added new tools along the way, but what I did essentially describes my approach over the course of my career: apply the fundamentals of exposure and risk assessment science to any sick building problem. This has allowed me to work with forensic teams to investigate and resolve hundreds of such problems, from a breast cancer cluster in a commercial office building to a concern about radon emitting from granite countertops. I've evaluated the environmental causes of 11 infant deaths on a US military base and led an investigation into the "Chinese Drywall" issue that plagued the Southwest United States for several years around 2010.

But let's get back to Grady Hospital. So there I was, sitting on that plane to Atlanta next to my new boss, having read every single important published research paper on *Legionella* since the 1970s over the past 24 hours. He had decades of experience doing this type of sick building work, and together we were, and remain, quite a formidable team. By the time the wheels touched down in Atlanta, we had a plan. Not just to stop the outbreak, but to be sure it never happened again.

I can't go into the details of what we did at Grady Hospital because of confidentiality concerns—so far I've only given you publicly available information—but I will tell you this: we stopped the outbreak. It was a multipronged strategy that used a combination of point-of-use water filters; additional shock treatments of the water system; a permanent chlorine dioxide water treatment system; a rigorous monitoring campaign for indicators of water quality like pH, temperature, and bacterial growth; and, ultimately, upgrades to the hot water heaters and water circulation system. The financial cost for all of this? Greater than $1 million but less than $5 million (I can't disclose specifics). But that's nothing compared with the human toll and the cost in lost revenue from closing two floors of the hospital for several months.

There were no new cases from the moment we were involved until the moment the contract ended a few years later (and as far as I know, no new outbreaks after we left). Of course, we didn't do this alone. We had a team supporting us, and we had a multistakeholder and multidisciplinary team from Grady Hospital of administrators, nurses, infection control experts, water disinfection experts, and doctors. And, most important of all, the building engineers.

Building engineers and facilities managers are the true heroes of our health. (As you'll see, they are the reason why I often say, "The people who manage your building have a greater impact on your health than you doctor.") At Grady Hospital, we spent countless hours in the belly of the beast, poring over the plumbing plans and mapping the pipes in the basement with these unsung heroes of Healthy Buildings.

I'm proud of our work at Grady Hospital. It was also a great period of growth for me. I was trained in exposure and risk assessment science, but what I didn't get in my graduate studies at a school of public health was formal training in a whole lot of building science. And yet, I was beginning to see firsthand that solving the problems of sick buildings required a merging of the skills of building science and health science. In the years following this Legionnaires' disease investigation, I learned building science on the job by being part of, and leading, teams of building engineers, mechanical engineers, toxicologists, epidemiologists, statisticians, and exposure and risk experts, solving complex sick building issues.

Consulting comes with an immediacy that is missing in academia, where we end every peer-reviewed paper with the sentence, "More research is needed." In the real world, the question is, "Is it safe for people to be in that hospital *right now*?" We are forced to make decisions with the best information we have at that moment. For me, the final test on each project was asking myself, "Would I give the same recommendation if my daughter or wife worked in this building?" If the answer was ever no, I never gave the all-clear.

Now, as a professor at Harvard, I'm trying to rectify what I saw as a short-coming in my own formal public health training. I teach a class that merges building science and health science, to give our public health students an understanding of the importance of the building that I never got. And I operate with the same great sense of urgency that I learned in consulting. I expect the same from everyone on my team. Written on the wall in my lab is, "How will your research impact the world?" We publish plenty of papers, teach many classes, and give frequent seminars. But how we judge ourselves is all about impact.

Along the way I picked up new tools and skills. The most important of these is the focus of this book: business science. And much like the Grady

Hospital *Legionella* outbreak, which opened my eyes to the power of my training in exposure and risk, it was a different Legionnaires' disease project at a different hospital that opened my eyes to the importance of paying attention to the economics of Healthy Buildings.

For this example, I can't give you names, places, or dates, because I was hired as an expert witness and the details remain confidential. But I'll give you big-picture details, with some names and places changed to protect the client.

The setting was the same—a hospital experiencing an issue with Legionnaires' disease. But this time, someone died. (This is not that uncommon with Legionnaires' disease outbreaks. It turns out that, in hospitals, about 40 percent of those exposed to *Legionella* develop Legionnaires' disease. This is what epidemiologists call the attack rate. Then, once someone is sick ["attacked"], he or she has about a 10 percent chance of dying from the disease. This is what epidemiologists call the mortality rate.[6])

As with Grady, I was hired as an expert to evaluate and advise the hospital on the case. By this point, though, I was further along in my career and a seasoned forensic investigator across many sick building issues, having led several *Legionella* outbreak investigations and many dozens of other projects. I reviewed the hospital's approach and data and confirmed that the hospital had taken appropriate corrective actions.

This hospital decided to settle the lawsuit with the patient's family for several million dollars. But what happened next shocked me. To this day, it is stuck in the forefront of my brain, and it is one of the primary motivations for my wanting to write this book.

Someone had died. The hospital had just spent millions of dollars settling this case, and a couple hundred thousand more on the many experts who were involved in the investigation, me included. Being a good public health scientist (and businessperson), I pitched the hospital on a proactive *Legionella* risk management plan. Because of my experience with previous hospital outbreaks, and the success of the plan we put in place at Grady Hospital that led to no new outbreaks over four years, I was essentially guaranteeing this hospital that they would not have another case of Legionnaires' disease while we were working for them.

The plan I pitched cost $20,000. That's it. Against the backdrop of a multimillion-dollar outlay (not to mention the damage to the brand from bad press), I told the owner of the company I worked for that the proposal

I submitted was a done deal. In fact, we both thought we were underpricing our service at $20,000. "This is too cheap for what we're offering," we thought. We rationalized that this would simply be one of many *Legionella* risk management plans the company could pitch to hospitals around the country.

We were dead wrong. To my shock, the hospital balked at our proposal. Why? They told me that the price was too high. What?! I was flabbergasted. The public health scientist in me could not understand this in any rational way. How could a hospital that had just had a patient die, a hospital that had just spent millions, not go for a $20,000 plan that would guarantee it would not happen again?

The answer, it turns out, is that I was naïve about the economic drivers of decision-making in buildings and business. What I failed to recognize, but learned after some digging, is that the millions of dollars in settlements were paid by the insurance company, but our $20,000 risk management plan would come out of the facilities budget.

An aha moment for me, for sure. The hospital wasn't paying the settlement to the family of the patient who had died. (Maybe in some way through higher insurance premiums, but the reality is that this one case is a small drop in the bucket in relation to the many factors that set their insurance premiums.) But the $20,000? Well, it turned out that was a big line item in the facilities team's budget, and it wasn't something they could afford. After all, "patient health" wasn't their charge—that was the purview of the doctors and nurses, right?

Thus came my introduction to the issue of split incentives. For this hospital, the issue reveals itself in misalignment between the goals of the facilities team and those of the business, and a split incentive between the business and the insurer.

Of course, the issue of split incentives is not the exclusive domain of hospitals. Split incentives pop up all over the place in this Healthy Buildings conversation. Real estate investors, owners, developers, and tenants all have different goals, which creates disincentives for investing in Healthy Building strategies. It's a topic that we will repeatedly come back to in this book, along with ideas for how to present win-win solutions designed to overcome split incentives.

Seeing these split incentives as a barrier to the adoption of Healthy Building strategies over and over is the primary reason why I have made it a goal to spend more time connecting my research on health to a business argument.

This is why I sought out John.

Driving Research into Practice

We partnered up and have been talking with business leaders together for several years now. It seems that with every new conversation, many of these leaders are surprised to learn about all of the information and tools that are at their disposal from the health and business worlds, information that could greatly help them but that has not permeated beyond the halls of academia— even some of what we consider the basics.

Here's an example. Joe was at a conference giving a speech titled "The Nexus of Green Buildings, Global Health and the U.N. Sustainable Development Goals." The presentation wound its way through scientific data showing how buildings are at the center of our sustainable urbanization efforts, covering everything from indoor health to environmental health. On the latter point, Joe mentioned that buildings were major contributors to air pollution, as most of the energy they use comes from fossil fuel sources. The story necessarily brings in the basics of outdoor air pollution and the health effects of one of the most studied air pollutants: $PM_{2.5}$.

At the end of the presentation, Joe was engaged by a C-suite executive from a company that is involved in selling air filters for buildings. This executive asked, with a straight face, "Is there any data on the health effects of $PM_{2.5}$?"

For those of us in the world of public health, this would be akin to someone asking an astronomer, "Is there evidence that the moon goes around Earth?" The scientific literature on $PM_{2.5}$ could quite literally fill a hundred-story building. PubMed lists over 7,000 scientific papers on $PM_{2.5}$ and health, with over 1,000 papers published in each of the past few years. (That's about 3 papers *per day*.) Here are some examples of what we know about $PM_{2.5}$:

- Five percent of lung cancer deaths globally are attributable to particulate matter (PM).[7]
- Mortality rates increase by 7 percent for every 10 μg/m^3 of $PM_{2.5}$.[8]

- Hospital admissions increase by over 4 percent for every 10 $\mu g/m^3$ increase in long-term $PM_{2.5}$.[9]

For reference, the current ambient exposure limit in the United States is 12 $\mu g/m^3$, and the annual average in Los Angeles for the past few years ranged from 13 $\mu g/m^3$ to 19 $\mu g/m^3$. In Beijing and New Delhi, $PM_{2.5}$ concentrations have exceeded 1,200 $\mu g/m^3$. (This notation is common for talking about the amount, or concentration, of air pollution in the air. This is read as, "10 micrograms of $PM_{2.5}$ for every cubic meter of air.")

Joe's mouth was agape for a full 20 seconds. But that's not the only time this has happened. Here's another equally shocking example, from someone who controls the health of millions of people each day. Or rather, millions of *kids* each day.

Former US Secretary of Education Betsy DeVos did an interview with *60 Minutes* in 2018 in which she said something that should make anyone reading this book fall off his or her chair: "We should be funding and investing in students, not in school buildings."[10]

What?! As if the two aren't directly related! There are over 200 scientific studies documenting how the school *building* influences student health, student thinking, and student performance.[11] The facts are astounding:

- Cognitive testing of students shows a 5 percent decrease in "power of attention" in poorly ventilated classrooms. The researchers equate this to the effect of a student's skipping breakfast.[12]
- In a study of over 4,000 sixth graders, lower ventilation rates, moisture and dampness, and inadequate ventilation were all independently associated with a higher incidence of respiratory symptoms. Inadequate ventilation was also associated with more missed school days.[13]
- A study of over 3,000 fifth-grade students showed that they had higher math, reading, and science scores in classrooms with higher ventilation rates.[14]
- In a study of exam records for nearly one million school students in New York City, the likelihood of failing an exam taken on a 90°F day versus a 75°F day is 14 percent greater. The researcher estimates that this leads to a 2.5 percent lower likelihood of the average New York City student graduating on time.[15]

- Third-grade students with "focus" lighting (1,000 lux, 6,500 K) for a full academic year had a higher percentage increase in performance on oral reading fluency than students in a standard lighting scenario (a 36 percent versus a 17 percent increase).[16]
- A study of nearly 300 students found that mouse allergen was detected in 99.5 percent of samples taken, and students with higher exposure to mouse allergen had a higher likelihood of having allergy symptoms and lower lung function.[17]

To be fair, DeVos is not alone in her lack of knowledge of the scientific literature. Most people don't have this type of scientific data at their fingertips. But most people can be forgiven for not knowing; DeVos was in a leadership position in an organization that *depends* on knowing this type of stuff. And you, as a reader of this book, are likely finding yourself in that same position—making key decisions about the health of people, and your business, without yet having a full understanding of how health science, building science, and business science can be leveraged to your advantage.

While these stories give us the opportunity to point to the folly of others, really the only thing these two examples show is our own failing. That's right. We are the ones who should be laughed at. Here we are, sitting on mounds of scientific data, laughing at others for not putting that data to use when, in reality, nearly all of that data is locked up in dusty scientific journals full of inaccessible jargon, caveats, uncertainty, and titles like this: "Cytotoxicity and Induction of Proinflammatory Cytokines from Human Monocytes Exposed to Fine ($PM_{2.5}$) and Coarse Particles ($PM_{10-2.5}$) in Outdoor and Indoor Air." This style of writing is great and informative for scientists, and in fact necessary—it's what we expect and want to see—so we don't mean to minimize the value of the scientific process. But it's no wonder that so much of this information can't be put to use by practitioners. Collectively we, the scientific community, need to work harder to translate the hard science into accessible language and actionable recommendations.

With this book, we aim to correct this failing. We have read the scientific papers and business case studies so you don't have to. Our goal is to now bring the rich science of our fields into the hands of practitioners and to make sure any future Secretary of Education, or anyone else in control of the health and productivity of millions of people in buildings, never again utters a phrase like, "We need to invest in our people, not our buildings."

How This Book Will Get Us There

To be clear, we won't just talk about the academic literature. We'll also draw on our knowledge gained from years of practice working with leaders in the building space. We will show you how to use all of this data and information to your advantage, so you will see that when you focus on optimizing buildings for health, your business wins, too.

We structured the book in two parts. In Part I, we make the case for Healthy Buildings. In Chapter 1 we began by sharing some motivations for our work together on this book and the value in having crosstalk between our two disciplines—health and business. In Chapter 2 we describe the challenges and opportunities in front of us all. To have a discussion about the role of health and buildings without discussing the gigantic forces that are shaping and reshaping this industry would be a fool's errand. We show how 10 global mega-changes are shaping our world, our businesses, our buildings, and our health:

1. Changing populations
2. Changing cities
3. Changing resources
4. Changing climate
5. Changing role of the private sector
6. Changing definition of health
7. Changing buildings
8. Changing work
9. Changing technology
10. Changing values

They all converge on one point: Healthy Buildings.

Grounded in the global forces at work, we will quickly move to the primary goal of this book: to make the business case for Healthy Buildings in a straightforward manner. We present the irrefutable evidence that the indoor environment is a key determinant of our health and productivity, and show that a business strategy that focuses on the people in your building drives bottom-line performance (Chapter 3). Then we show you how to put the building to work for you (Chapter 4). We give you the economic evidence demonstrating how even just one building factor—ventilation—can lead to significant enterprise-wide gains, and show you how to create and capture this value (Chapter 5).

Once you are well versed in these 10 global mega-changes and the straightforward business case for Healthy Buildings, you will be right to ask, "So what else matters, and what do I do now?" We know you'll ask that because everyone does.

In Part II, we expand our discussion of what it means to have a Healthy Building and give you tools to operationalize A Healthy Building Strategy. In Chapter 6 we bring to life the science behind the 9 Foundations of a Healthy Building, putting the tools and knowledge of health science and business science at your fingertips, complete with recommendations you can implement today for each foundation. In Chapter 7 we explore the products we place in our buildings and how they influence health, and in Chapter 8 we explore how buildings can make us sick, or protect us from infectious diseases. Then we explore Healthy Building certification systems, the economics behind them, and what we think are the key elements that should define any Healthy Building certification (Chapter 9). Last, recognizing that we can't improve what we don't measure, we move to a discussion about how to use Health Performance Indicators, or HPIs, in tandem with Key Performance Indicators (KPIs) and new sensor technologies, to track the impact of your Healthy Building strategy (Chapter 10).

We close our book with two chapters that are really about expanding the winner's circle around the Healthy Building movement. In Chapter 11 we expand the Healthy Buildings conversation to include health impacts beyond the four walls of the building. We will dive into the building-energy-health-climate-resilience nexus and explore the business opportunities, and challenges, around quantifying the social performance of real estate and making decisions about resiliency in the face of a changing climate. In Chapter 12 we explore how to scale the Healthy Buildings movement from flagship projects to business as usual by asking, "What's now?" and "What's next?" Finally, we conclude with a synthesis of the key arguments and a clear demonstration of how everyone wins in this Healthy Buildings movement.

CHAPTER TWO

The Global Mega-changes Shaping Our World, Our Buildings, and Us

We shape our buildings and afterwards our buildings shape us.
—WINSTON CHURCHILL

THE WORLD IS CHANGING around us, and buildings are at the center of that change. So much so that the decisions we make today regarding our buildings will determine our collective health for generations to come. Winston Churchill's famous quote has never been more apt.

You may know that quote; many in the building world do. But you may not know that Churchill wasn't making some grand statement about the societal impacts of our urban fabric when he uttered this now famous phrase. After all, he lived at a time of abundant natural resources and natural capacity to deal with pollution (or so they thought). Population growth and urbanization were not occurring at the scale they are today.

What Churchill had in mind was something very specific and relevant to him: how the parliamentary chamber had shaped Britain's government, and therefore its people (the "us" in "our buildings shape us"). This story, even though it's about the UK Parliament, is very interesting—and we promise it will be useful to you. Stick with us for a few more paragraphs here.

The British Parliament is split into two houses—the House of Lords and the House of Commons—and their chambers are on opposite ends of the

FIGURE 2.1   Historical image of the British Parliament chambers. i.Stock.com/whitemay.

Palace of Westminster. In 1943, the Commons Chamber was destroyed after a German Luftwaffe sortie dropped incendiary bombs on it during the Blitz. If you're not familiar with the British Commons Chamber pre-1943 (why would you be?), it was a fiercely intimate setting. Lawmakers sat shoulder to shoulder on benches, within feet of their political adversaries. The prime minister stood in the center. It was so small and intimate that the chamber didn't even have enough seats for all of its members.

The intimacy was in fact its key feature. In this room, there was nowhere to run or hide. You made your argument face-to-face with your colleagues. Friend and foe alike could see fear or conviction in your eye. They could smell your breath. The convenings were, by design, a raucous affair (and often filled with colorful vitriol).

The fire from the Luftwaffe's incendiary bombs tore through the chamber, turning it to rubble. There was immediate discussion of replacing it with a bigger, more expansive chamber hall. (One with enough seats for all, for starters!) The idea of a vast chamber with semicircular seating was floated.

That's when Churchill made his famous declaration, "We shape our buildings and afterwards our buildings shape us." Churchill recognized that the building had shaped their debate, their society, them. The intimate quarters of the Commons had shaped Britain. He was vehemently opposed to the semicircle idea.

Now compare this with the US House Chamber.

Expansive, regal even, and lacking in intimacy: the semicircle that Churchill disdained. The room is not a boxing ring like the British Parliament. The US chambers inspire civil, comfortable, but wholly detached debates. The people in the back are a hundred feet from the person speaking. They definitely can't see the speaker's conviction, fear, or passion. The building shapes the debate.

We all know it's easier to say something bad about someone when you're not toe-to-toe with that person. That's why as kids we used to say, "I dare you to say that to my face." It takes real conviction and chutzpah to stand face-to-face with someone and spout vitriol. It's easy to do it when you're across the room (or online). Speaking in the US House Chamber is more akin to talking behind someone's back.

Back in Britain, Churchill won the day. The British Commons Chamber was rebuilt to its original form and is essentially a rectangular boxing ring—still without enough seats for everyone. Eighty years later, the building continues to shape the country.

We shape our buildings and afterwards our buildings shape . . . our health, our businesses, and our planet. So much so that, of the ten megachanges shaping the world right now, buildings are at the center of them all.

The First Four Mega-changes: Changing Populations, Changing Cities, Changing Resources, and a Changing Climate

Think about this: we are living on a planet of over 7 billion people, a number that is rapidly moving to 9 billion. And as a group, we are getting older. Much older. Driven by advances in global health that have significantly extended the average life expectancy, the shape of the age distribution of the human population is changing dramatically. In 1900, 4 percent of the US population was over the age of 65. Today we are at 16 percent, headed toward 20 percent in 2050. Many countries in Europe, such as Italy, France, and Germany, already have 20 percent of their population over the age of 65, and in Japan they are at 28 percent. More striking is what's happening at the upper end of human longevity. On a global scale, 100 years ago very few reached the age of 80 (0.2 percent), but today it's an order of magnitude greater (2 percent), and we are on pace to hit over 4 percent by 2050.[1]

The global population is also on the move. For the first time in history, more of us live in cities than do not. To put this in perspective, consider India, where it is projected that over 400 million people will move into Indian cities by 2050.[2] Four hundred million! That's roughly the equivalent of adding a city the size of Paris every two months from today through 2050. That's a lot of new buildings. In fact, 70–80 percent of the infrastructure needed in India to meet this demand is not yet built.[3]

The capacity to meet this demand in India and around the world is strained by limits on our natural capital. Simply put, we have overshot the capacity of Earth's systems. Gone are the days of "Dilution is the solution to pollution," when we thought we could forever dump pollutants into our air and water and watch as they dispersed, thinking that the problem was solved. Rachel Carson's book *Silent Spring*, written in 1962, was our first wake-up call about the perils of this approach.[4]

Nearly 60 years later we have had another wake-up call, and this time it has to do with our consumption of natural resources and the changing capacity of Earth to sustain life. You have likely heard that we currently consume 1.5 Earths. For those of us in the United States, it's more like four Earths. Famed Harvard biologist E. O. Wilson warns in his book *Half-Earth* that the loss of biodiversity from overconsumption and overdevelopment is such a monumental catastrophe that we need to reserve half of Earth right now.[5] For anyone about to argue that this is some tree-hugging notion of leaving nature pristine for nature's sake, you're wrong. Wilson argues that nothing less than the survival of the human species is at stake. Taken together, the constant release of pollutants and overuse of natural stocks and space mean that our current overconsumption of resources is not sustainable.

But you didn't buy this book for a lecture on natural capital. You bought this book because of your interest in buildings. Guess what? Likely no surprises here—buildings play a dominant role in depleting these resources, and Healthy Buildings can play a role in counteracting this depletion. Buildings represent the largest consumer of materials of all industries on Earth.[6] And after the building dies, where does all of that converted natural capital go? Most of it becomes landfill waste, used once and then buried forever.

Demolition debris from buildings in the United States generates more waste than the total amount of garbage (municipal solid waste) that goes into land-fills each year.[7]

The impact of the collision of these first three mega-changes—population growth, urbanization, and resource consumption—is compounded by a fourth mega-change: global climate change. Buildings play a key role here, too. Approximately 80 percent of global energy comes from fossil fuel com-bustion, and as consumers of 40 percent of that energy, buildings influence our health indirectly by contributing to (or in the case of energy-efficient buildings, by reducing) the amount of air pollutants and greenhouse gases produced by our energy generation.[8]

Climate change will alter social dynamics, population migration, ecosys-tems, and agriculture and ultimately cause a cascade of adverse health impacts. John Holdren, the scientific adviser to President Barack Obama for eight years, summed it up best at a Harvard University Center for the Environment event.[9] His key points are paraphrased here:

- The climate is changing.
- The cause is human activity.
- Impacts are already emerging.
- Adverse impacts are baked into the system.
- The extent of future impacts depends on what we do now.

Taken together, these first four mega-changes—changing populations, changing cities, changing resources, and a changing climate—are the con-sequence of this era of human-dominated influence on the environment—dubbed "the Anthropocene." The profound impact of human activity on Earth's life-support systems is fundamentally shifting how we must think about how our decisions concerning our built environment affect our natural environment and, ultimately, our health.

The Fifth Mega-change: Changing Role of the Private Sector

An observer might assume that it's a core function of government to recog-nize the threat posed by these first four mega-changes and to plan ahead, presumably using logic, science, cost-benefit analysis, taxing power, bond-issuing capabilities, and consensus to create the infrastructure we all need—roads, bridges, power, water, sanitation, parks—to get to outcomes we all want: jobs, homes, schools, hospitals, arts, and more for a healthy citizenry.

Yet there is no escaping the glaring inability of government, in particular federal government, to do any of this. Political stalemates from Brazil to Nigeria to Malaysia to Italy underscore the gap. Right here in the United States, our political gridlock prevents us from making a long-overdue investment in infrastructure, despite widespread agreement from both political parties that this is necessary and a sound economic investment. The same infrastructure investment is needed from Bolivia to Ethiopia to Myanmar, but financial shortfalls prevent action. The popular press is full of accounts of how bad air in Delhi or Shanghai sickens people every day. If we are not going to have a planet of dirty slums, what can the private sector do to invest in and improve these situations? It turns out the answer is "quite a lot." And we'll show how in this book.

The Sixth Mega-change: Changing Definition of Health

The old definition of health as "the absence of disease" is rightfully being replaced with something more like this from the World Health Organization: "state of complete physical, mental, and social well-being, and not merely the absence of disease or infirmity."[10] Businesses are getting into the mix. Companies are recognizing that there is value in not just a *disease avoidance* strategy for their employees but also a *health promotion* strategy. In academic and medical jargon, this is articulated as moving from studying pathogenesis, or the origins of disease, to studying salutogenesis, or the creation and promotion of health. (The term "salutogenesis" was coined by medical sociology professor Aaron Antonovsky.)[11] It's great PR and HR strategy, and to many companies this is central to their core values, but the main driving incentive is economic.

Consider this: in an article published in the *Journal of the American Medical Association,* consistently ranked as one of the top medical and scientific journals in the world, our former Harvard colleague Ashish Jha (now Dean at Brown University School of Public Health) and others report that the United States spent a staggering 17.8 percent of its gross domestic product on health-care costs. This is twice as high a percentage as those of 10 of the other highest-income countries around the world, despite American utilization rates being similar (and many health outcomes being demonstrably worse).[12] In the United States, where most people's health care is tied to their employment and the employer contributes to the costs of that care (often upwards of $14,000–$20,000 per employee per year), companies should have a strong economic incentive to keep their employees healthy.[13]

It shouldn't be shocking to learn, then, that companies spend millions on some form of health or wellness programs. But when you look at all of these efforts to promote the health and productivity of employees, you will be shocked (shocked!) to learn that, for many companies, there is no mention of buildings in their wellness strategy. But we see signs of change in the air. Two prime examples: Harvard and Google.

In 2016, Harvard Business School and the Harvard T. H. Chan School of Public Health held a joint colloquium. This was unusual for Harvard: to convene a significant number of alumni, faculty members, researchers, and industry experts from two separate professional schools. (Most people might think this type of thing happens every day, but it is not routine and took special effort.) The topic? The possible contributions of both disciplines to the concept of "a Culture of Health," which was billed as a "Business Leadership Imperative." The colloquium was funded by the Robert Wood Johnson Foundation, drawing together CEOs and academics alike to consider how businesses could take intentional action to drive health results across four domains: consumer health, employee health, community health, and environmental health.[14] Both of us participated, and executives from many of the companies we work with every day were there, too.

The event was a resounding success. One key deliverable: a massive online open course called Improving Your Business through a Culture of Health. The goal was to offer free lectures to anyone in business around the world interested in learning how to build a culture of health.

That course went off in the spring of 2018, and it was a success: nine weeks of content with some of Harvard's most renowned experts delivered to thousands of online students. The course covered many aspects of how health can drive the bottom line of your business. Buildings were mentioned, but they weren't a focal point.

Now that is changing. Joe is now co-directing a new initiative at Harvard's T. H. Chan School of Public Health aimed at forging closer ties between business leaders and health researchers. The program, called Public

Health and Business Leadership, includes healthy buildings as a focus area; in it, Joe and John teach the health and business case study "A Tower for the People," about the construction of a new tower at 425 Park Avenue in Manhattan. Most important, from our perspective, is the opportunity to reach a next generation of leaders through our students. Harvard has established a new joint degree program between its graduate schools of design and public health. Further, we have been teaching "home and away" lectures on each other's campuses—with John teaching real estate finance to Joe's public health students, and Joe teaching Healthy Building science to John's business students. The key point here is this: hundreds of future executives and design and health leaders are being trained to understand the power of Healthy Buildings and learning both rigorous science and comprehensive finance tools.

This change is not just happening within the confines of academia. Change is in the air at major global companies, too.

No organization is more adept than Google at creating a brilliant workplace culture that continues to attract talent and produce outstanding innovations year after year. So when Eric Schmidt, the former CEO of Google, wrote a book with Jonathan Rosenberg called *How Google Works*, we read it with intense interest.[15] Along with everyone in the world, we hoped to pick up insights from the person who worked with Sergey Brin and Larry Page, the cofounders of Google, to create this technology juggernaut.

It turns out the "secret sauce" at Google is a focus on . . . people. And it's a focus on a particular set of people—the "smart creatives," as they call them.

Imagine our delight when we read this sentence in the opening chapter of the book, which tells you how to get the most out of these smart creatives: "The only way to succeed in business in the 21st century is to continually create great products, and the only way to do that is to attract smart creatives and put them in an environment where they can succeed at scale" (p. xv). The book doesn't explicitly mention buildings (we wish it did), but Google has sent a clear message through its actions that the environment in which people work matters.

In other outlets it has made it crystal clear that the building, and the people in them, is at the heart of a healthy, thriving, and innovative business. Take this story. During a project meeting with students and technologists from the University of California, Berkeley, Page pulled out his particle counter to show them something. (You read that right—"his" particle counter. In other words, Page *owns* an air-quality sensor and apparently carries it around with him!) As Google recounts, Page then began to pound a piece of carpet in front of this group to show everyone how the airborne particle numbers dramatically spiked. The message: we are all walking around in these potentially toxic little dust clouds—in other words, our environment matters.[16]

The high levels of particles in the demonstration were shocking, and the implications were immediately clear to everyone watching. That included the Google Real Estate and Workplace Services team. When the founder brings up air quality in a public presentation, it sends an important signal that this is a priority. No wonder, then, that this is how the team views their work: "For Google real estate teams, buildings are the product and the people in them are our users," as Kate Brandt, Google chief sustainability officer, told us. "Our goal is to build sustainability in from start to finish, prioritizing our planet and the health and well-being of future occupants."[17]

When your CEO carries around a particle counter, it tends to sharpen your focus. Change is quite literally in the air at Google.

The Seventh Mega-change: Changing Buildings

Have you seen a car ad on television that shows the noisy chaos of the world outside the car before it pans to the driver inside the quiet, luxurious interior of said car, protected from the elements outside? The message you're supposed to take from this juxtaposition is that this car is "tight"—sealed off from the world outside and all its perils.

This sealing up is done for a few reasons: it provides a quiet interior, for sure, and it makes your air-conditioning and heating more efficient because the car is less "leaky." But it also comes with an unexpected side effect: the pollutants inside the car have nowhere to go, leading to a buildup of potentially toxic pollutants emitted from materials inside the car, and a buildup of carbon dioxide (CO_2) emitted from the car's occupants. We regularly see levels of CO_2 inside cars that are as much as four to five times higher than what we allow in buildings.[18] Ever get sleepy while on a long drive with the family or friends? The high carbon dioxide levels in your car are contributing to that—it's one of the reasons why you've likely heard the recommendation to roll down your windows if you feel sleepy while driving.

Buildings are the same. Like humans, they need to breathe. But, as with cars, we've done one hell of a job over the past 40 years of cutting off their air supply.

For over a hundred years there have been efforts to figure out the proper amount of fresh air that needs to be brought into a building. Beginning around the time of the energy crisis in the late 1970s, we did our best to tighten our building envelopes and reduce ventilation rates in an effort to conserve energy. The goal for our homes and offices and schools was to make them less leaky. (We'll talk about this in detail in Chapter 4.)

We were very successful in these efforts. Kudos to the energy engineer pioneers in the 1970s for helping to alleviate the energy crisis in buildings. But maybe they should've consulted some health scientists along the way. The result of sealing up our buildings, as you likely guessed from the car story: a buildup of pollutants indoors. And with it, the birth of a phenomenon known as Sick Building Syndrome. So there you have it—if you don't feel well in a building, you can thank a set of energy engineers who decided that the best way to tackle the energy crisis was to choke off your air supply.

Sick Building Syndrome first started appearing in the literature and news in the early 1980s. What is it? We'll use the *Merriam-Webster* definition here because it is pretty good: "a set of symptoms (such as headache, fatigue, and eye irritation) typically affecting workers in modern airtight office buildings that is believed to be caused by indoor pollutants (such as formaldehyde fumes or microorganisms)."[19]

The few edits we would make are these:

- Sick Building Syndrome doesn't just affect workers in a building; it can affect visitors, too.
- Sick Building Syndrome doesn't just occur in "modern" buildings; it can occur in any building.
- Airtight buildings are often the culprit, but other factors can create a sick building, such as a water leak that leads to mold or *Legionella*, and others that we'll explore in the 9 Foundations of a Healthy Building in Chapter 6.
- While formaldehyde fumes and microorganisms are two examples of indoor pollutants, there are many causes of a sick building beyond these. (Also, sorry for the nerdiness, but "fumes" are technically solid

particles suspended in air, like fumes from metalworking or even smoke; formaldehyde is a vapor or gas.)

- Sick Building Syndrome can be attributed to time spent in underperforming environments where the symptoms often resolve after leaving that underperforming environment.

The Eighth Mega-change: Changing Work

Greg O'Brien, CEO of the Americas at JLL, a leading commercial real estate services firm, succinctly captured the essence of our eighth mega-change when he told us this: "Driven primarily by the Digital Revolution, the nature of how, when and where employees work is undergoing a seismic shift."[20] The gig economy is expanding, more companies are offering flex time and work-from-home options, and some companies have gone to "hoteling," where employees don't get a fixed desk but rather get assigned on upon arrival each day. For what it's worth, he said all this *prior* to Covid-19 and the great realignment and blurring of home and work that ensued for many.

In their *Harvard Business Review* article "Thriving in the Gig Economy," Gianpiero Petriglieri, Susan Ashford, and Amy Wrzesniewski report that there are approximately 150,000 employees engaged in this type of part-time or independent contractor work in North America and Western Europe alone.[21] Guess which type of worker this is affecting most? The authors cite a McKinsey report that found that *knowledge workers* and *creative workers* are the fastest-growing segment of the freelance economy—in other words, the smart creatives that Google and others are in a global competition for.[22] They also happen to be the exact type of expensive workers for whom the building has the biggest impact on the bottom line. Enhance their performance and you will enhance your business performance.

So how can you protect these workers? In a presentation at Harvard in 2017, the head of the US National Institute for Occupational Safety and Health, John Howard, lamented the difficulties involved in studying this group of workers. How can we study and help workers if we don't even know where they are? The US Occupational Safety and Health Administration has weighed in too, indicating its concern that employers may not be meeting all of the Occupational Safety and Health Act requirements with temporary workers.[23] Essentially, some companies may be "off-shoring" some risk by not having workers do certain work on-site, or by only employing them temporarily. Who, then, is responsible for their work environment? The Occupational Safety and Health Administration says the temp agency and the company have joint responsibility. That's fair, but what about the many people working in the gig economy, who aren't operating through a temp agency? These questions are unresolved.

And what about relatively new approaches to work that are gaining traction, such as hoteling and open floor plans? Both can save companies massive amounts of money, as they allow them to maximize space use. It is certainly cheaper to allocate 100 square feet of office space per person than the more typical 250 square feet. There are also savings from only having to build and maintain one large area instead of paying for interior corridors and countless walls, doors, and air supply and air return components. And for many jobs, work can be done remotely from home or a coffee shop with only occasional and temporary space in the office needed.

But it comes with risks. If not done right, the experience can drive away talent or hamper productivity. A recent publication by our Harvard Business School colleague Ethan Bernstein and Stephen Turban has attracted much interest.[24] In their study of workers in a corporate headquarters transitioning to an open floor plan, they found a *decrease* in social interaction and an *increase* in email use, the opposite of what was predicted.

Research shows that one of the keys to making open floor plans successful is to provide a variety of work environments to match the variety of work styles of different individuals, and to account for the changing nature of their day-to-day work. Put more simply, some people prefer a quiet library space and some like the loud coffee shop environment, and some days you need time to concentrate alone and some days you need to collaborate. The building is your best friend in helping to create these environments—and these needs go well beyond aesthetics.

Businesses are not just sitting around watching these "seismic shifts" occurring. As one would expect, they are adapting in a strategic way. O'Brien at JLL has seen this firsthand, telling us, "This changing world of work is impacting real estate decisions. Businesses are responding with workplaces *centered on the human experience,* with employee health and well-being as a core component."[25]

The Ninth Mega-change: Changing Technology

To date much of the industry's description of its buildings relies on anecdotes and subjective surveys. Architects and developers can be the most visible, offering beautiful descriptions of their designs and personal stories about how the building makes people feel better. Here's one colorful quote from a developer that is featured in a Harvard Business School case study that John and his colleague wrote: "Fortune-Creating Vedic Architecture is the world's most ancient system of architecture. It is the knowledge of how to construct and design buildings in accord with Natural Law, in perfect harmony with all the laws of nature. Laws of nature are the universal principles of intelligence with nature that administer, with perfect order, everything from our human physiology to the whole galactic universe."[26]

Sounds good as a marketing pitch, and at some level it's hard to argue with—who wouldn't want to design a building "in perfect harmony with all the laws of nature"? But is it backed up by hard data? Is any of this quantifiable or verifiable?

The answer is yes. With the proliferation of low-cost environmental sensors and wearable technologies, both of which can objectively measure the performance of humans and the environment to a high degree of specificity, we can get to a point where we move from qualitative to quantitative. Buildings are now entering the "big data" era. Much like the field of genetics, which has rapidly transformed with the advent of new metagenomics tools that let us understand that our DNA is much more interesting than our discrete genes, the field of building science is changing thanks to new technological tools. New sensor technologies are making the invisible visible, allowing us to see, in real time, how buildings and the indoor environment fluctuate from minute to minute. It used to be the case that evaluations were done annually (if at all), at which time a course correction could be made. Now, this can be instantaneous, with environmental sensors communicating directly with the building management system to provide an autonomous reaction to changing conditions indoors.

The outstanding question is whether these new "smart" buildings will be smart *and* healthy. Big companies are betting that they will be both: "With technology as an accelerating and fundamental enabler," says Jim Whalen,

Chief Information & Technology Officer at Boston Properties, "the coming decade for buildings will be a data journey in proactively balancing health, comfort and energy consumption—an equation that occupants and guests expect to be solved and is now amplified more than ever."[27] A Chief *Technology* Officer talking about *health* is a market signal not to be ignored.

The Tenth Mega-change: Changing Values

The tenth mega-change is the uptick of focus on firms' environmental, social, and governance (ESG) performance by the investing world. The idea behind it is this: the investment decisions we make are not only economic decisions; they are also ultimately decisions about our values. If we invest in companies that do bad things (for example, tobacco companies or big industrial polluters), then we are contributing to the harm they cause. If we invest in companies that do good, then we are contributing to the benefits they bring. It's that simple.

Investors are demanding that their investments be put toward companies that do good. And we're not talking about individual investors with relatively modest savings and investments. As individual investors, we have chosen to account for ESG in our investment strategies, and maybe you have, too. And we'd all like to think that, collectively, our modest investment decisions are having an impact. That may or may not be true, but what is definitely true is that when the big investment players start talking ESG, companies sit up straight and start listening. We're talking about the big pension funds and state-run sovereign wealth funds—like Norway's sovereign wealth fund and the Japanese Government Pension Investment Fund—that control trillions of dollars of investment decisions globally. In an article in *Harvard Business Review,* Robert Eccles and Svetlana Klimenko reported that, as of 2018, 1,715 investment companies, representing $81.7 trillion in assets under management, have signaled a commitment to incorporate ESG into their investment decisions.[28]

That's why BlackRock, another gargantuan player in the investment world, with more than $6 trillion of assets under management, sent shockwaves through the investment community in 2018 when it sent a letter to all of the companies in its portfolio that basically said this: we want to know what your social purpose is.[29] Shortly thereafter, in 2019, nearly 200 CEOs who are part of the Business Roundtable, representing some of the biggest companies in the world—Apple, JPMorgan Chase, Walmart—got together to redefine the purpose of a corporation. The goal? The end of the era of shareholder primacy. The group wrote a statement that said that in addition to creating shareholder value, a corporation "must also invest in their employees, protect the environment and deal fairly and ethically with their suppliers."[30]

Wow. Imagine that. Rather than focus on the usual quarterly performance metrics, 200 of the leading business executives in the world decided it was time to focus on long-term ESG, too.

The movement is picking up momentum. Consider the follow-up op-ed in 2019 by Marc Benioff, the CEO of Salesforce (Saleforce's mission is "doing well by doing good"): "Every C.E.O. and every company must recognize that their responsibilities do not stop at the edge of the corporate campus. When we finally start focusing on stakeholder value as well as shareholder value, our companies will be more successful, our communities will be more equal, our societies will be more just and our planet will be healthier."[31]

What does this mean for buildings? We can learn a lot about what this means by first reflecting on the green building movement of the past 20 years. Building a "green" building used to be a leading edge and progressive approach; these days it is simply business as usual in many markets. (We discuss the green building movement in detail in Chapter 9.) The invisible hand demanded green buildings because they are a good investment. And the market responded. Well, now the invisible hand is signaling that it is time to invest in healthy people and healthy businesses. This has left the real estate market wondering, "What is the social performance of real estate assets?" It turns out that the positive social performance can be a line-item in your financial statement already. Better buildings come with a health co-benefit that can be quantified back to a financial value. We explore this in depth in Chapter 11, but the takeaway for now is this: being able to quantify the social performance means that this can be added as a line item in the financial statement, tying real estate decisions into impact-weighted investing. Buildings will undoubtedly be front and center in this era of changing values for business. Are you ready?

The Solution: Healthy Buildings

We opened this chapter by saying that the decisions we make today regarding our buildings will determine our collective health for generations to come. In the face of these 10 mega-changes, in which buildings are at the epicenter, this is undeniable. What is also undeniable is that Healthy Building strategies represent a solution to many of the challenges brought on by these mega-changes. And this gets us to the central premise and promise of this book: Healthy Buildings represent, without exaggeration, one of the greatest health—and business—opportunities ever.

CHAPTER THREE

Why Are We Ignoring the 90 Percent?

> In a modern society, total time outdoors is the most insignificant part of the day, often so small that it barely shows up in the total. The finding that emerges is that we are basically an indoor species.
>
> —W. R. OTT

"WHY ARE WE IGNORING the 90 percent?" This is the question with which Joe likes to start most presentations, to get the audience thinking about the importance of the buildings we live and work in for our health and the bottom line. There are two parts to his equation: time and money.

Let's start with time: studies have found that in North America and Europe we spend 90 percent of our time indoors.[1] It isn't a perfect formula—some jobs have you out and about more, and kids tend to spend a little more time outside than adults—but for most of the developed world, it is more accurate than you might think. (In some places and in some seasons, that 90 percent is actually an underestimate. Joe once quoted the 90 percent figure while presenting in Abu Dhabi and heard chuckles in the audience—in the United Arab Emirates, it can be more like 99.9 percent indoors for some people.)

To put this 90 percent figure in perspective, it's useful to think of what it means in terms of our own lives. By the time we hit 40, most of us have spent *36 years* indoors. Try it for yourself: take your age and multiply it by 0.9. That's your indoor age. If we are lucky enough to live to 80, most of us will have spent 72 years inside! We spend nearly all of our time indoors—so much so that Velux, a Danish company that specializes in skylights, cleverly branded us as "the Indoor Generation."[2] When we look at it this way, in terms of years, it becomes obvious and intuitive that our indoor environment would have a disproportionate impact on our health.

So let's break down that 90 percent and see where we spend our time. (Note that this section is based on research in the United States; the specific numbers will vary from country to country, but the basic facts don't change in most parts of the world.) We tend to split our time among our homes, our offices, our cars, and an assortment of other indoor places like restaurants, stores, gyms, and airplanes. For kids, this looks very different. By the time they graduate from high school, they will have spent 15,600 hours inside a school. (Incidentally, as Harvard professor Jack Spengler likes to point out, schools are one of two types of buildings where we *force* people to spend time indoors. The other is prison.)

Sometimes we think that all we really need to do to advance the Healthy Buildings movement is mention this "90 percent" fact. After hearing that, how could anyone conclude that the indoor environment does *not* impact our health? Heck, we spend a third of our lifetimes in one little box on this planet—our bedrooms!

Here's a weird but helpful way to think about all of this indoor time, courtesy of Rich Corsi, dean of engineering and computer science at Portland State University, an outstanding building scientist with a clever take to put this in perspective: "Americans spend more time inside buildings than some whale species spend underwater."[3]

What?! It's kind of hard to wrap your head around this—that whales spend more time on the surface than we, as land mammals, spend outdoors—but it's true. We would never go about trying to understand whales by studying the air they breathe when they are at the surface; we study them where they live, underwater.

And yet that's exactly what we do with humans. For all this time spent indoors, we tend to focus much more on outdoor air quality than on indoor air quality. Check any newspaper or news site on any given day and you are likely to see a story about the hazards of outdoor pollution, but how often do you see a story about building health?

Our regulatory system is also geared toward the outdoor environment, too. In the United States we have the Clean Air Act, which set National

Ambient Air Quality Standards establishing limits for the six so-called criteria air pollutants: particles ($PM_{2.5}$ and PM_{10}), lead, ozone, sulfur dioxide, nitrogen dioxide, and carbon monoxide.[4] Many other countries have similar standards for outdoor air pollution.[5]

But what about a "National *Indoor* Air Quality Standard"? No such thing. The only things akin to this in the United States are the legally enforceable limits set by the Occupational Health and Safety Administration (OSHA) for exposures to pollutants indoors. But before you start thinking that this means we're all set, you should know that very few scientists, if any, would argue that the OSHA limits are truly protective of health. Even OSHA admits this. From its own website: "OSHA recognizes that many of its permissible exposure limits (PELs) are outdated and inadequate for ensuring protection of worker health."[6] That's because OSHA was created in 1970, at which time "permissible" exposure limits were set for many chemicals based on a report from 1968, and those existing, unprotective limits were grandfathered into the new law. And as for *new* permissible exposure limits, OSHA has only created 16 since 1970. The last one was in 2006, for hexavalent chromium, a toxic heavy metal that is linked to respiratory cancer, asthma, skin irritation, and liver and kidney damage. This is not protecting us. And quite frankly, if you encounter any of these regulated hazards in an office building at the OSHA "permissible" limits, something is really amiss.

Why Are We Ignoring the 90 Percent? Part II—Money

The second 90 percent that we are ignoring is the true cost of operating our buildings: the people inside. Most companies spend as much as 90 percent of their budgets on human resources, a figure largely driven by their salaries and benefits—and as we'll see in Chapter 4, their productivity.

The 3-30-300™ rule of real estate was created and popularized by the global facilities management company JLL.[7] It's intended to show a company's relative per-square-foot costs across three factors—utilities, rent, and people. The rule goes like this: for every $3 a company spends on utilities like electricity and heat, it spends $30 on rent and $300 on payroll. This realization can make a focus on miserly utility spending, say, for ventilation, look pretty silly if the expensive assets—the humans—are not functioning at their best.

This rule of thumb can be corroborated through multiple sources. For example, the Building Owners and Managers Association International *2018 Office Experience Exchange Report* indicates average office gross rents of $30.35 per square foot for private-sector office buildings, average utility costs of $2.14, and total space per employee of 288 square feet (inclusive of corridors and lobbies).[8] As offices get smaller, a number like 250 square feet per person is becoming more typical. From a salary point of view, in Massachusetts, the gross wages for job titles like advertising sales agent, tax preparer, and computer user support specialist—the kind of people who would make up the bulk of typical office users—are about $65,000 per year, per US Bureau of Labor Statistics.[9] After including other costs paid by the employer, the fully loaded cost per employee would be about $75,000 per year. This divided by 250 square feet works out to $300 per square foot per year as the compensation component. While the 3-30-300 rule of thumb is a generalization and a simplification, the order of magnitude is appropriate and useful. Some professions pay much more. When higher salaries are considered, the impact of productivity becomes greater and the impact of energy savings becomes even smaller.

Just as we pointed out earlier in the context of how much time modern people spend indoors, once again the building industry discussion has missed the key 90 percent—the impact of the big expense, the people. Financial types tend to focus on the 10 percent: the rent and utilities spend. Don't get us wrong, these costs are critically important, but this has been the sole focus of the building sector for far too long. Think about it this way: the entire green building movement, with billions of square feet of office space registered globally, was largely built to chase a small subset of that 10 percent—the 1 percent costs of energy, waste, and water when looked at in terms of total cost of occupancy.

The reason for this focus on the 1 percent is largely that these are easy targets. They are easy in two ways. First, it's simple to calculate a return on investment based on energy savings. If you invest in an energy recovery ventilator, for example, an owner can quickly see that the upfront capital costs for the equipment will be recouped in a few years. It's a straightforward calculus—executives can literally do the math on the back of an envelope. (To be fair to those who do energy modeling, it's not exactly "easy" in the absolute sense; considerable sophistication and expertise go into building these models, but it is certainly more easily quantifiable than health.)

Second, it's easy to meter a building for energy, waste, and water. Take the building you're sitting in or that you own or manage, and we bet with just a little effort you could find out precisely how much energy it uses in a typical year. That's because it essentially only takes one or a handful of cheap sensors and a couple of utility bills to understand energy use in your building. That means that the return-on-investment calculus can be supported by hard data, which means it can be traded, financed, and guaranteed, as energy service companies do every day.

But now consider the people in your building, that crucial 90 percent of your costs. How do you "meter" the health of people in a building? Or even on one floor, or in one room? This is not a trivial undertaking. And because it's hard, it has been a barrier to advancement. We measure energy really well, so we manage it. But we've ignored the people side of the equation, and, as predicted, we've failed to manage this opportunity. This is something the two of us have been thinking about for some time, and in Chapter 10 we will give you tools for metering the health of people in a building.

We're certain you don't need this, but we'll do it anyway to drive the point home. That 90 percent represents a massive opportunity going forward. Said simply: *The indoor environment matters for health and wealth.*

Full stop. You can probably close this book right now.

The Indoor Environment's Three-Pronged Assault on Our Health

Now that we have the basics covered, we want to broadly explore the indoor environment and how it impacts our health. (We'll get into the important details of the financial impacts in Chapter 4.) In the remainder of this chapter, we will talk about what the science says, and then we'll give you a framework for how to think about minimizing your exposure and risk.

Indoor Assault 1: The Dirty Secret of Outdoor Air Pollution

We want to share something that will likely shock you: the majority of your exposure to *outdoor* air pollution can occur *indoors*. It's the dirty secret of outdoor air pollution.

Don't believe us? Let's do some basic math to prove it.

Let's say we are in Los Angeles, where the outdoor concentration of a major air pollutant called $PM_{2.5}$ periodically hits 20 µg/m³. For background, PM stands for "particulate matter" and is, essentially, airborne dust. The "2.5" stands for particulate matter that is 2.5 microns (µg) or smaller. The size of the particle matters because particles of this size penetrate to the deepest parts of our lungs, the alveoli, where gas exchange occurs. Larger particles are captured by nasal mucosa or the upper respiratory system, where we get rid of them when we blow our noses, or after our lungs bring them up to our mouth via a mucociliary escalator to be harmlessly swallowed. The notation "µg/m³" refers to the mass of $PM_{2.5}$, in micrograms, in a cubic meter of air (m³).

What most people don't fully recognize is the extent to which outdoor air pollution can penetrate inside a home or building.[10] As you might expect, there are a lot of factors that determine just how much outdoor air pollution enters a building, or what we call infiltration factors. Things like the year of construction and leakiness of the building, whether there are operable windows (and whether they open or not), and the type of ventilation and filtration system in your building are the obvious ones, but wind direction, pressure, and other meteorological factors also play a critical role. A review of different infiltration factors in homes shows that a stable median estimate for infiltration in homes is ~50 percent.[11] In commercial buildings, which typically use a MERV 8 filter, the $PM_{2.5}$ removal efficiency is about the same as this estimate. (MERV stands for Minimum Efficiency Reporting Value, a tool developed to evaluate filter performance.)

Using these facts, and for demonstration purposes, we can take the outdoor air pollution number in our Los Angeles example and estimate that, on average, the *indoor* concentration of *outdoor* air pollution is half of that, or 10 µg/m³.

Now we need to figure out how much air we breathe, because ultimately we want to know the total amount of air pollution that enters our body each day, what we call a "daily dose" in public health. We take about 1,000 breaths per hour, and that means we typically breathe in about 0.625 m³ of air per hour, or 15 m³ per day.[12]

Now that we know *how much* air pollution from outdoors is inside, and *how much* air we breathe each day, we need to know *where* we are breathing that air. For that, let's turn back to our "where we spend our time" data at

TABLE 3.1   The dirty secret of outdoor air pollution.

	Outdoor Air Pollution	Breathing Rate	Time Spent Indoors	Total *Outdoor* Air Pollution Breathed per Day
Outdoors	20 µg/m³	0.625 m³/hour	2.4 hours (10% of 24 hours)	30 µg/day
Indoors	10 µg/m³	0.625 m³/hour	21.6 hours (90% of 24 hours)	135 µg/day

the beginning of this chapter. Because we spend 90 percent of our time indoors, this means that we spend over 21 hours of each day inside and less than 3 hours outside. (For some of us it will be less than 1 hour.)

Now, the math is very straightforward. Multiply this out and you'll see the proof behind the counterintuitive fact that the majority of your exposure to *outdoor* air pollution occurs *indoors*. In this example, the amount of outdoor air pollution breathed indoors is four times as high as the amount breathed outdoors. Dirty secret no more!

Every single day, you can find a news story somewhere about how bad outdoor air pollution is in places like Mexico City, Seoul, New Delhi, or Beijing—and it truly can be bad, dangerously so. That news story is typically accompanied by a picture of a parent and young child walking hand in hand outside with dust masks over their noses and mouths, engulfed in a haze of air pollution. But we challenge you to find a news story that talks about what happens when that parent and child go inside. You will never find this "dirty secret of outdoor air pollution" in the news. We look forward to the day when a news story about outdoor air pollution is accompanied by a picture of a family sitting on the couch wearing dust masks. (A public health side note to readers: those paper dust masks don't actually work well against this type of pollution; they'd have to be on their couch wearing an N95 mask.)

Indoor Assault 2: Indoor Sources

In addition to outdoor air pollution penetrating indoors, we also have indoor sources of air pollution. In fact, a frequently referenced estimate from the Environmental Protection Agency says that indoor levels of some contaminants can be 3–5 times higher than outdoors. For many pollutants, the number can rise as high as 10 times or more.[13]

These higher indoor levels of pollutants happen because we tightened up our buildings to limit how much fresh air came in, in our efforts to save energy. Then, after we trapped ourselves in these airtight chambers and became appalled at the odors we started to notice, we started to use sprays, candles, and scented cleaners to make that stuffy indoor air smell just a bit better, without realizing that those sprays can create a whole other set of attacks on our health. And then we doused ourselves in underarm deodorant, cologne, perfume, and scented shampoo so we would smell good in all of these stuffy boxes we created. Not to mention all the building materials and furniture that off-gas pollutants into our sealed-box homes and offices.

There are all sorts of potential indoor contaminants, some of which you may be familiar with, and some of which you probably haven't thought much about. Perhaps the most well-known indoor contaminants are a class of chemicals called volatile organic compounds (VOCs). As the name suggests, they volatilize, or off-gas, from the products they are in. VOCs are a broad class of chemicals, emitting from paints (the VOCs evaporate, leaving the pigment behind), building materials, surface cleaners, dry-erase markers, furniture, and even dry cleaning. In your home, VOCs also come from laundry detergent, dryer sheets, couches, and soaps. One of the most notorious VOCs, formaldehyde, is a known carcinogen that is used to bind wood together in some cabinetry and laminate flooring that can off-gas into our homes and offices. A high-profile example was an issue with Lumber Liquidators in 2015, when they sold flooring imported from China that was emitting formaldehyde into homes. (In 2019 Lumber Liquidators settled a $33 million lawsuit for misleading investors on this issue.)[14]

Another set of infamous VOCs are the BTEX compounds (benzene, toluene, ethylbenzene, and xylene) that come from gasoline. We encounter BTEX when we breathe in our cars, and if your house has an attached garage, the BTEX chemicals can find their way into your home.[15] This also happens in offices and schools when the air intakes or open windows face streets or parking lots. Elevated levels of benzene (and formaldehyde and particles) can be found in schools during the end-of-day pickup time, when school buses are idling adjacent to the building.[16] If you live in a community ringed by traffic corridors—particularly if there is frequent congestion—BTEX chemicals are likely in your life as well.

And then there are the VOCs in personal care products. VOCs emit from perfume, lotion, hand sanitizer, shampoo, and deodorant. A study of high schoolers in Texas by Corsi and his collaborator Atila Novoselac found a VOC signal from one brand of teenage body spray, Axe, in all of the class-rooms studied![17]

VOCs also include things like limonene, a sweet-smelling chemical nat-urally found in oranges that is added to household cleaners to give them a pleasant scent. Sounds innocent enough, but limonene reacts with ozone to form formaldehyde and indoor particles.[18] So not only do we have outdoor sources of particles penetrating indoors, we have our own indoor particle sources, too.

Indoor particle generation doesn't end with VOCs reacting with ozone, though. We have other indoor sources. Smoking is an obvious one. Candles also emit a steady stream of particles indoors, as does cooking a stir-fry on the stovetop. A research team led by Delphine Farmer and Marina Vance, who simulated particle generation during cooking of a Thanksgiving dinner as part of their House Observations of Microbial and Environmental Chem-istry study, found that indoor particle concentrations can be 10 times higher than outdoor maximums.[19]

Our bodies are also part of this equation. Just like the Charles Schulz cartoon character, we are all our own little versions of Pigpen. (For those who don't know the *Peanuts* comic strip, Pigpen is one of the characters, a prototypical messy kid swirling in his own personal dust cloud.) As we walk, sit on couches, and fold laundry, we resuspend particles that have settled out on surfaces all around us, creating a cloud of invisible particles that surrounds us.

While the main problem comes from breathing them in, pollutants find their way into our bodies through what we eat (ingestion), through hand-to-mouth contact, and even through our skin (dermal absorption). Take this fascinating set of new studies by Gabriel Bekö, Charlie Weschler, and others at the Danish Technical University that asked, "Are we breathing through our skin?"[20] The researchers sat for several hours in a room with elevated concentrations of a common indoor pollutant. They were fully stripped down to their shorts, so nearly all of their skin was exposed, but they were breathing "clean" air through breathing hoods that covered their heads. Then they tested their urine to look for the chemical or its metabolites in their urine. A few days later they repeated the scenario, but this time with no hoods, to disentangle the relative importance of the different pathways that chemicals take to get into our bodies. Surprisingly, they found that dermal uptake of some plasticizers (and even nicotine) is as important as the inhalation route. In other words, we are definitely "breathing through our skin." They also found that clothing can act as a barrier, or as a source. If your clothes have these chemicals in them, they may trap them close to your skin, creating a constant source of exposure over an extended period of time. If the source is somewhere else in the room, a clean set of clothing can help limit that exposure, simply because less skin surface area is exposed.

When we think about buildings and exposure to pollutants, the conversation in the building world tends to revolve around indoor air quality, or IAQ. We see the shorthand IAQ now being used to mean basically any hazard in the indoor environment, and that needs to be corrected. A more apt term that some of us use as a replacement phrase for IAQ is IEQ: indoor environmental quality, which is a bit more encompassing. Here's why.

In addition to VOCs, there are a whole host of other indoor pollutants to think about and other routes of exposure beyond inhalation. There are things like the heavy metal lead, which can be found in old paint and old water pipes or tracked indoors on our shoes. Lead gets into our bodies through ingestion, as well as inhalation of suspended dust. Or as we saw with the preventable catastrophe in Flint, Michigan, it can get into our drinking water, which we then ingest. The term IAQ does not work here; it's too narrow.

There's also an insidious set of chemicals that are used in furniture, carpets, and other products that wreak havoc on our hormone system. (Fast-forward to Chapter 7 if you want more on toxic chemicals from products.) Some of these are what we call semivolatile organic compounds (SVOCs). You might think of SVOCs as multi-talented VOCs—they can be a gas or attach themselves to airborne dust, or they can be in dust on the floor, or on walls, or on our skin or clothing. The scientific term for what we are talking about here is "partitioning." Where these SVOCs reside in the air or dust depends on their physical and chemical properties and environmental conditions like temperature, humidity, and airborne dust levels.

The multi-talented SVOCs are also clever about how they can get into our bodies—through our lungs, through our skin, or through our GI tract as we transfer small quantities from the surface of our hands to our mouths when we eat with our fingers or touch our lips. We call that transfer of dust via hand-to-mouth contact "incidental ingestion." And would you ever guess that this "incidental" ingestion can be up to 100 milligrams of house dust per day?[21] It might make you think about the dust in your office or home a bit differently . . .

All this is to say that the products we use in our offices, homes, and cars, and the activities we perform there, all contribute to this indoor cocktail that our bodies are constantly absorbing and ingesting. The problem goes beyond IAQ. It's a question of total IEQ, of which air quality is a subset. And our building plays an important role in creating, or mitigating, these conditions.

Indoor Assault 3: What Is Your Neighbor Doing?

We've now talked about two assaults on your health—indoor sources of air pollution and outdoor air pollution coming inside, but indoor health hazards are actually a three-pronged assault for many people. It turns out that even if you do your best to stop outdoor pollutants from penetrating inside and you are super careful about what's happening inside your own space, there's another thing to be concerned about. And that "thing" is your neighbor.

Anyone living in a high-rise or multifamily dwelling is all too familiar with the experience of smelling your neighbor cooking. That's telling you that the air inside the building is communicating between apartments. You might want to ask what your neighbor is doing, because it turns out that in many buildings, on average, 9 percent of the air inside your apartment is coming from a neighbor.[22] (If you're in an older multiunit building, this can be as high as 35 percent.)

Take a good look at your neighbors next time you're in the elevator or stairwell and ask yourself, "Do I really want to be breathing their air?" If they smoke, you're smoking. If they have cats, you have cats. If they have laminate flooring that emits formaldehyde, you're getting a bit of that, too.

This issue of the neighbor isn't just one to think about for multitenant residential buildings. You can, and should, also think about the word "neighbor" for any space adjacent to yours that can impact your indoor environmental quality. So for a commercial office building, your neighbor could be the building next door. There are many instances of one building's ventilation exhaust feeding almost directly into the adjacent building's air intake. When a restaurant exhaust billows up into the adjacent building's air intake system, it's noticeable because of the distinct grease smell; if a renovation is happening next door, the smell of freshly cut wood may waft into your building. That's an indication of just how much air transfer there can be between buildings.

A common example of this problem can be found in buildings whose air intakes are right at street level or by a parking lot. Any idling car in the vicinity of that intake supplies a steady stream of pollutants that gets sucked up by the air intake and efficiently distributed around the building. Take a look around you the next time you walk by a set of buildings in the downtown district in your hometown—you'll find that, amazingly, the practice of having the air intake close to the street or in a parking lot is not that unusual.

Joe's favorite example comes from an office building where people noticed an occasional whiff of air that smelled like rats and mice. The owners hired a pest management firm and searched the building but couldn't find evidence of any pest infestation. After a thorough investigation inside their own space, they could not figure out why there was a rodent smell—until they started looking at their neighbor. It turns out that the air *intake* for their building was in an alley and the *exhaust* air for the adjacent building was feeding into that same alley. That second building happened to be the home of an animal toxicology program with many hundreds of . . . mice and rats.

Understanding Risk

With this three-pronged assault on our health, you might be forgiven for thinking that all is lost and you should spend the rest of your life living in the mountains or in a hermetically sealed bubble. That's not necessary. There is good news here: your building can actually help mitigate the impact of this assault.

To understand how these assaults may impact us and how our buildings can help requires that we understand the basic concepts of exposure science— that is, we need to know how the *concentration* of a pollutant, the *duration* of exposure, and the *frequency* of that exposure can combine to create an adverse health effect—and then figure out how to intervene to stop that from happening.

Take the example of the short, infrequent exposure to the BTEX chemicals while filling your car's gas tank. You can be exposed to a high concentration of benzene while you are filling up at a gas station, but the overall risk is quite low because the duration of that exposure is brief and infrequent. (If you have an electric vehicle, it's never. If you're a worker at the gas station, that's another story altogether.)

Using the Building to Break the Chain of Exposure and Risk

In public health, when we try to understand the different building factors that influence health, one useful model to consider is what we call the "conceptual model for exposure-related disease," first introduced to Joe by one of his doctoral thesis advisers, Michael McClean, now associate dean at Boston University School of Public Health. (We promise to make this part interesting, but we're academics, so we have to talk about conceptual models too. Bear with us; this will be useful to you.)

This model is great because it is really simple in concept and really useful in practice. As we work from left to right, we move from sources of pollutants in buildings to personal exposure to those pollutants to potential health effects, with a couple of steps in between. Why is this useful? *If we break the chain* before personal exposure, we have eliminated or at least minimized the risk of a downstream health effect. A key aspect of this model that's right in the name but needs to be highlighted anyway is that this model is about *exposure-related* disease, not other factors that influence health, such as genetics, which is why it's so relevant to our buildings. This is all about the environment. And that's why and how buildings can be used to break that chain.

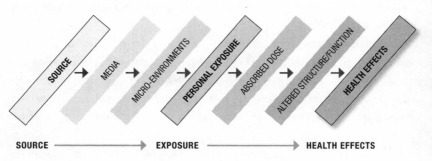

FIGURE 3.1   Conceptual model for exposure-related disease.

Let's go through an example and walk through the various subboxes to make it clear. And to make it interesting, we will use a high-profile case from a few years ago.

"What's Lurking in Your Countertop?"

In 2008 the *New York Times* published a story with the alarming title "What's Lurking in Your Countertop?" The story started a national scare by "breaking" the news that granite countertops can emit radon.[23] What's radon and why should I care, you ask? It's a radioactive gas that is commonly reported as the second leading cause of lung cancer.

Radon is a ubiquitous gas that forms from the natural decay of uranium from granite in the ground. It's a hazard that we think about mostly in relation to our homes, as it can permeate through the soil and find its way into our basements through cracks and fissures, and then to the rest of the house, where we spend our time. The *New York Times* story taught us that another source of radon indoors was granite in people's homes.

Radon is interesting from a risk perspective because, unlike for other environmental pollutants, we "accept" an unusually high level of risk for radon. To put numbers on this, whereas the Environmental Protection Agency regulates other pollutants to keep risk at 1 in 1 million (10^{-6} risk, spoken as "ten to the minus six"), the goal is to keep radon below 4 picocuries per liter of air in our homes, a level associated with a nearly 1-in-100 lifetime risk for lung cancer for nonsmokers (10^{-3}) and a truly astounding nearly 1-in-10 risk for smokers (10^{-2}). In short, we "accept" a much higher level of risk for radon than we do for other environmental pollutants.

Back to our conceptual model for exposure-related disease, where we'll use radon to explain the other boxes in the model. The source of radon, as that *New York Times* article pointed out, is the granite countertop. The next step in our model is environmental media, which is the annoying public health way of saying air, water, or dust. Radon is gas that is emitted from the granite countertop (the source) into indoor air (the environmental media).

Next up in the model is micro-environments. This is our way of saying *where* you encounter the pollutant. Most of the time granite is used in the kitchen in a home, but the gas migrates around the home, so the different micro-environments where you could encounter radon are places like the kitchen, your bedroom, the basement, and even outdoors. This is critical, because understanding risk requires you to understand the different micro-environments where we are exposed.

If we want to figure out the next part of our model, personal exposure, we need to match up where we spend our time (the micro-environments) with the concentration of the pollutant in air (the environmental media). It's all very logical if you step back from the terminology for a minute—a pollutant can't have a meaningful impact on our health if we rarely encounter it (the BTEX at the gas station, for example).

In the radon from countertops example, you would rightly anticipate that the personal exposure concentration would be highest in the kitchen, where the source is. But what are the frequency and duration of that exposure?

To figure that out, we go back to "where we spend our time" and learn that we spend about 2 percent of our time in the kitchen and 34 percent of our time in the bedroom. So while the radon concentration may be highest in the kitchen, the duration and frequency of exposure there may be quite low.

An interesting side note to get you thinking about the role of the building here: In homes with central air-conditioning, the radon concentrations aren't that much higher in the kitchen than in the rest of the house, even though that's where the countertops are. Why? It's because these central air-conditioning systems draw air from all areas of the home, cool it, and then redistribute that cooled air evenly around the home. Essentially, the central air-conditioning takes that higher radon concentration in kitchen, mixes it with air from everywhere else in the home, and then spreads that mixed air around the home. The result is lower radon in the kitchen but higher radon elsewhere. This makes that time in the bedroom more consequential from an overall exposure standpoint because the central air takes some of that radon from a place where we don't spend much time and delivers it to a place where we spend a good portion of our time. (This same thing happens often in commercial office buildings, hospitals, and schools, where the ventilation system sometimes acts as an efficient system for distributing a pollutant all around the building.)

Now that we understand the elements of the left side of this conceptual model, it's easy to target our interventions. If you wanted to lower your personal exposure to radon from countertops, you could remove the source, attempt to lower the pollutant concentration in the air (environmental media) through filtration or building-ventilation strategies, or reduce time spent in different micro-environments. In fact, you must use this model when thinking about a building-related exposure. All too often, the mere presence of a potential hazard is used to say there is risk, without understanding how that potential hazard migrates out of the source and creates exposure.

(The right-hand side of the model goes beyond the scope of this book, but it covers what happens to pollutants after they enter our body. In Toxicology 101, this is described by the handy acronym ADME [absorption, distribution, metabolism, and excretion]. The penultimate box in the model is altered structure and function, which is the way we highlight that it's not always enough to have an absorbed dose [the amount that enters the body]. Rather, that absorbed dose has to lead to some altered structure or function of one of our biological systems to have the potential to cause a health effect.)

So What's Lurking in Your Countertop? Nothing

We didn't think it was right to end this chapter without telling you what happened with the radon-in-granite-countertops scare. Joe led the team that was hired to work on this project after the *New York Times* story broke, performing a series of investigations with colleagues in his former consulting company.

The ensuing forensic investigations essentially followed this conceptual model of exposure-related disease, beginning with measuring the emissions, or flux, of radon from the countertops into air in the home. Sure enough, the testing confirmed that some granite countertops can emit radon.

And this is where the *New York Times* story failed. It essentially reported this finding, that radon comes out of granite countertops, without taking into account the rest of the conceptual model. Had the "expert" the reporter interviewed done so, he would have figured out what Joe and his team did when they simulated 1 million granite countertop purchases and installations, accounting for things like varying ventilation rates in homes and where people spend their time. They found that 99.99 percent of scenarios generated radon levels that were below what's typically found in US homes from radon coming from the ground. The formal conclusion in the peer-reviewed paper: "The findings presented in this study demonstrate that the probability of a granite countertop leading to a meaningful radon exposure in a home is negligible. These *de minimus* risks would be considered acceptable based on risk limits used by the EPA in regulating potential environmental hazards (10^{-5}–10^{-6})."[24]

So if you were thinking about ripping out your granite countertop, think again.

The Opportunity Moving Forward

So far we've aimed to make it clear that the buildings where you spend your time have an impact on your personal health. In Chapter 4 we will discuss *specific* steps you can take to optimize for health and performance, and we'll show you how this directly translates to bottom-line performance.

Here's what's at stake: In the preface we mentioned that $7 trillion in real estate institutional capital tracks green building performance, and as of this writing, there are over 100 green building councils around the world and millions of square footage of office space certified as green. In this chapter we showed the massive opportunity in front of us when we begin to shift from thinking about green buildings (which largely focuses on the 1 percent of costs associated with energy, waste, and water) to thinking about Healthy Buildings (which focuses on the 90 percent of the costs of our buildings—the people). John Mandyck, the former chief sustainability officer at United Technologies and now CEO of Urban Green Council, has put the challenge succinctly: "Can you imagine how much farther and faster we can go when we start to focus on health?"[25]

In Chapter 4, we will do exactly that—we will show the quickest, easiest way to unlock the power of buildings to drive health and wealth.

CHAPTER FOUR

Putting the Building to Work for You

> I am persuaded that no common air from without is so unwhole-
> some as the air within a close room that has been often breathed
> and not changed.
>
> —BENJAMIN FRANKLIN

BUSINESSES ARE IN A GLOBAL competition for talent. How do you attract the best and brightest, and how do you retain them? Then, once you've hired them, how do you give them the opportunity to perform their best? It turns out that your building has a role to play in all of this, acting as a differentiator for recruitment and retention and optimizing employee productivity. From an individual point of view, what environment helps you be "the best you"?

In Chapter 3 we saw that time spent indoors is a big driver of health, and that the human capital in buildings is the biggest driver of business costs. We argue, then, that the person who manages your building has a bigger impact on your health than your doctor. And this person just may have as big an impact on your bottom line as your CFO.

The natural follow-on question is, What specific actions can we perform to start putting our building to work for us? *The answer is literally right under our noses.*

Tomes have been written with tips and tricks for improving worker productivity—standing meetings, work-from-home strategies, employee bonuses, and engagement programs, to name just a few. What's always missing from this list is the easiest one: the impact of air quality on worker productivity.

Let's look at one critical factor: the amount of fresh air being supplied to people. In many of the hundreds of forensic investigations of sick buildings that Joe was involved in, the root cause of the problem could be traced to inadequate ventilation. In fact, in 100 percent of those cases, even if ventilation wasn't the root cause, it had to be fully understood to solve the problem.

When we talk about ventilation, we are talking about the amount of fresh air brought into a building—outdoor air ventilation. Decades of research have shown that ventilation is a key determinant of health indoors. But we didn't really need decades of research to know this when we've known it anecdotally for hundreds of years. As Benjamin Franklin once professed, "I considered fresh air an enemy and closed with extreme care every crevice in the room I inhabited. Experience has convinced me of my error. I am persuaded that no common air from without is so unwholesome as the air within a close room that has been often breathed and not changed."[1]

Ventilation and Cognitive Function: The COGfx Study

Take recent work by Joe's Healthy Buildings research team that examined the effect of air quality on cognitive function, a useful indicator of productivity in knowledge workers. In the first COGfx Study, a study that was simple in concept but sophisticated in design, we enrolled office workers to spend six days over two weeks with us in a highly controlled, simulated office environment at the Syracuse Center of Excellence. We asked them to show up at this office space instead of their regular offices and spend their nine-to-five day with us, doing their normal work routines.[2]

What is unique and interesting about this study is that each day, without their knowing, we changed the air quality in that office space in subtle ways. This was very much akin to an animal lab study in which different things are injected into the cage, except this time we did it with humans. (Lest you be concerned with this "humans as guinea pigs" study, this testing was governed by Harvard's Institutional Review Board, which makes sure study participants are protected in public health research. All of our protocols were reviewed and approved by the board, and at no time was anyone placed in a condition that would even remotely be considered dangerous to his or her health.)

At the end of each day, we administered a cognitive function test while the subjects were still in their offices. This test was developed by Usha Satish and her colleagues at the State University of New York Upstate Medical Center and has been used on thousands of participants. It allowed us to quantify performance across nine cognitive function domains. We're pretty sure you'll agree that this is a list of performance skills that are relevant and valued in knowledge workers:

1. Basic activity level
2. Applied activity level
3. Focused activity level
4. Task orientation
5. Crisis response
6. Information seeking
7. Information usage
8. Breadth of approach
9. Strategy

Each person was compared with him- or herself—we didn't really care if John scored higher than Joe. We just cared how people scored against their own baselines. Importantly, this was what we call a double-blind study: the participants didn't know how we changed the air in the room each day, and the data analysts weren't aware, either.

So what did we change about the air each day? We tested the impact of three different factors on cognitive function performance: ventilation, volatile organic compounds (VOCs), and carbon dioxide. To be clear, we didn't test exotic conditions or weird VOCs—we tested levels of these three factors that are or can be encountered in nearly every building. For ventilation, we tested what would happen if we doubled the ventilation rate from the current standard.

When workers were in an optimized indoor environment ("green+" in this figure), meaning high ventilation rates, low VOCs, and low carbon dioxide, we found a dramatic improvement in higher-order cognitive function across all nine cognitive function domains.

Think about that for one second—simply increasing the amount of air brought into an office, something nearly every office can easily do, had a quantifiable benefit to higher-order cognitive function in knowledge workers. When John Mandyck, the CEO of Urban Green Council, saw these results,

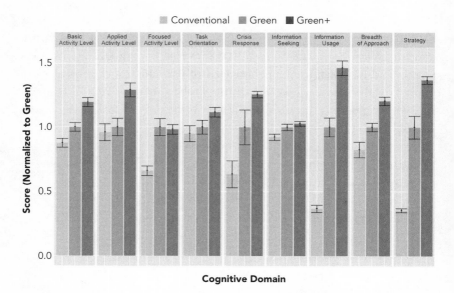

FIGURE 4.1 Cognitive function test scores for nine domains across three building conditions. Reformatted from Allen et al., "Associations of Cognitive Function Scores with Carbon Dioxide," *Environmental Health Perspectives* 124, no. 6 (2016): 805–812, figure 1.

he immediately grasped their economic significance. He recognized that, unlike rolling out a new enterprise-wide system to improve worker performance, where it can take a year or more to see results once everyone is trained, there was no learning curve for the COGfx Study—all you had to do was breathe. Even better, from a practical standpoint, VOCs and carbon dioxide can largely be controlled in a building through higher ventilation rates.

These results aren't really all that surprising. Just like Ben Franklin, we have all experienced a poorly performing indoor environment. Ever get on an airplane in the middle of the day only to fall asleep immediately, even though you're not tired? That's because most planes do not have their ventilation system on at the gate. Ever feel sleepy in a stuffy conference room? Many are underventilated. Your mind focuses on the lack of air, the odors, the temperature, and . . . the clock. When that door finally opens, you can feel the life breathe back into the room.

All we did in our study was quantify the impact of what we have all experienced. Sometimes we think we are really just academics in the field of common sense. Casinos figured this out a long time ago, pumping in extra fresh air and keeping the temperature cool to keep you awake and at the gaming tables and slot machines longer.

The results of the COGfx Study were published in 2015 and immediately grabbed the attention of the commercial real estate press. The *Wall Street Journal* headline proclaimed, "Scientists Probe Indoor Spaces for Clues to Better Health," and the *New York Times* celebrated as "A Greener, More Healthful Place to Work." Even *National Geographic*, which traditionally focuses on the outdoor environment, ran a piece called "5 Surprising Ways Buildings Can Improve Our Health." COGfx also landed on the cover of *Newsweek*, which went with a scare-tactic title—"Your Office Air Is Killing You"—complete with a picture of the grim reaper at the water cooler. We mention this not to brag about the reach of our research but rather to illustrate just how much the concept of objective measures of a Healthy Building is starting to permeate into the mainstream. These ideas are no longer exclusively confined to academic circles.

All of this attention from the commercial real estate sector inspired Joe to write an article for *Harvard Business Review* that quickly summarized the results of the study and identified the economic potential of Healthy Buildings ("Stale Office Air Is Making You Less Productive").[3] The goal was to engage and educate business executives on the link between indoor air and cognitive performance. The COGfx research is now a series of studies; the latest was a global study of over 300 office workers in six countries tested for an entire year. Real-time air quality sensors were placed at every desk, and workers were periodically prompted to complete short cognitive function tests right at their desks through an app on their phones. With this unprecedented insight into immediate affects, we saw, yes, a link between office air quality and cognitive function. That was expected at this point. But the data added more to the body of evidence: it revealed a linear relationship between ventilation and cognitive function, even in buildings with good air quality. In other words, there was no threshold of benefit to higher ventilation: even people in buildings with "good" air quality performed better with "great" air quality. But in truth, the results weren't all that surprising to us. That's because over the past 30 years, study after study has shown that the amount of fresh outdoor air brought inside—what's known as ventilation—is a critical determinant of health. This steady stream of research has demonstrated that enhanced ventilation has been shown to reduce sick building syndrome, cut absenteeism, and even reduce infectious disease transmission.[4]

Acceptable Is Not Acceptable

What exactly is ventilation, and if the public health benefits are so clear, why are buildings chronically underventilated? The history is worth exploring here because it tells us how we got to this point and what we can do going forward. The invention of air-conditioning by Willis Carrier in 1902 forever altered how, when, and where we can work. The modern mechanical system governs how fresh air is brought into a building, how it is filtered for outdoor pollutants, how it is dehumidified (or humidified), how it is thermally conditioned, and how it is delivered to occupants. Most importantly, it governs not just how outdoor air is brought indoors but also how *much* outdoor air is brought in.

Some readers may be aware that there are industry-accepted guidelines as to how much outdoor air should be brought into a building. This is determined by a standard-setting body called the American Society of Heating, Refrigerating and Air-Conditioning Engineers (ASHRAE, pronounced "ash-ray"). But even those who know a lot about these standards seldom recognize that they have a critical flaw.

The ASHRAE standard is called "Ventilation for Acceptable Indoor Air Quality."[5] The key word here is "acceptable." This is not a standard for "healthy" indoor air quality, nor is it a standard for "optimal" air quality. It is a bare-minimum standard, by name and definition. (ASHRAE is quick to acknowledge that it's a minimum standard.)

Think about this for a minute. We have learned that ventilation is critical for health and productivity, yet nearly every indoor space where you spend your day—from multifamily homes to offices to restaurants and schools—is guided by this *minimum* standard for ventilation, despite study after study showing the benefits of increasing ventilation above this minimum. This standard of "acceptable" is not acceptable!

The False Choice of "Energy versus Health"

How did we get to this point? Well, it's been a 100-year odyssey. The "acceptable" ventilation rate has fluctuated up and down over the past few decades, trying to find a balance between energy conservation and comfort—in other words, between tightening up our buildings and increasing the amount of fresh air coming in. ASHRAE itself can't seem to make up its mind on this point. For the past 30 years it's been involved in an internal debate about whether it is a "health-based" standard, or whether it's just about energy (its latest opinion is that yes, it's health based).

For decades, ASHRAE has published "comfort tables" (or to be more technically accurate, psychrometric charts). The standard offered by these tables was created before it was easy to measure many of the components of air that we can look at today, such as particulates, metals, or gases like CO_2. The intent was simply to target set points for temperature and humidity and to help engineers size and specify equipment that could deliver that temperature and humidity on most days of the year, with the exception of a few very hot or very cold days.

For the first hundred years or so of mechanical air-conditioning, this scale was well aligned with what humans perceived on their own: "I'm hot (or cold)," "It's too humid (or too dry)." But our ability to assess what's in the air we breathe, and to measure its impact beyond "I'm not shivering" or "I'm not perspiring," has moved on as sensors and data management have advanced. For the most part, buildings have not moved on with that capability. They should.

We have this 100-year journey of ventilation rates fluctuating up and down, trading off health for energy. Where are we now? ASHRAE has settled on a recommended ventilation rate for commercial buildings of approximately 20 cubic feet per minute per person (cfm / person). In our COGfx Study we tested performance at 20 cfm / person and 40 cfm / person, and we saw significant benefits in cognitive ability across a wide range of functions from doubling the standard rate of ventilation.

Here's another big problem with the current ASHRAE standard for acceptable indoor air quality. Nearly every building is *designed* to this minimum, because that is the standard. But it's not uncommon to find that many buildings are not *operating* at the minimum standard. So not only is this a standard aiming for a mere acceptable level of indoor air quality, it is only a *design* standard, not an *operating* standard. All too often a building may be meeting this minimum acceptable level when the doors open on day 1, but by day 2, no one is verifying performance.

To put some numbers on this, consider the use of CO_2 as a proxy for ventilation. (Indoor CO_2 levels come largely from human respiration.) If you're meeting the minimum ASHRAE standard, you should expect CO_2 levels in an office to be less than 1,000 parts per million (ppm). It turns out that in many offices, CO_2 levels creep above this threshold frequently. In one study of 100 nonproblem buildings in the United States, the 95th percentile CO_2 concentration was about 1,500 ppm.[6] This means that many buildings were above 1,000 ppm, and 5 percent of buildings were grossly missing the minimum ventilation standard—by a full 50 percent.

Low ventilation rates are not solely a problem in office buildings. It is common to find CO_2 levels above 1,500 ppm or higher in schools.[7] To put some specifics on this, Mark Mendell and colleagues at Lawrence Berkeley National Laboratory studied 162 classrooms across 28 elementary schools in California and found that the average CO_2 concentration was above 1,500 ppm.[8] (In one district the average was closer to 2,500 ppm.) California is not an aberration. In Texas, one in five schools tested had peak CO_2 concentrations above 3,000 ppm.[9] These are just two examples of dozens of studies showing similar findings. Taken together, the full body of scientific evidence paints a problematic picture—up to 90 percent of schools in the United States are not meeting the *minimum* ventilation standards.

The same low ventilation can be found in your bedroom at night, your car, and most airplanes. Side note on airplanes (another indoor environment that also follows design-based, not performance-based, guidance on ventilation rates from ASHRAE): Joe and colleagues studied airplane cabin air quality as part of an FAA-funded Center of Excellence. Our measurements of CO_2 in airplanes show that it can reach as high as 2,500 ppm during boarding (1,500 ppm was typical at cruising altitude).[10] This may help explain why you may find yourself falling asleep after boarding, even in the middle of the day. Perhaps more interesting, after seeing the results of the COGfx Study, Joe and his team did a similar study but this time with airplane pilots and flight simulators. In that study, varying levels of CO_2 were injected into the cockpit of a flight simulator while active commercial airline pilots were challenged with 21 simulated advanced flight maneuvers, like avoiding a midair collision, aborting a takeoff after an engine fire, or landing the plane with one engine inoperative. The result: pilots were more likely to fail these advanced maneuvers when CO_2 concentrations were elevated in the cockpit.[11]

In short, all day long we find ourselves in environments that fail to meet even minimum acceptable ventilation rates, and the scientific evidence shows that this is impacting our performance.

TABLE 4.1   Pro forma income statement for Health & Wealth, Inc. (H&W).

BASELINE COMPANY ASSUMPTIONS

Number of Employees	40
Average Salary	$75,000
Payroll as Percentage of Revenue	50%

	Baseline	Percentage of Revenue
Revenue	$6,000,000	
Payroll	$(3,000,000)	50.0
Rent	$(300,000)	5.0
Utilities	$(30,000)	0.5
Other Expenses	$(1,000,000)	16.7
Net Income before Taxes	$1,670,000	27.8
Taxes (30%)	$501,000	8.4
Net Income after Taxes	**$1,169,000**	19.5

The Impacts of Higher Ventilation on Your Income Statement

We want to show you what the science on ventilation rates interlaced with measurable cognition results (notably focus, information usage, and strategy) all means for your business. To do that, let's take a hypothetical 40-person consulting company, Health and Wealth, Inc. (H&W). Here is an illustrative pro forma income statement.

At H&W, as in many knowledge worker firms, payroll accounts for more than two-thirds of the firm's total expenses. Returning to the 3-30-300 rule of thumb from Chapter 3, payroll is $3,000,000 per year; rent is $300,000 per year; and energy and utilities, at $30,000 per year, are a tiny item on the income statement at 0.5 percent. (Here, revenue is modeled at two times payroll, although some service firms enjoy higher ratios.)

In the first era of green buildings, many companies focused most of their attention on energy efficiency. While that is a worthy quest, energy efficiency does not really contribute much to the bottom line of a typical office tenant.

For example, what if the utility cost (mostly energy) at H&W is cut by a quite substantial 20 percent, as in our next example?

TABLE 4.2   Pro forma income statement for H&W with energy savings.

BASELINE COMPANY ASSUMPTIONS

Number of Employees	40
Average Salary	$75,000
Payroll as % of Revenue	50%

(X) WHAT IF?	IMPACT
OpEx Cost (energy)	−20%

	Baseline	*(X)* ITEMIZED IMPACTS OF HEALTHY BUILDING DECISIONS OpEx Impacts		Baseline + Energy Savings
Revenue	$6,000,000			$6,000,000
Payroll	$(3,000,000)			$(3,000,000)
Rent	$(300,000)			$(300,000)
Utilities	$(30,000)	−20%	$6,000	$(24,000)
Other Expenses	$(1,000,000)			$(1,000,000)
Net Income before Taxes	$1,670,000			$1,676,000
Taxes (30%)	$501,000			$502,800
Net Income after Taxes	$1,169,000			$1,173,200
Change				0.36%

This changes the *bottom* line by less than half of one percent. No wonder many tenants don't want to go through a lot of effort to seek these relatively minor savings when there are so many other things for office managers to worry about.

Now let's look at some of the payroll-related items. After all, this is the largest single cost by far.

Starting with the cost side, suppose that these employees were a little healthier thanks to higher ventilation rates. If so there should be fewer sick days. But are we making this up? Is there evidence for such an effect?

It turns out that, yes, there is. This brings us to the work of Don Milton, professor of environmental health at the University of Maryland, who showed that healthier buildings were associated with 1.6 fewer days of absenteeism

TABLE 4.3   Pro forma income statement for H&W with absenteeism savings.

BASELINE COMPANY ASSUMPTIONS

Number of Employees	40
Average Salary	$75,000
Payroll as % of Revenue	50%

(X) WHAT IF?	IMPACT
Payroll Effect: Health*	–1%

Bolded item is new in this model

	Baseline	*(X)* ITEMIZED IMPACTS OF HEALTHY BUILDING DECISIONS		Baseline + Healthy Buildings
		OpEx Impacts	Payroll Effect: Health	
Revenue	$6,000,000			$6,000,000
Payroll	$(3,000,000)	–1%	$30,000	$(2,970,000)
Rent	$(300,000)			$(300,000)
Utilities	$(30,000)			$(30,000)
Other Expenses	$(1,000,000)			$(1,000,000)
Net Income before Taxes	$1,670,000			$1,700,000
Taxes (30%)	$501,000			$510,000
Net Income after Taxes	$1,169,000			$1,190,000
Change				1.8%

due to sickness each year.[12] What constituted a "healthy building" in that study? You guessed it—higher ventilation rates.

One way to look at this is in the context of about 250 workdays per year (50 weeks × 5 days per week = 250 days). Rounding up, if a worker has 2 fewer sick days, this is just about 1 percent of his or her total workdays for the year. Take a look at the income statement now with the added "Payroll Effect: Health," which uses this 1 percent figure to help understand what this could mean to our hypothetical company, H&W.

Even with this conservative estimate, the cost savings from avoided sick days already equals the total utility spend. And since the savings flow through to the bottom line, net income increases by almost 2 percent.

Now suppose that the documented improvements in thinking—notably in measurable cognitive domains like focused activity, information usage, and strategy—led to true revenue increases from more billable hours, more client assignments, and more engagements sold. This would be material for any business. In addition to the impact on cognitive function, others have conducted studies that estimate productivity gains of anywhere from 2 to 10 percent with better indoor air quality.[13]

To return to our example, let's take the low end and assume that just 2 percent of this added impact flows to the top line as a "productivity boost."

TABLE 4.4   Pro forma income statement for H&W with productivity boost.

BASELINE COMPANY ASSUMPTIONS

Number of Employees	40
Average Salary	$75,000
Payroll as % of Revenue	50%

(X) WHAT IF?	IMPACT
Payroll Effect: Health	−1%
Revenue Effect: Productivity Boost*	**2%**

*Bolded item is new in this model

(X) ITEMIZED IMPACTS OF HEALTHY BUILDING DECISIONS

	Baseline	OpEx Impacts	Payroll Effect: Health		Productivity Boost: Health		Baseline + Healthy Buildings
Revenue	$6,000,000				2%	$120,000	$6,120,000
Payroll	$(3,000,000)		−1%	$30,000			$(2,970,000)
Rent	$(300,000)						$(300,000)
Utilities	$(30,000)						$(30,000)
Other Expenses	$(1,000,000)						$(1,000,000)
Net Income before Taxes	$1,670,000						$1,820,000
Taxes (30%)	$501,000						$546,000
Net Income after Taxes	$1,169,000						$1,274,000
Change							*9.0%*

Improving this one aspect of a Healthy Building—ventilation—becomes a very substantial business advantage, increasing the bottom line by 9 percent.

Let's take this a step further. To ward off any energy conservation critics, a proper analysis would have to project a net increase in energy usage to achieve these gains. But what would a doubling of the ventilation rate cost in terms of energy? Research led by Joe's Healthy Buildings program modeled the energy costs from increasing the ventilation rate from 20 cfm / person to 40 cfm / person in buildings across the continental United States to cover all climate zones and common building types. The worst-case scenarios, in

TABLE 4.5   Pro forma income statement for HB—all costs and benefits included.

BASELINE COMPANY ASSUMPTIONS

Number of Employees	40
Average Salary	$75,000
Payroll as % of Revenue	50%

(X) WHAT IF?	IMPACT
OpEx Cost (energy)*	**$40/person/yr**
Payroll Effect: Health	–1%
Revenue Effect: Productivity Boost	2%

Bolded item is new in this model

(X) ITEMIZED IMPACTS OF HEALTHY BUILDING DECISIONS

	Baseline	OpEx Impacts	Payroll Effect: Health		Productivity Boost: Health		Baseline + Healthy Buildings
Revenue	$6,000,000				2%	$120,000	$6,120,000
Payroll	$(3,000,000)		–1%	$30,000			$(2,970,000)
Rent	$(300,000)						$(300,000)
Utilities	$(30,000)	$(1,600)					$(31,600)
Other Expenses	$(1,000,000)						$(1,000,000)
Net Income before Taxes	$1,670,000						$1,818,400
Taxes (30%)	$501,000						$545,520
Net Income after Taxes	$1,169,000						$1,272,880
Change							8.9%

the hottest or coldest climates, were $40 per person per year. (When a building uses energy-efficient technologies, that cost is usually driven down to single dollars per person per year.)[14]

Suppose we assume that no energy efficiency measures were taken and that H&W increased the ventilation rate to 40 cfm / person and incurred that cost of $40 per person per year. This would cost it $1,600 per year in

TABLE 4.6   Pro forma income statement for H&W with benefits distributed to multiple parties.

BASELINE COMPANY ASSUMPTIONS

Number of Employees	40
Average Salary	$75,000
Payroll as % of Revenue	50%

(X) WHAT IF?	IMPACT
OpEx Cost (energy)	$40/person/yr
Payroll Effect: Health	−1%
Revenue Effect: Productivity Boost	2%
Rent Increase*	**10%**

*Bolded item is new in this model

(X) ITEMIZED IMPACTS OF HEALTHY BUILDING DECISIONS

	Baseline	Rent/OpEx Impacts		Payroll Effect: Health		Productivity Boost: Health		Baseline + Healthy Buildings
Revenue	$6,000,000					2%	$120,000	$6,120,000
Payroll	$(3,000,000)			−1%	$30,000			$(2,970,000)
Rent	$(300,000)	10%	$(30,000)					$(330,000)
Utilities	$(30,000)		$(1,600)					$(31,600)
Other Expenses	$(1,000,000)							$(1,000,000)
Net Income before Taxes	$1,670,000							$1,788,400
Taxes (30%)	$501,000							$536,520
Net Income after Taxes	$1,169,000							$1,251,880
Change								*7.1%*

additional operating expenses (OpEx). The net impact of higher ventilation rates would still be highly positive to the tenant occupier company.

Finally, there is room in this equation for gain sharing. Suppose the economic gains in this model were shared with the landlord. Sharing gains with the landlord can help to align the parties around first cost of construction, who pays for what in the tenant space, and allocation of operating costs.

TABLE 4.7 Pro forma income statement for H&W with full productivity and health boosts.

BASELINE COMPANY ASSUMPTIONS

Number of Employees	40
Average Salary	$75,000
Payroll as % of Revenue	50%

(X) WHAT IF?	IMPACT
OpEx Cost (energy)	$40/person/yr
Payroll Effect: Health	−1%
Revenue Effect: Productivity Boost*	**3%**
Rent increase	10%

Bolded item is new in this model

(X) ITEMIZED IMPACTS OF HEALTHY BUILDING DECISIONS

	Baseline	Rent/OpEx Impacts		Payroll Effect: Health		Productivity Boost: Health		Baseline + Healthy Buildings
Revenue	$6,000,000					3%	$180,000	$6,180,000
Payroll	$(3,000,000)			−1%	$30,000			$(2,970,000)
Rent	$(300,000)	10%	$(30,000)					$(330,000)
Utilities	$(30,000)		$(1,600)					$(31,600)
Other Expenses	$(1,000,000)							$(1,000,000)
Net Income before Taxes	$1,670,000							$1,848,400
Taxes (30%)	$501,000							$554,520
Net Income after Taxes	$1,169,000							$1,293,880
Change								10.7%

In this example, the revenue gains from productivity, the cost savings from health, and the net added energy costs could allow the landlord to ask for a 10 percent *increase* in rent—and still leave room for this company to add more than $75,000 to its bottom line. That's a lot for a firm whose profit was just over $1.1 million at the start. This illustration allows for gain sharing with the landlord—the kind of win-win alignment that helps to solve the "healthy real estate investing paradox" mentioned in Chapter 1. Of course, some firms might instead want to share the added revenue with employees through a bonus or profit-sharing system. (In Chapter 5 we will dive deeper into the issue of split incentives in real estate and why this negotiated distribution of value is so thorny—and so important.)

Now, recall that the scientific evidence suggests that higher ventilation is associated with gains ranging from 2 to 10 percent. What if we were to project a more optimistic 3 percent productivity and health realization?

This is a shocking result. Why? Because it shows that bottom-line net income for this brainpower-dependent consulting firm *increases* more than 10 percent—from $1,169,000 to $1,293,880—even while paying more for energy (mostly ventilation) and paying the landlord more for rent (since the space was designed and engineered for healthy air, the landlord can attract higher-value tenants and charge a premium for the added benefits).

This broad "what if" kind of analysis is common in the real estate industry. Landlords frequently need to decide on other improvements like changing the carpet or replacing the roof or putting marble in the lobby or a daycare center in the common area or electrical vehicle chargers in the garage. These one-time capital investments are almost never directly traceable to a specific increase in rental rates, but tenants quickly get a sense of the expected price range for features like windows, finishes, noise, and more that contribute to the overall appeal of a lease. Landlords and investors go by these calculations in deciding what to put in and what to leave out. We are proposing that quantification of the benefits of a Healthy Building should become a critical part of landlord and tenant math.

The figures in the pro forma are intuitively logical. But readers may think, "Come on, how will revenue go up by that much?" What if objective measures of health and well-being beyond ventilation could be proved and implemented? In the rest of this book, we'll argue that they can, even in the rough-and-tumble world of commercial real estate.

CHAPTER FIVE

Creating and Capturing Value

> Organizing is a process; an organization is the result of that process.
>
> —ELINOR OSTROM

IF THE OPPORTUNITY IS SO GREAT even for just one factor, ventilation, why hasn't the market attempted to capture the value of Healthy Buildings? We think the answer has to do with split incentives—"Why would I incur higher energy costs, as landlord, if the productivity benefits go to you, the tenant?" This disconnect exists in commercial office buildings, in public buildings like schools and city halls, and even in institutional settings like universities, hospitals, and multifamily residential buildings. We think it can and should be easily overcome, but there are obstacles to surmount.

To really understand how this works, it's worth stepping back for a minute to look at all of the stakeholders involved in the decision-making process around buildings. The motivations are complex, but the lack of market response comes down to four factors: *information, inertia, incumbents,* and *incentives.*

The information component is straightforward: people just don't know how large the beneficial impact of healthy indoor air really is. That's what we have covered so far, and we will cover throughout this book. Here is a look at the other hurdles.

Inertia: A Complex, Trillion-Dollar Market

The real estate and construction industry is one of the largest business sectors and investment classes in the world. New construction globally is almost $9 trillion per year and rising; for reference, this is equal to about half the size of the gross domestic product of the United States.[1] Homes, commercial buildings, airports, roads, power plants, and more represent hundreds of trillions of dollars in assets. For most people who own a home, it's their largest asset. Yet the industry is also very complex. Scores of entities are involved in almost every building project—ranging from permit givers to excavators to elevator installers to painters to mortgage brokers. And unlike the output of any other industry, the product of construction cannot be easily moved. Buildings are a lot harder to ship than cars or phones.

Additionally, these are very big-ticket items. The average sale price of a home in the United States is almost $400,000 (the median is about $190,000), according to the Federal Reserve Bank of St. Louis.[2] But it's not unusual to see an office tower or airport or power plant costing more than a *billion* dollars. Most products in the built environment are unique, the result of custom designs for clients in nonhomogeneous locations. Unlike starter homes or fast-food restaurants or warehouses, only a small percentage of office towers or major construction projects are carbon copies of other buildings. Finally, homes and buildings last a long time, so the fleet does not get "retired" in favor of new models as with mobile phones, cars, or computers. The average age of an owner-occupied house in the United States is 37 years, with half built before 1980.[3]

These factors contribute to an industry that is capital intensive, fragmented (that is, many smaller players), and risk averse. These are characteristics of a system that will be hard to budge, as there is inertia among the players. To unpack this phenomenon, it's useful to segment the real estate and construction market across several key variables in order to identify the right action for each.

First, consider geography. Is the structure located in the developed world or emerging world? In a city or in a rural area? In a jurisdiction with clear land title and laws or without them? In a dense and dirty city or an open and clean setting? These factors all contribute to thinking about an investment in Healthy Buildings.

Second, consider usage type. Most of the construction in the world is single-family housing. Five other common asset classes are multifamily housing, office, retail, hospitality, and industrial (warehouses). Many government and nonprofit organizations own offices and housing; they might also own hospitals, classrooms, libraries, courthouses, laboratories, prisons, and more. There is also heavier infrastructure like roads, bridges, pipelines, water treatment plants, power plants, seaports, and airports. All of these assets have different characteristics with respect to structural systems, external facade, interior finishes, parking needs . . . and of course ventilation and energy.

Readers will have noticed some conflation of owner types and building types. The owner classes frequently used in industry classifications and in investing are, broadly, single-family homes; multifamily buildings (apartments or condos); museums, universities, schools, and hospitals (MUSH); and government buildings (from the local town hall to the Pentagon). The final configuration is nonresidential nonbuildings such as roads, power plants, canals, and bridges. Again, the perspective of a single-family homeowner is different from that of the Pentagon, which is different from that of a toll road operator. The importance of healthy indoor air, the ability to recognize healthy indoor air, and the ability to pay for the elements that create healthy indoor air vary quite a bit.

Incumbents: Making Sense of the Motivations

These classifications help builders, owners, investors, and lenders to develop marketing plans. But another characteristic of the building industry is even more important to understanding how innovation happens, how best practices evolve, and what goes into a decision regarding air quality. One needs to understand the structure of the industry value-added system. This can help with strategy and tactics, and it can also illuminate where to nudge entrenched players and overcome slowness to change.

An industry value-added system is sometimes called a supply chain or value chain. A simple example, taken from the agribusiness industry, involves the flow of products:

Seeds are purchased → Farmer plants, tends, and harvests → Grain is stored → Grain is shipped to factory → Breakfast cereal is manufactured and boxed → Boxes are shipped to stores → Stores stock shelves → Families buy and consume cereal.

The product flows from left to right in this sketch, and the money from right to left. The family pays the store, the store pays the manufacturer, the manufacturer pays the farmer, and so on. In the food industry, the system runs pretty much continuously, since consumption of breakfast cereal is largely constant (storage is needed at the other end because grain grows seasonally).

But supply chains can be made much more complex. For example, the farmer also had to acquire or rent the land at some point, and the farmer probably purchases and uses fertilizer, pesticides, farm equipment, and fuel. Maybe there is debt involved in the chain. Since these are all contracts, there are lawyers, insurance companies, banks, and brokers to be paid. And this is just to get your cornflakes to the kitchen table.

Now think about a major new office tower. The key players are, broadly speaking, led by a developer or promoter who assembles and controls the land, secures financing, engages a designer or architect, hires a builder or general contractor, and rents the finished space to tenant companies (who employ the people who will spend much of their waking time in this building). At the Salesforce Tower in San Francisco, for example, Salesforce is the anchor and "name" tenant, but Boston Properties and Hines are the developers, Hathaway Dinwiddie and Clark Construction are the general contractors, CBRE is the leasing broker, the Herrick Corporation fabricated 10,000 tons of structural steel, and Conco was the concrete contractor.

Of course, it's still more complicated than that. The general contractor will hire scores of specialty contractors ranging from excavation and foundations through steel and concrete, as well as bricks, windows, roofing, plumbing, heating, ventilation, and air-conditioning—all finished with carpets, stone and wood flooring, and walls of wood, brick, glass, and gypsum coated with paint. Heating and ventilating has its own key subspecialties like ductwork, piping, wiring, insulation, controls, air balancing . . . and of course the provision of big equipment like pumps and chillers and small equipment like fans, louvers, and switches. The manufacturers of pumps and chillers might seem far down in this value-added system, but building product manufacturers like Carrier, Trane, and Johnson Controls are large corporations in their own right that sit atop their own value chains of sheet metal, cylinder blocks, spark plugs, bolts, bearings, and so on.

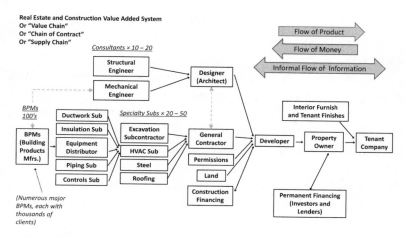

FIGURE 5.1   Real estate and construction industry value-added system for a typical new office building.

Another branch of the value-added system, at least in the US commercial construction model, is design. A billion-dollar office building like the Salesforce Tower might have a "design" architect with a big name like Pelli Clarke Pelli, an "architect of record" (creating the actual contract documents) like Kendall Heaton, a structural engineer specializing in this seismic zone like Magnusson Klemencic Associates, a mechanical design team like WSP, and dozens of specialty consulting firms in landscaping, curtain walls, security, acoustics, lighting, food service, elevators, and more.

The design and construction team would be subject to building codes (and American Society of Heating, Refrigerating and Air-Conditioning Engineers [ASHRAE] standards) covering dozens of characteristics from seismic concerns to shadows to parking to egress to accessibility. In practice, overlaying this system of product flow and cash flow is a large cadre of oversight, regulation, and inspection regimes. Hundreds of thousands of professionals work in established industry groups that are not shown in the "chain of contract" but that are nonetheless credentialed and powerful. These include roles like building inspectors, zoning code writers, commercial lenders, consulting engineers, insurance brokers, lawyers, accountants, actuaries, insurance companies, and more. While all of these players help organize and standardize the overall industry, and at the micro-level also help facilitate project delivery, the presence of this vast secondary ecosystem adds to the inertia of the industry—and strongly favors incumbents, thanks to their specialized knowledge and existing web of relationships.

At the other end of the industry value-added system is a second chain represented by the money. A small office building in a suburb might have a single owner, a single tenant company that is the occupant, and a mortgage from a single local bank. But for a billion-dollar building in a big American city, there are dozens to hundreds of tenants; the contractual ownership might be allocated among dozens of partnerships or corporations; and the mortgage might be split into layers where different nonbank lenders have different rights to the cash flow, or even made into financial product like commercial mortgage-backed securities. Boston Properties, for instance, lists Vanguard, Fidelity, JPMorgan Chase, Schwab, and Putnam among its biggest stockholders. Financial investors like these have fiduciary considerations, and they are interested in the performance of their investment portfolio; they are not directly interested in the health or productivity of the people who work in the building—unless this will impact their bottom line.

Perhaps most critically, this dance is done only once per project: the relationships are built, the contracts are signed, the materials are made, the labor is performed, and after completion of the project, the parties break up and move on. The provision of a billion-dollar building, once, is thus far different in terms of ability to standardize from, say, the provision of 25,000 cars at $40,000 each annually and forever.

Why Does This Matter to Healthy Buildings?

The configuration of this constellation of players matters for two main reasons: money and risk. At the simplest level, if it costs someone else (the landlord) more money to help me (the tenant), why should I expect him or her to do that? We have proposed one answer in Chapter 4, where we have shown that the impact on the people who use the building is so positive that some of the gains can be shared. A 1.7-million-square-foot building like Wells Fargo Plaza in Houston probably houses about 6,000 people . . . each of whom spends most of his or her waking hours in the building; that's the target population for these ideas.

The second aspect is risk. Engineers and air-conditioning installers want to litigation-proof themselves by meeting building codes, and they don't want to be called back to fix faulty equipment. Some of the air-conditioning equipment may be relatively inexpensive at first but very costly to repair once it's been installed in the ceiling and connected to the pipes and ducts, and the users are in the space. It's much safer for a firm to stick to tried and true than to innovate if it might take on more exposure if something were to go amiss; so the industry continues as it has before. Inertia is powerful.

But Healthy Buildings don't necessarily require new and unproven technologies. Often they just require an upsizing of capacity to exceed code—which can be accomplished with standard technology. We hope that the evidence in this book regarding the health and productivity benefits of indoor air quality will ultimately drive user requests, accelerate the demand for healthy air . . . and lead to a greater willingness to pay a little to push these requests upstream so that people can benefit here and now.

(Split) Incentives: Who Wins and Who Loses?

Let's look at the most challenging situation from an incentive point of view: commercial real estate. This is difficult because a landlord is primarily looking to build or operate a building at the lowest possible cost. If the tenant is responsible for energy costs (and employee health costs), there is no incentive for the landlord to spend more on any of this if it can't be recovered somehow in rent or direct payments. This is the classic split-incentive problem that has been discussed frequently in the energy efficiency space: "Why don't landlords just build a more energy-efficient building from the start?" Answer: "Because there is no benefit to them in spending the money and effort." Only the most sophisticated landlord-and-tenant combinations realize the mutual benefit in getting "better" space in a "better" building (because that kind of tenant recognizes the importance of, and is willing to pay for, a "better" space).

The relationship between the tenant Li & Fung and the landlord Empire State Building is a well-publicized case in point.[4] Tenant and landlord collaborated to finance base building improvements like better windows and more insulation; and the tenant also invested in its own electricity-reducing engineering, such as more efficient light fixtures, automatic plug switch-offs at night, and an interior design that allowed daylight to reach farther into the office space.

But that's a best-in-class, well-capitalized global firm with a long-term lease working in New York City with an enlightened landlord in a big structure that is probably the most famous office building in the world. In the rest of this large, locally oriented, fragmented industry, it's a long way from elite landlords with "Class A" investments in elite cities to the smaller, "Class C" buildings in smaller cities occupied by smaller firms with smaller balance sheets that really can't be bothered with some of the energy details. This, of course, is where our book comes in: those are exactly the companies that should care most about the health of their employees. More productivity and better health go right to the bottom line (with some in employee bonuses) not just in high-profile buildings but in fact in all buildings.

A different sort of split incentive can be found in some owner-occupied buildings. The understandable commercial landlord-tenant split incentive—where the two are totally separate economic entities—disappears. But within big organizations like hospitals or universities, decision-making and incentives are often devolved into different departments. Take the case of a large research university in the Boston area (not Harvard) that was considering energy-efficiency investments several years ago. The construction group was responsible for capital costs and was measured on how competitively projects were designed, bid, and delivered. There was only passing consideration for the life-cycle costs. In another office, operations staff had a budget for maintenance, repairs, cleaning . . . and energy for lighting, heating, cooling, and lab equipment. They had no influence on the construction side but were still responsible for the cost of energy.

For simplicity, this organization billed all departments on a square-foot basis for lighting, heat, and cooling regardless of the age and condition of the department's particular building (desktop and lab bench electricity was billed separately). This seems fair at first blush since faculty and departments don't necessarily get to select their space. But as a result, when researchers, department heads, or grant writers sought funding, it was never for energy efficiency: Why should they allocate their hard-won funds to a capital expenditure whose benefit would be spread across all users? That's not just a split incentive, it's a *reverse* incentive—where using funds for energy efficiency in the space you control winds up with a negative financial impact.

Harvard encountered a similar misalignment of incentives, and it addressed the issue in part with its Green Revolving Fund.[5] Originally capitalized by discretionary funds from the Office of the President, the concept was to loan funds directly to academic departments so they could make investments that made economic sense—usually with a three- or four-year payback period. The department could fund the capital improvements (using a loan from the fund to pay for the general construction and cover the repairs budget). The energy savings were measured and the savings went toward interest and principal on the loan. When repaid, the funds could be used again.

This was, in practice, mostly a matter of accounting. The "loan" to one entity was "repaid" by savings from another piece of the same large financial statement. But the presence of the fund highlighted the issue, overcame the silo problem, and led to more energy efficiency.

This approach to energy-efficiency finance is mentioned here for three reasons. First, the productivity and health benefits of better indoor air quality arguably outweigh the financial benefits of energy efficiency. Second, it shows that the issue of misaligned incentives is not limited to commercial landlords and corporate tenants, and that it can be found among capital budget, operating budget, and department budget within the same university (or hospital or museum). Third, the "revolving fund" tool can work in other ways to help account for improvements in the built environment that lead to demonstrable improvements in health, wellness, and productivity.

I'm Still Worried about Costs

So far we have contemplated the economic value of health and productivity and looked at the strategic implications of split incentives (in the commercial world) and misaligned incentives (in the museum, university, school, and hospital world). But what kind of costs are we talking about here?

The cost has two components—real and perceived. Let's look at the real cost of one simple fix—higher ventilation. As we discussed in Chapter 4, our modeling and that of others suggests that across the United States, the cost of doubling the ventilation rate from the ASHRAE "acceptable" level is about $10–$40 per person per year (reduced to $1–$12 with energy-efficient technologies in place).[6] That covers all climate zones and many of the most common commercial building types and mechanical systems. However, the *perceived* costs are quite a bit higher. In a study of building managers asked about the estimated cost of doubling ventilation rates (and upgrading to higher-grade air filters), these managers estimated the costs to be in the range of $100 per person per year. In other words, their estimates were anywhere from 2.5 to 100 times more than actual costs.[7] But even if their estimates were off by a factor of 3 or 4, it should not have mattered. Why? Look back at Table 4.2 and see that even a 20 percent swing in energy costs only impacts the bottom line by less than half of one percent—yet the perceived cost is used as the barrier to adoption. Accurate information is not out there yet.

The obstacles raised in this chapter boil down to four issues: information, inertia, incentives, and incumbents. To recap:

- **Information is incorrect or lacking.** On the cost side, it's a lot less expensive to implement healthy indoor air than people think. On the benefits side, the cognition, productivity, and health benefits are material, objective, quantifiable, and significant. The first objective of this book is to share information.
- **Inertia is powerful.** As always, it's easier to keep doing what one has always done than to change. In a large and nonhomogeneous industry like real estate and construction, with a long and complex value-added system featuring thousands of tenants, owners, contractors, engineers, and vendors, it's not simple to push through even small innovations. We believe that with a growing awareness of measurable health benefits, this will change—starting with the big, sophisticated user groups and dispersing to the rest. The second objective of this book is to overcome inertia.
- **Incumbents are hard to move.** Influential organizations like ASHRAE, the US Green Building Council, the American Institute of Architects, and many other ratings or accreditation groups have their own patterns, systems, hierarchies, and revenue streams. It can be very hard for them to adopt and promulgate a new system when the old one has broad acceptance. For established groups whose influence is linked to static building codes or proprietary point systems, moving to modern, sensor-based measurements and cost-benefit-adjusted, benchmarked outcomes can be a major disruption. As with other innovations, forward-thinking building occupants—and landlords—will gravitate to a better system without regard for the fate of incumbent associations. The third purpose of this book is to show how to do that.

- **Incentives are misaligned.** Most design and construction decisions are not made by the people who will breathe the air: choices reside with engineers who won't occupy the space, construction budgeters who aren't measured on long-term productivity of occupants, landlords who don't benefit from their tenants' results, and numerous different departments in large organizations that are set up to be at cross-purposes. Plan A is for all the parties to "get it" about indoor air and health and spring into action collectively (this is, arguably, much easier at a university or hospital or museum, where someone at "the top" can decree modifications across multiple departments). But what if the parties don't get it? Our final purpose is to propose incentives, initiatives, and innovations that can help frame a plan B and push for improvements on the merits.

Now That We Have the Basics Down, What Do We Do Next?

Until recently, these arguments (particularly about improving the corporate bottom line by spending more for occupancy and energy) seemed like so much hand-waving broker talk, since productivity and health benefits were not quantifiable. But that has changed. These benefits are now objectively quantifiable. Going forward, we will describe what it means to have a Healthy Building, going well beyond the simple example of better ventilation. We'll give you tools to start capturing these enterprise-wide health boosts, and we'll give you ideas for how to scale these solutions and benefits.

PART II

A Healthy Building Strategy

CHAPTER SIX

The 9 Foundations of a Healthy Building

As I look back on it now from this changed world of "safety first," . . . . it astonishes and amuses me to see how very well this primitive method often worked.

—ALICE HAMILTON

AS WITH MANY FIELDS, there are deep silos in the world of indoor environmental quality. It's not uncommon for a scientist to declare that he or she is a "water person" or an "air quality person." Very often, there is little communication across the disciplines. To be successful, the Healthy Building movement will require a new, holistic approach that jointly looks at a range of factors and systems, forcing interactions among various fields of expertise. This approach has been successful in the biological sciences, with the advent of various "-omics" fields, such as metagenomics, proteomics, transcriptomics, and epigenomics. (Sometimes simply naming it helps to advance the field.) The question then is, How do we do this for buildings? We have previously proposed the field of "buildingomics"—the study of the totality of factors in buildings that influence our health, well-being, and productivity.[1]

But what are those factors, and what is the scientific evidence supporting each? *The 9 Foundations of a Healthy Building* is the title of a short report created by Joe and a multidisciplinary team of experts from his Healthy

FIGURE 6.1   The 9 Foundations of a Healthy Building.

Buildings program at the Harvard T. H. Chan School of Public Health that distills 40 years of research on the key determinants of health in a building.

The idea for the 9 Foundations arose from many interactions over the past several years with real estate professionals, building owners, hospital administrators, facilities directors, homeowners, and academic colleagues. Two things stood out. First, during these discussions, Joe would often say, "The idea of a Healthy Building has been made too complicated. There are just a handful of things we need to do to make a building healthier." This of course led to the very fair, on-the-spot request to name them. In the ensuing discussions, it became clear that the public health community has often failed to translate our research into actionable information.

Second, Joe would often hear some variation of the refrain, "Your research is very interesting, but I can't take a scientific paper into my meeting on Monday and convince a building owner or manager to do things differently. I need a short summary." Thus, the 9 Foundations project was born.

We won't regurgitate the report here in this book. Instead, we will take it a step further—we will give you our opinion on the essential takeaways and then some recommendations for each of the 9 Foundations. We recognize that this is a dense chapter, so feel free to skip around it and pick a topic or two to read now before continuing on with the rest of the book—you can always come back and pick another foundation to read about later.

Foundation 1: Ventilation

We won't go into much detail here on how ventilation impacts health, as we spent most of Chapter 4 spelling this out. You now know that the current ventilation standard specified by the American Society of Heating, Refrigerating and Air-Conditioning Engineers (ASHRAE) of about 20 cfm / person is a bare-minimum standard. Many studies show the benefit of higher ventilation rates, but collectively they have not identified the optimal rate. We do know that it should be greater than 20 cfm / person, and our studies and those of others have seen benefits at 40 cfm / person and above.[2] Some Healthy Building certification standards, discussed in detail in Chapter 9, give a building "credit" for going 30 percent over the minimum ventilation rate. We think most buildings can attain 30 cfm / person today with little cost and very little effort (beyond a mind-set shift as to what gets counted in the cost-benefit analysis).

When the Air Is Turned Off, So Is Your Protection

Since we've already covered *how much* outdoor air needs to be delivered, let's keep this interesting by talking about another key aspect of ventilation and health: *when* that air is delivered.

In an office building with mechanical ventilation, a typical run-time schedule for the air-handling equipment might look something like a ramp-up beginning at six or seven o'clock in the morning to prep the building for worker arrival, and then a shut-off at around five or six in the evening.

If you're like us, and millions of other workers, the end of that sentence should have jumped out at you.

"Wait, building ventilation systems shut down at five or six o'clock in the evening? I'm still in the building at that time!"

That's not all—many people work on the weekends, and it's really uncommon to find a commercial building that has its mechanical system running full bore seven days per week.

The consequences are exactly what you'd expect in some respects, and surprising in others. On the obvious front, this means that there might be very little or no outdoor air coming into most office buildings outside of traditional nine-to-five working hours. Also not surprising, there is often a corresponding increase in reporting of odor complaints, hot or cold complaints, or sick building issues at precisely those times.

To show how common this is, and how it leads to problems, just today, as Joe was writing the first draft of this section, a colleague contacted him asking for advice about what to do. She said she'd started to smell cigarette smoke in her office over the past few days. Joe asked a series of basic questions, including the time of the odors. She said that it was right about five o'clock in the evening. (We're not making this stuff up, we swear.)

The culprit? A smoker outside the building, and a building that shut down its ventilation system at precisely five o'clock. But *why* did this happen? you may ask. The smoker was outside, not inside.

When mechanical systems shut off, the building loses two key defenses against outdoor air pollutants. Once that system is off, the building is (1) no longer positively pressurized relative to outdoors and (2) no longer filtering incoming air and recirculated air. The result? A million pathways for outdoor air pollutants to penetrate through cracks and crevices, doorways, and windows. And then, once inside, airborne particles are not effectively captured in the building's filters. So what our colleague was experiencing was a building that had turned off its defense system at five o'clock, allowing cigarette smoke to penetrate right back into the building.

There are also more insidious examples, such as pollution from a parking garage or restaurant exhaust reentering the building once that positive pressure is gone. In one fascinating project, Joe led the forensic investigation of an unexplained accumulation of thick dust on the office desks of an urban high-rise building. The investigation was prompted by an employee who reported the dust as a health concern. The forensic investigation involved setting up real-time air-quality sensors around the building, "sniffing" the air with specialized probes to explore in the walls and ceilings, and using a "fingerprinting" technique to compare the thick dust in that office with other known dust matrices. It revealed that this normally pristine Class A commercial office space was being impacted by subway soot traveling from the subway station below. We discovered that with every train arriving in the station after hours, a plume of subway dirt shot up through poorly sealed penetrations around the steel columns and found its way into the office building through electrical outlets and the ceiling plenum. At the end of each day, the workers left a clean office space, only to arrive the next morning to find a layer of dirt and grime on desks, walls, and every other surface.

But why would this phenomenon only happen *after hours,* even though the subway was running all day? The answer is that the mechanical system in this building was turned off for the day around six o'clock, and the office areas were thus no longer under positive pressure relative to the subway (and the recirculated air was not being filtered). As trains rumbled by overnight, the building no longer had enough positive pressure to keep those subway particles at bay. The remedy? In the short term, running the mechanical system 24/7 to keep the building under positive pressure and the air continuously filtered. We also installed an air quality monitoring system with real-time alerts to verify that the air quality was safe for the workers at all times. The longer-term solution was serious work on the building to seal off all of the air penetrations from the subway.

The Fine Details of Capturing Fine Particles

On a related note, another key component of any ventilation system is the level of filtration of the air stream. We know that airborne fine particles ($PM_{2.5}$) are a serious threat to our health, and we showed in Chapter 3 that these particles infiltrate our buildings. Mechanically ventilated buildings allow for the control of many of these particles because, with a central point of entry, the building can filter outdoor air before it's distributed all around.

But the devil is in the details. The typical filter used in a building with a central mechanical ventilation system is a MERV 8 filter. Recall that MERV stands for "Minimum Efficiency Reporting Value," and the higher the MERV value, the higher the particle removal efficiency.

To help make sense of this, let's first think about high-efficiency particulate air (HEPA) filters. It's likely you've seen a product with a HEPA filter that has this written on the packaging: "99.97% efficiency." Well, HEPA is actually nearly 100 percent efficient across most particle sizes, so why the

99.97 percent rating? It's because filters are rated based on the particle size for which they are *least* effective. For HEPA, they are least effective for particles of 0.3 microns—99.97 percent effective, to be precise. Thus the rating.

Now let's go to a MERV 8 filter, the one most commonly found in buildings, which might only remove 50 percent of $PM_{2.5}$. It's a boulder catcher, really, designed to capture large particles that can damage the mechanical equipment.

So what to do? If you're in an area with high levels of outdoor pollution—or in any building in a major city, for that matter—we strongly recommend upgrading to MERV 13 or higher. This is the level of filtration recommended for "superior office buildings," and it removes almost 90 percent of $PM_{2.5}$. If you live in an area like Shanghai or Cairo or in areas impacted by wildfires, like San Francisco, where $PM_{2.5}$ levels have been known to reach 100 $\mu g/m^3$ or sometimes as much as 1,000 $\mu g/m^3$—levels that are immediately dangerous to health—you should definitely be using a MERV 13 or higher. You pay an energy penalty for the higher filtration (and a slightly higher filter cost), but this is trivial compared with the health benefits.

Giving Your Building a Regular Checkup

One last point on ventilation: if you want to be sure your mechanical system is operating in a way that protects your health, the single best recommendation we can give you is to commission your mechanical system. Our commissioning recommendation is straightforward, but if you're not familiar with commissioning, it's worth your time getting up to speed quickly. Commissioning is the process by which you make sure your building is performing the way it was designed to. (Or for new buildings, it's the process by which you verify you are getting the building you paid for.) This recommendation for continuous commissioning stems from years of observations by John during his building projects, by Joe during his forensic investigations, and by nearly everyone who knows anything about buildings. Buildings don't always perform as designed (actually, they never do), and they change over time. Commissioning is like going to the doctor for an annual checkup. It helps you catch things early, before your building ends up in the emergency room, where you'll spend 10 times as much fixing the problem. With the advent of new sensor technologies, it's also possible to do continuous commissioning, thus ensuring that the building systems are performing optimally every minute of every day.

Our Recommendations

- Increase the ventilation rate to a minimum of 30 cfm / person.
- Verify ventilation performance with real-time monitoring of CO_2.
- Run the air-handling system during all hours the building is occupied, preferably using demand control ventilation.
- Upgrade to MERV 13 filters on incoming and recirculated air. (For more information on selecting the right filter for the location of your building, check out the terrific report by Brent Stephens, Terry Brenna, and Lew Harriman, "Selecting Ventilation Air Filters to Reduce $PM_{2.5}$ of Outdoor Origin.")[3]

Foundation 2: Air Quality

What's the first thing you would do if you ever found yourself in the unfortunate position of discovering an inch of water in your basement or a puddle of water in your bathroom? If you have any sense, you won't start mopping up the water until you have tried to find the source. In other words, you turn off the spigot. Then you get to cleaning.

The same logic applies to air quality in your building. The very first step in maintaining good air quality is to control indoor sources. You have to turn off the spigot of indoor air pollutants. (Think back to our conceptual model for exposure-related disease in Chapter 3; if you control the source, then there is no exposure and also no chance of adverse health effects.)

For chemicals like volatile organic compounds (VOCs), this means choosing things like no-VOC paints and formaldehyde-free products. It also means avoiding scented sprays and cleaning agents with high VOC content. Not only are the VOCs potentially harmful, they can react with ground-level ozone to generate formaldehyde and particles. Speaking of particles, avoid the use of incense or candles (and we hope this is obvious and doesn't need to be stated, but just in case—no smoking in or around buildings). Then you can worry about controlling infiltration of outdoor pollutants, including those that penetrate from the ground, like radon and even some VOCs.

There can be hundreds of different sources of indoor air pollutants—in this case, there's no one spigot to turn off. And even when you do get rid of a source, sometimes that can lead to a new and unexpected source taking its place.

Joe once led a forensic investigation of a doctor's office where workers were reporting symptoms consistent with formaldehyde exposure. But all of the wood products were certified as "formaldehyde-free," and the builder was adamant that he had purchased all "green-certified" products. How could that be? Well, the investigation showed that the wood products were indeed formaldehyde-free, as described, but it turned out they were screaming hot with other aldehydes that had been used as a replacement for formaldehyde.

So even if you do everything you can to limit common sources of VOCs and other indoor pollutants, there is only one way to know if you've been successful, and that's to test the air regularly. Air quality in a building can change frequently, based on everything from the building's systems to out-door conditions to what the people bring into the space and the work they do in the space, so we strongly recommend continuously monitoring air quality in real time, supplemented with more traditional "industrial hygiene" assessment methods.

You should be monitoring for indicators of indoor air quality in your building at all times. This includes carbon dioxide, temperature, relative humidity, and particles, and if you have combustion sources like a boiler in your home, then you should also be measuring carbon monoxide. New sensors are coming on the market every week, so this list will expand as the quality and availability of new sensors continue to expand. Measuring these is akin to having a smoke detector in your office or home—the real-time sensors are your first-alert warning system that something may not be right.

But real-time monitoring is not the endgame, as some may have you believe. Real-time monitoring *must* be supplemented with more targeted sampling on an annual basis, at a minimum, using traditional air-sampling approaches (industrial hygiene methods). These are validated and standard-ized techniques that allow you to make specific measurements that real-time monitors cannot reliably make at this time, such as collecting air samples and sending them to a lab to test for 70-plus VOCs, or sending water samples to a lab to test for the presence of lead or bacteria in the water. (We discuss *who* should do this testing in Chapter 9, and we further discuss *what* you should be testing for in Chapter 10.)

Controlling Indoor Pollution When You Can't Control the Source

What if you can't control these indoor sources of pollution and your environmental monitoring tells you that the levels of a particular pollutant are high? Well, then it's worth revisiting the ventilation and filtration section earlier in this chapter. For mechanically ventilated systems like those in office buildings, you can add enhanced filtration on the recirculated air stream. In some cases you could consider fortifying your MERV particle filter with a tool to capture gaseous pollutants like VOCs—such as a carbon-based filter. These can be expensive, and they require some skill and expertise to use well because carbon filters can saturate. When a *particle* filter gets dirty, it performs better because there is more physical junk in the way of the air stream, but when a *carbon* filter saturates, VOCs pass right through. So having it in place may give a false sense of security. Not to mention that carbon filters also preferentially bind certain VOCs. There is an art to using carbon filters, but they can be effective when done right.

For the home or office kitchen, making sure you have a vent over the stove to capture particles generated during cooking is critical—and make sure that vent is ducted to the outside, or else you're just recirculating the pollutants in the building. Last, portable air purifiers can be effective at controlling airborne particles from either indoor or outdoor sources. Just make sure they are sized right for the room. New portable air purifiers include a carbon-based filter to capture VOCs, along with the traditional filter for particles, and they also have embedded sensors that control when the filter activates.

Our Recommendations

- Turn off the spigot by selecting low- or no-VOC materials and avoiding scented cleaners and candles.
- Supplement real-time air-quality monitoring with targeted analysis for speciated VOCs and other air pollutants (see Chapter 10 for a more complete list).

- Consider air cleaning using enhanced filtration techniques in your mechanical system (or portable air purifiers) if sources can't be removed and if the air-quality testing reveals unacceptably high concentrations of pollutants.

Foundation 3: Thermal Health

Ask any building manager, "What is the number one complaint you hear about a building?" and we guarantee that he or she will say, "Calls from employees about feeling too hot or too cold." If you address this one issue in a building—and granted, it can be hard—you will be far ahead of most everyone else when it comes to employee satisfaction.

Traditionally, indoor environmental quality practitioners and ASHRAE refer to this issue as "thermal comfort." We hate the use of the word "comfort" and prefer the term "thermal health" for two reasons: (1) using "comfort" places the onus on the individual and suggests the issue is about complainy types rather than the building, and (2) it fails to acknowledge that this is a health issue, not merely a "being uncomfortable" issue, as you'll soon see.

Several factors go into thermal health, but only a few that the building controls. Outside the purview of the building, the person's activity level (metabolic rate), clothing, genetics, and gender all play a role in thermal health. But the building controls four key factors: air temperature, relative humidity, radiant temperature, and air movement.

Thermal Health and Human Performance

To get a sense of how buildings can factor into human performance, take a look at this inverted U-shaped curve from a 2018 study published by Joe's Healthy Buildings team at Harvard, led by research associate Jose Cedeno-Laurent.[4] This was a study of students in dorms with and without air-conditioning before and during a heat wave, and their resulting performance on simple cognitive functions, as measured by the Stroop Test. (The Stroop Test is commonly used in psychology to test selective attention. In the test, you *see* the color red but *read* the word "green." The person in the test is asked to report the color they see, not the color they read. Your brain

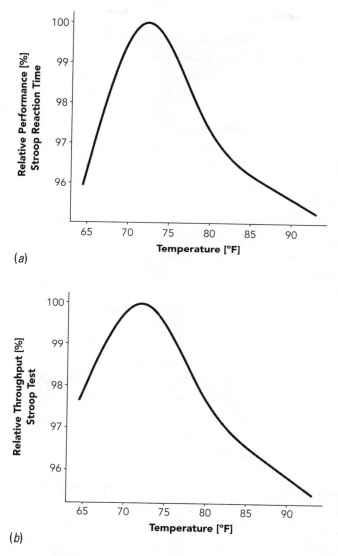

(a)

(b)

FIGURE 6.2   The impact of temperature on (a) reaction time and (b) throughput. Data source: J. G. Cedeño Lauren et al., "Reduced Cognitive Function During a Heat Wave among Residents of Non-Air-Conditioned Buildings: An Observational Study of Young Adults in the Summer of 2016," *PLoS Med* 15, no. 7 (2018): e1002605, https://doi.org/10.1371/journal.pmed .1002605, figure 3.

pauses because of this dissonance. The test records your reaction time, or the length of your "brain pause," and the number of questions you get right.)

Here's the quick and dirty interpretation—for every 2°F variation from the optimal temperature, there was a 1 percent reduction in throughput on the Stroop Test. You read that word right, "throughput." Synonyms include "capacity," "productivity," "yield," "bandwidth," "production" . . . you get the point. This is impacting worker performance.

This relationship between thermal health and performance is now well known, at least in public health and building science circles. Researchers at Lawrence Berkeley National Laboratory found a 10 percent relative reduction in performance when the temperature fell out of this narrow optimal range.[5] What's amazing here is that these two studies show a remarkable consistency, despite being performed using different tools nearly two decades apart. The specifics of the studies and methodologies are less important than the key takeaway: there is actually a very narrow range of temperature conditions that promote optimal performance. And this narrow range is smaller than what is specified for "comfort" by ASHRAE.

To see what this means to the economics of your business, let's say you let that optimal level of about 72°F stray a bit in your building, and the indoor temperature reaches 76°F. (Joe once worked in an office where it regularly hit 80°F and higher.) On that one factor of thermal health alone, temperature, the data from the Harvard study indicates that you would see a 2 percent hit to productivity. If you think back to the pro forma for Healthy Buildings Inc. in Chapter 4, a 2 percent productivity boost led to 9 percent in bottom-line gains, *even after* accounting for additional energy costs and paying a premium on rent. On the flip side, this means that the 2 percent *lower* throughput equates to a decline of 9 percent in the bottom line. Just from having your temperature stray by 4°F!

This might make you think a bit harder about those seemingly annoying "too hot" and "too cold" complaints—they aren't red flags about complainy employees; they are indications that these people's productivity is being hit. Imagine going to your boss and telling him or her you could boost bottom-line performance by almost 10 percent with a flip of the switch!

Thermal health is a complex dance of many factors, and one factor we haven't touched on yet is humidity and the uncomfortable sticky feeling that comes on muggy days in summer. Air-conditioned buildings provide us with some relief (while also ensuring that indoor humidity does not reach levels that promote mold growth). On the flip side, there is a prevailing notion that we are overcooling buildings in the summer—when people feel cold air coming out of vents, it is common to hear a comment along the lines of, "It's so cold in here I have to bring a sweater to work." What most people don't realize is that in humid climates, this "overcooling" is actually a necessity and is not really overcooling at all. The air-conditioning system needs to cool the outside air to the dew point in order to extract all that humidity from the air, and that means cooling the air to some pretty cool temps. Let's say your target indoor temperature is 72°F with 50 percent relative humidity. In that case the dew point is 52°F (this is all from a psychrometric chart). The cooling coils in your mechanical system therefore must cool the outdoor air to 52°F to get water to condense out of the air and then reheat the air so that it will come out of the diffusers at around 55°F. Then, factoring in a few different factors that generate heat indoors, like solar heat gain, body heat, and heat from electronics, the air will be a comfortable 72°F by the time it reaches you at your desk. That reheating uses energy and comes at a cost, so it is not uncommon for building operators to keep the air temperature very cool, so as not to have to do too much reheating—thus the icy-cold air coming out of the vents in your office or in stores.

Of course, temperature and humidity are just two components of thermal health, albeit the easiest to control and fix. But comfort levels vary with each person, the type of activity being performed, and even over time and across seasons. There is no "one size fits all." One of our favorite places to explore the interaction of these factors is the CBE Thermal Comfort Tool, created by the Center for the Built Environment at Berkeley. We recommend going to its website and playing around to see which combinations of inputs keep you in an "acceptable" thermal health zone and which ones push you out.[6]

There is one aspect of thermal health that deserves some special attention, because it often gets brushed aside, and that factor is differences by gender. A study published in *Nature Climate Change* in 2015 brought this gender-difference issue to the forefront when it showed that the current thermal comfort standards were originally based on the metabolic rate, and clothing choices, of men . . . in the 1960s![7] When these researchers tested women, they found that their metabolic rate was up to 32 percent lower than men's. The *New Yorker* published a piece in 2015 based on that research titled "Is Your Thermostat Sexist?," and women who work in offices were finally given research-based affirmation of what they had been experiencing firsthand for decades.[8] Alas, this research was not without controversy. ASHRAE quickly pushed back, saying that the thermal comfort standard it sets is actually based on a large sample of men and women. So what's really going on?

If you explore ASHRAE's rebuttal, you'll see that the ASHRAE standard has indeed been updated since the first iteration in 1966. The updates do rely on a study of men and women, true, but the fine print shows that it was first updated in 1982. Not exactly the male-dominated workplace of the 1960s, with men wearing three-piece suits, but not that far from it, either. ASHRAE argues that its thermal comfort standards are now based on men and women equally and do get updated regularly (the latest version was 2017). What is really at issue, it argues, is clothing choices, with women dressing more appropriately for outdoor conditions each season, but indoor temperatures still catering to men in suits.

Looking at more updated science, we do, in fact, see a gender divide with regard to temperature. More than half of the studies of gender and temperature reveal that women show a higher level of dissatisfaction than men when they are in the same thermal environment. Ignoring this science would be to ignore the voices of millions of women working in offices who will tell you that this is a fact based on their own experience. It is time for us to start listening. The current ASHRAE thermal comfort models have several variables that can be adjusted to help find an optimal condition, including one for clothing choice. Why not just acknowledge the science, and the experience of millions, and add in another factor—gender? There is a business imperative for this, too. A recent study that reviewed the entire body of evidence on gender and thermal comfort concludes with this point: "Females are more sensitive than males to a deviation from an optimal temperature and express more dissatisfaction, especially in cooler conditions."[9]

Looking forward, optimizing indoor conditions is going to require a future of hyperpersonalization and hyperlocalization of thermal conditions to create zones of "personalized indoor health" that satisfy the unique preference of each person. This is already starting to happen. Some buildings have systems where each workstation has controls for its own temperature and airflow, and systems that disaggregate ventilation from temperature control. The future of personalized indoor health is not far off.

Indoor Heat Waves

For most buildings, maintaining good thermal health requires the use of air-conditioning. While it has been partly demonized because of its contribution to greenhouse gases, we feel that it's unrealistic to tell people to forgo air-conditioning. For one thing, it's not going to happen. More importantly, in many places it is absolutely necessary.

This is particularly relevant for places prone to extreme heat, like India, but maybe a bit surprisingly this is also extremely relevant for traditionally cold-weather climates, like those in the Northeast United States and northern Europe, where buildings were designed to capture and retain heat—a terrific strategy in the winter but terrible in the summer in a warming world. These buildings were built with materials with high thermal mass, such as brick and concrete. When outdoor temperatures rise, sustained high indoor temperatures can occur, as these buildings have a hard time "shedding" heat, in particular when nighttime temperatures do not drop. The result is an indoor heat wave—a period of elevated and sustained indoor temperatures that continue after the outdoor heat wave has technically ended. This gives people a false sense of safety: the heat wave warnings may have subsided, but the indoor heat wave continues.

As our planet continues to warm, and as standards of living improve globally, the use of air-conditioners is expected to rise dramatically. By one estimate, 4 billion air-conditioning units will be installed by 2050 (on top of the 1.6 billion that already exist). Air conditioners consume energy, and we talk about the implications of the building-energy-health-climate-resiliency nexus in Chapter 11, but it's worth touching on this here, too, because there are things we can do right now to limit the greenhouse gas emissions associated with all of this air-conditioning. The solution does not have to be "use fewer air conditioners." As an example of one clever solution, consider the work of the Center for the Built Environment at Berkeley, which found that you could maintain acceptable levels of worker satisfaction with thermal conditions in warm or wet climates even if indoor temperatures were raised by 8°F, simply by using fans to increase air movement.[10] Another thing we can and must do relates to improved technology. In an op-ed Joe and a colleague wrote last year called "Want Air-Conditioning and a Healthier Planet?," they pointed out that there is one thing we can do right now to dramatically lower the environmental footprint of air conditioners:

swap out the refrigerants. Air conditioners rely on hydrofluorocarbons, a refrigerant that is 3,000 times more potent than CO_2 in terms of its greenhouse gas potential. Swapping out hydrofluorocarbons could eliminate an estimated 0.5°C of global warming by the end of the century (that's a full 25 percent of the 2°C limit that the Paris Agreement calls for). The good news: replacement refrigerants are already available and coming on the market.[11]

Our Recommendations

- Maintain temperature and relative humidity within ranges selected for optimal performance rather than just "comfort" ranges.
- Proactively monitor thermal conditions and respond to upset conditions quickly.
- Be responsive to employee hot and cold complaints.
- Reduce solar heat gain (and save energy and reduce environmental impacts) by following the "energy-free" tactics suggested by the Lawrence Berkeley National Lab:[12]
  - Improve insulation.
  - Improve external shading (for example, by adding tree cover).
  - Upgrade window energy efficiency (for example, by installing dynamic glass).
  - Add cool-roofing coating that absorbs less solar radiation.

Foundation 4: Water Quality

In Chapter 3 we spent some time talking about what health scientists call exposure pathways—the air we inhale, the chemicals that permeate through our skin, and the dust we ingest unintentionally. Then there's the stuff we willfully put into our bodies—namely, food and water. We'll leave the food issue to our colleagues in the Nutrition Department, but water quality is central to buildings, so that's in our domain.

Most of us have heard that we should drink eight glasses of water per day. Staying hydrated is one of the keys to good overall health. We need water to stay alive, of course, but what might surprise you is that staying hydrated also helps regulate mood, performance, and even thinking.

Take our study mentioned in the section on thermal health, where those suffering from an indoor heat wave performed worse on cognitive function tests. What we didn't tell you was that some of the negative impact of heat stress was offset in those young people who drank more water. Put another way, drinking water had a protective effect against the dangers of indoor heat waves.

You likely didn't pick up this book just to be told that water is good for you, so let's dive into how buildings influence water quality and, therefore, our health. Overall water quality in a building is determined by measuring some basic indicators, such as the turbidity of the water, total dissolved solids, and total coliform. These indicators tell you about how "clean" the water is: turbidity is an indicator of how transparent the water is, governed by the amount of suspended particulates, or dirt; total dissolved solids is everything in the water besides actual water (for example, minerals, salts, and organic matter); and total coliform is an indicator of fecal contamination of the water (coliform bacteria are present in the feces of all humans and other warm-blooded animals, and while largely innocuous, their presence indicates that some other harmful pathogen may also be in the water).

Beyond these basics, there are drinking water standards that have to be met, and these vary by country. In the United States the National Primary Drinking Water Regulations set maximum contaminant levels for six groups of contaminants: microorganisms, disinfectants, disinfection by-products, inorganic chemicals, organic chemicals, and radionuclides.[13]

Despite these protections, there are always "new" issues cropping up—and a lag from the time we discover a water hazard until there are regulations in place. One current example is the issue of "Forever Chemicals" that are now in the drinking water of millions. Only recently have we had discussions about defining a "safe" level. (We discuss these Forever Chemicals more fully in Chapter 7.) There are also more localized issues in areas where industrial waste gets into our bodies of water, such as carcinogenic trichloroethylene from dry-cleaning operations or perchlorate near military bases (perchlorate, which is used in rocket fuel, interferes with your thyroid).

When Water Arrives Clean, but the Building Makes It "Dirty"

That said, overall these drinking-water standards do a pretty good job of ensuring that the water delivered to your building, home, or school meets some basic safety criteria. The catch here is that they ensure water quality right up to the point it enters your building. After that, all bets are off and the quality of the water is up to the building owner. We will give two quick examples—of *Legionella* and lead—to show what can happen after that water reaches your building, and we'll briefly discuss how controlling one factor, pH, will help with both.

Another Legionella Example

Many people think of cooling towers when they think of *Legionella*, and maybe rightly so, considering the high-profile outbreaks that have occurred—most notably in the Bronx, where cooling towers were implicated when 130 people were diagnosed with Legionnaires' disease in 2015. Controlling *Legionella* in rooftop cooling towers is important, and it's straightforward enough with the use of disinfecting chemicals and regular monitoring, so in this chapter we want to focus on *Legionella within* the building. While cooling towers are the culprit in many outbreaks, in some instances the source of the outbreak is an interior decorative fountain, a hot tub, a shower, or even an ice machine.

Buildings can help control *Legionella* and other bacteria in interior water systems by controlling water temperature, limiting stagnation, ensuring an adequate level of residual disinfectant, and controlling pH. (There is also now an ASHRAE standard, ASHRAE Standard 188, that requires all human-occupied commercial, institutional, multiunit residential, and industrial buildings to have a *Legionella* risk management plan. If that describes your building and you don't have one, you should.)[14]

The reason for controlling water temperature and stagnation is intuitive—bacteria like to grow in lukewarm water that sits idly for long periods. The second two—residual disinfectant and pH—are intertwined, and interesting.

When your municipal water supplier treats water at its treatment facility, it adds a residual disinfectant like chlorine so that bacteria won't grow in the water on its way from the plant to your building. That's a good thing. What you may not know is that the effectiveness of that disinfectant is dependent on the pH of the water. (We're going to get a little technical here, but stick with us.) Here is the so-called chlorine dissociation curve.

Chlorine exists in balance in water as hypochlorous acid (HOCL) and hypochlorite ion (OCL⁻). Notice that the relative amount of each depends

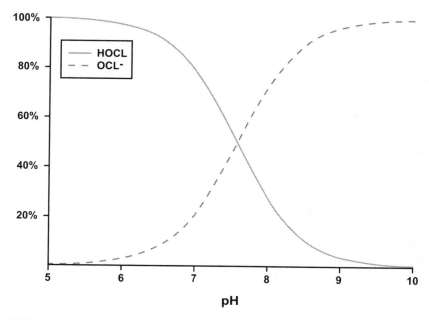

FIGURE 6.3   Chlorine disassociation curve at varying pH.

on the pH; at low pH (acidic), it's almost entirely HOCL, and at high pH (alkaline or basic) it's all OCL⁻.

Why does this matter? It turns out that one of these is much more effective at killing bacteria—HOCL. Most of the time this works out well for buildings, where water is generally at a pH of 7 (neutral). Looking at the chart, if the pH is right at 7, about 80 percent of the chlorine exists as the highly biocidal HOCL. Now look what happens if that water becomes more basic, moving to pH 8 or higher. Big problems ensue; the balance shifts to OCL⁻, which is a disinfectant, but a disinfectant that reacts more slowly than HOCL and is 80–100 percent less effective.

This leads to problems because sometimes the only thing a facilities team measures and tracks is the amount of chlorine (measured as "free" and "total"). If the water is tested and a target chlorine level is reached, some building managers assume everything is A-OK. As you now see, based on the chlorine disassociation curve, this concentration of chlorine doesn't mean much unless we also know the pH. (This isn't rocket science. Ask any college kid who has ever had a summer job as a swimming pool lifeguard. They know this well. They test the swimming pool water every day. And they *always* test for both chlorine *and* pH.)

Get the Lead Out

Now let's move to lead, another water contaminant that can come from *within* the building (and is also influenced by pH). We have known about the toxic effects of lead for millennia, literally since the age of the Roman Empire, when lead-lined pots and aqueducts caused chronic mass poisoning of the population. Fast-forward a few thousand years to the 1970s and 1980s, when we learned about the effect of low-level lead exposure on children's IQs and mental development. This time the culprit was the use of leaded gasoline and lead-based paint in homes.

Most recently, lead has been back in the news because of the tragedy in Flint, Michigan, where high levels of lead in drinking water were discovered, then covered up. Testing for lead is required under the US Lead and Copper Rule. Briefly, under this rule, after collecting water samples from homes, a 90th-percentile concentration is calculated and compared with a limit of 15 parts per billion (ppb). In Flint, officials from the Michigan Department of Environmental Quality excluded two high samples from the data set, which had the effect of keeping the 90th-percentile concentration below the limit required for action. Had they included those two samples in the analysis, as they should have, it would have shown that lead levels exceeded the limits set by the Lead and Copper Rule and action would have had to be taken at that time. The continued poisoning of the population could have been avoided.

Unfortunately, Flint is the tip of the iceberg. There are many communities affected by high levels of lead in water in the United States and around the world. Right here in Boston, where we live and work, as of 2017 an astounding one-third of schools had their water fountains turned off because of high lead levels.[15]

Even if the lead isn't coming from the water supplied by water districts, it can come from the historical use of lead as a solder for plumbing fixtures. Laws passed in 1986 and amended in 1996 make it illegal to use plumbing materials that are not "lead-free," but many older buildings, including schools and homes, still have lead in the pipes.

Here's where pH comes into play: At low pH, the acidity of the water can cause the lead to leach into the drinking water. In that way, even lead-free water coming into your building can be contaminated by the time it reaches the tap. (The chemistry involved in this process is fascinating and involves complex interactions between biofilms and scale, pH and alkalinity, organic matter, and more. For a nice summary on this, and the Lead and Copper Rule, check out this US Environmental Protection Agency report: *Optimal Corrosion Control Treatment Evaluation Technical Recommendations for Primacy Agencies and Public Water Systems.*)[16]

The takeaway on pH is this: too low and you run the risk of leaching and corrosion; too high and you lose some of the biocidal properties of the residual chlorine in your water. Like thermal health, there is a sweet spot that you need to hit, and the only way to know if you're there is to measure and monitor it.

Our Recommendations

- Test water quality annually at point-of-use taps in the building, and verify that you are meeting the standards set by the US Safe Drinking Water Act.
- Monitor water temperature, residual disinfectant (for example, chlorine, chloramine, copper-silver), and pH.
- Measure *Legionella* concentrations in cooling towers quarterly to ensure treatment is effective.
- Filter the water in your building or home, if necessary.

Foundation 5: Moisture

One of the top priorities in building design and operation is moisture control. There is no bigger issue a building faces than water damage. (This may not be entirely true; as the builder in John points out, fires and building collapses are bigger issues . . . but they are rare and water infiltration is common.)

The task of controlling water and moisture dominates our design and construction of the building—everything from rooftop drainage to the curtain wall, to vapor barriers in the basement and dehumidification in the air handler, to placement of water pipes. (There's a reason washers and dryers are traditionally in the basements of homes.)

A major water event can be extremely costly. This is both because of the cost of tearing out, remediating, and replacing walls, floors, and other damaged material and also because of the cost of business disruption. Joe worked on a project for a major health-care provider where a water pipe leaked on a Friday but was only discovered on Monday morning as employees arrived for work. The building had to be closed for 16 days to do the water recovery, cleanup, demolition, and rebuild. This was, to be sure, a massive disruption to the company's business. One way to think of the economics here is simply as a percentage of revenue. With roughly 240 business days in a year, 16 days of a closed office represents ~7 percent of annual revenue lost. For this ~$20 million operation, that's roughly $1,300,000 in lost revenue, not to mention the cleanup and renovation costs.

Major water events are one thing, and we'll also cover extreme weather-related events in Chapter 11, but for the vast majority of buildings, water issues are much more sneaky: it's the water damage you can't see from slow leaks or condensation.

While these are mostly subtle issues that miss notice, there are telltale signs of water damage, such as discolored ceiling tiles. It's one of the things you can look for in every building you enter—"Are the ceiling tiles stained?" It's a classic sign of current, or past, unaddressed water issues. You can also look for paint on walls near the ceiling that looks saggy, or sniff the air for musty odors. (Water issues are the subject of one of the most common questions in home transactions—during the home inspection, when you get to the basement, the home inspector is looking for water damage. And he or she will ask about it, too, no doubt.)

Growing (M)old Together

The reason we care about untreated moisture or water issues is that they create the potential for mold growth. Three conditions need to be present together for mold to grow: moisture, temperature, and nutrient source. You have all three in buildings—plenty of water, an office building with temperatures in a range that many molds like, and the organic matter on the surface of wallboard and carpets acting as a nutrient source.

Mold is a health issue for two reasons: it can cause allergic reactions, and it can be an irritant. As an allergen, mold has been shown to be an asthma trigger and promoter; it can cause upper respiratory symptoms like coughing and wheezing. As an irritant, mold can act on the mucosal membranes of our eyes, nose, and throat, with some people experiencing headaches after being exposed to mold.

It's also just gross. No one wants to be working in an office building and see mold growth along the corner walls or on ceiling tiles, and no one wants to be in a space with that characteristic pungent mold smell, most often described as "musty" or "damp," or the dead-on accurate, "It smells moldy in here." In extreme cases, mold can even eat away at underlying material, such as the wood used for structure in a home, causing irreparable structural damage.

Our Recommendations

- **Prevent it:** Design the shell of your building right, from the roof flashing to foundation waterproofing, to prevent water from coming in, and check indoor plumbing and HVAC regularly for signs of leaks or standing water, respectively.
- **Detect it:** Keep your eyes open for signs of water damage from internal or external sources; trust your nose; consider floor sensors to detect water leaks in areas with plumbing fixtures.
- **Fix it:** Address water and moisture issues ASAP, because these are problems that cost significantly more to address with every passing hour.
- **Clean it:** If you have water-damaged porous materials, dry them fast or get them out. Then clean the nonporous materials that were in contact with the wet porous materials.

Foundation 6: Dust and Pests

Let's get your attention right away:

Dust mites are microscopic pests that feed on shedded human and animal skin cells, typically burrowing in bedding, mattresses, and furniture upholstery. While dust mites do not bite or sting, their feces and body parts create a harmful allergen (Der p1) that can dramatically impact human health. Mites have been associated with asthma, immune responses such as allergic rhinitis (hay fever), and allergic reactions ranging from mild symptoms like runny nose and watery eyes, to more severe responses such as asthma attacks.

Among asthmatic children, the rate of dust mite allergen sensitivity can range from 48–63%, and high allergen exposure among these individuals increases their risk of hospital admission.[17]

This reads like a horror movie—microscopic pests found in nearly every bed that feed on shed human skin and whose feces cause an allergic reaction! Nasty.

And dust mites are just the beginning of what we find in dust. We also find allergens from cockroaches, mice, rats, cats, and dogs. Some of these allergens are primarily from saliva and dander (dog, cat), some are from urine (rat or mouse), and some are from saliva, feces, and shedding body parts (cockroach). These allergens can cause itchy eyes and skin, coughing, and sneezing, and they can also cause wheezing and shortness of breath.

Are you thinking that you have a clean office or home, and this doesn't impact you? Or maybe you're thinking, We're not one of those Silicon Valley companies that let people bring dogs to work—no issue for us! If you are thinking along those lines, there are some studies you might find enlightening. In one study that looked at dog allergen in public spaces, it was found in lots of places where it's not common to find dogs—for example, schools, pubs, and movie theaters. How about cats? It turns out cat allergen is even worse because it is super "sticky." It can be found quite literally everywhere, including places that aren't very likely to have cats in them—offices, schools, airplanes, and so on. We collect these allergens on our clothes, carry them around wherever we go, and then shed or deposit some of them. Our clothing is a vector, in public health parlance, and mediates exposure to particles and chemicals.[18]

Dust as a Chemical Reservoir

Biological allergens aren't the only thing that's in dust. Dust also carries lead from lead paint and chemicals from our consumer products, building materials, and furniture. It's also the home for all of the dirt we bring in from the outside on our shoes. One of the most effective things you can do from a public health standpoint is to take your shoes off at the door at home, and have walk-off mats in offices.

This mix of potential allergens and chemical hazards in dust is why a company like Dyson, despite marketing itself as an engineering company, is actually a health-care company (in our view). It makes a suite of products that help to clean the dust (and air) in your home—vacuums and air purifiers. But here's why we think it should be marketing itself as a health company rather than an engineering company: If you think of a several hundred dollar vacuum as a tool to clean your kids' Cheerios off the floor, that seems exorbitant. But if you reframe that vacuum as a tool to protect you and your kids from chemicals and allergens in dust, well that investment in a good vacuum now looks cheap. And it is. No one in their right mind should be spending a few hundred bucks for a sexy vacuum, but everyone should be spending that much for a vacuum that keeps your home or office healthier. Joe spent a few years working with Dyson to get it to think about itself as a health company first and an engineering company second.

How Dust Gets into Our Bodies

For us to be exposed to the allergens or chemicals in dust, it has to get into our bodies in one of three ways: through the air we breathe, through our skin, or through incidental ingestion. We might stir some floor dust up, thus making it airborne and inhalable (the previously referenced Pigpen effect). Some fraction of dust lands on our skin, where some chemicals may permeate through into our bodies. And we may eat the dust. Not intentionally, of course, but we eat it just the same. It turns out adults consume about 45 milligrams (mg) of house dust each day. On the high end, it can be as much as 100 mg.[19]

To put that in perspective, the recommended daily allowance for sodium for an adult is ~2,000 mg / day, so the amount of dust you ingest is 2–5 percent of that by mass. We intentionally consume salt in our food or drinks, but how does dust get into our bodies? As we go about our normal everyday activities, we start to accumulate dust on our hands. Then when we touch our lips, or eat a sandwich or snacks with our bare hands, we transfer some of that dust into our mouths.

Fortunately, much of this exposure to dust can be controlled in an office environment and home. Before we get to our recommendations, if you're really interested in dust (and who wouldn't be . . .), we recommend a book by Paul Lioy called *Dust*. (Yes, there's a book called *Dust*.) Lioy wrote this book after examining the hazardous concoction of chemicals and materials found in dust in the aftermath of 9 / 11.[20]

Our Recommendations

- Wash your hands frequently (fine, this isn't a building recommendation, but it's Public Health 101, and we feel obligated to say this at some point).
- Clean floors regularly with a HEPA vacuum. (Double-check that it's HEPA, or else you may just be picking up large dust particles, shredding them into millions of smaller particles, and blowing them all over your house or office.)
- Cleaning with a HEPA vacuum should be supplemented with periodic cleaning of other surfaces beyond the floor to help control dust and allergen accumulation from settled dust. And when we say surfaces, we don't just mean desks. We mean *all* surfaces, including walls, picture frames, molding, partitions, and doors, which are all covered with a fine layer of dust. (As people move around, they create, and are surrounded by, a dust cloud. Those particles eventually settle, and not just on the floor.)
- To help control the source of animal allergens, the use of an integrated pest management plan can be effective at controlling pest infestations without the introduction of harmful pesticide and rodenticide chemicals into your home or office.

Foundation 7: Acoustics and Noise

Exposure and health concerns surrounding noise have traditionally focused on noise-induced hearing loss. In fact, occupational health standards are *specifically designed* to evaluate and protect against hearing loss. There's more to the story of acoustics and noise than hearing loss and protection, but let's start there because it will help ground us in the ways we talk about noise and give us some upper tolerable limits.

In the United States, the Occupational Safety and Health Administration sets the noise limit at 90 dBA over an eight-hour time period. "dBA" refers to A-weighted decibels, where decibels are a unit of measurement for the intensity of sound, and the A-weighting refers to a scaling system designed to most closely approximate the noise heard by the human ear. Other internationally recognized worker health organizations like ACGIH set it at a more protective 85 dBA. (ACGIH used to stand for the American Conference of Governmental Industrial Hygienists, but they now just go with ACGIH.) There is also a ceiling limit of 130 dBA, which means that workers should not be exposed to sound at this level for even one second.[21]

To put these sound levels and exposure limits in perspective, libraries are about 40 dBA, normal conversation is typically in the range of 60 dBA, leaf blowers are in the range of 95 dBA right at the worker's ear, an airplane at takeoff can exceed 90 dBA from over a mile away, and a gunshot can hit 140 dBA or higher. Importantly, dBA is measured on a logarithmic scale. A *New Yorker* story published in 2019, "Is Noise Pollution the Next Public Health Crisis?," points out that the effect of this logarithmic scale is that a 100 dBA noise isn't twice as intense as 50 dBA noise; it's 100,000 times as intense![22]

So for workers for whom the ACGIH noise limit is applicable, the allowable exposure duration is halved for every increase of 3 dBA. This means that if the average daily noise is 88 dBA, workers can only be exposed for 4 hours rather than 8 hours at 85 dBA. Similarly, if the noise level were to be lowered to 82 dBA, the allowable exposure duration would increase to 16 hours. This is called the "exchange rate" or "equal-energy rule."

Interestingly enough, if you read the fine print, you will see that when calculating allowable worker exposure to noise, any noise exposure below 80 dBA is *not counted* toward the daily limits. That's because the goal is to protect from hearing loss, and there is little evidence that levels below 80 dBA lead to long-term hearing loss.

Impacts of Noise Beyond Hearing Loss

There are many work environments where noise levels reach this 80 dBA threshold (for example, on airplanes or on construction sites), but in an office, home, or school it is rare for noise to reach these levels for any sustained amount of time (at least it *should be* rare). Worker exposure limits tell us we should not be concerned, but that's because the regulations are focused only on noise-induced hearing loss. But noise and acoustics matter at levels well below 80 dBA.

Studies of student performance in schools offer quite compelling evidence of what noise can do to our performance. For example, a study of more than 500 children in primary schools in France showed that standardized test scores were 5.5 points lower for each 10 dB increase in noise level over the average noise level of approximately 50 dB.[23]

So what is the mechanism of action where noise impacts test performance? There are a few factors that are worth discussing. First, there is the background noise the teacher has to speak over. The current standard specifies that this background level should be 35 dBA or lower. Second is the direct sound coming from teacher, which should be 15 dBA over background (you want a +15 dBA signal-to-noise ratio). Third is how far away the student is from the teacher. For a teacher speaking at 65 dBA measured at 3 feet away, the sound level at the back of the classroom, 24 feet away, will be 47 dBA (sound level decreases 6 dBA with each doubling of distance, based on the inverse-square law). In this scenario, a student in the front of the classroom is hearing the teacher well because the teacher's voice is greater than +15 dBA above background at that location, but the student in the back falls below this signal-to-noise ratio. Fourth is the issue of reflectance and reverberation. In addition to the direct sound from the teacher, sound reflects off interior surfaces, arriving at the student's ear sometime after the direct sound. If the reverberation time is too long, this can cause the talking to sound muddy or inaudible. Sometimes a little reverberation is wanted, like in a concert hall, but in other environments, like offices and schools, the goal is to keep this low.

Perhaps the most interesting developments related to noise exposure are studies showing that the health concern around noise goes well beyond hearing loss and learning. Adverse noise exposure has been associated with sleep disorders (not surprising), and it can affect blood pressure and stress response, including increased levels of adrenaline and noradrenaline. Most surprisingly, newer research is showing a link between noise and cardiovascular health. In one study of homes around airports, the researchers found that people living in areas with higher aircraft noise had a 3.5 percent increase in cardiovascular admission rate in hospitals for every 10 decibel increase in noise.[24] The "highly exposed" group was well below the 80 dBA cutoff used in calculations for noise-induced hearing loss.

Our Recommendations

The issue of noise, like many things, is multifactorial—it's affected by location, mechanical system noise, window and wall design, and acoustical properties of the materials inside. It's also a question of the type of building and its intended use; certainly conference rooms need to be quieter than kitchen areas in an office, just as the school library needs to be quieter than the lunch room. For this reason, making broad recommendations for noise can be tricky. But we'll try it anyway.

- Define "noise zones" for different areas of the building, each with different targets for acceptable noise levels based on the intended use and users.
- Minimize noise transmission across these zones, and noise infiltration from outside, by focusing on walls, doors, and windows (that is, keep the zones distinct; otherwise, they're not really zones, right?).
- Use building materials that absorb sound and minimize reverberation.
- Consider technologies for noise cancellation or masking if and only if noise can't be adequately controlled through an engineering solution.
- Provide office workers with designated quiet areas for work that requires deep concentration, and areas with soundproof rooms for private conversations and telephone calls.

Foundation 8: Lighting and Views

Just as the invention of air-conditioning forever altered *where* we work, the invention of electric lighting forever altered *when* we work. With the exception of the past 140-some years since Thomas Edison invented the light bulb, our relationship with light has been governed by the natural day-night cycles created by Earth rotating on its axis. Our bodies evolved under this daily rhythm of celestial bodies.

The approximately 24-hour cycle observed in humans and many other organisms is what we call our circadian rhythm. It is largely regulated by imperceptible, nonvisual effects of light that allow our brains and bodies to get in alignment with the day-night cycle. When all is aligned with our circadian rhythm (meaning, when we get light at the right amount, in the right spectrum, and at the right time), we see positive benefits to sleep quality, mental health, and performance. When we don't, we see adverse impacts. Consider research showing that shift workers (the ultimate circadian-disrupted workers) are less alert, perform worse in their jobs, and are more likely to experience accidents.[25] That might seem obvious—it's intuitive that working overnight shifts might lead to more slips, trips, and falls, as a result of tired or unfocused workers. But if that doesn't surprise you, this might: shift workers also experience higher rates of chronic disease and even cancer. In fact, shift work is being considered as a probable carcinogen.[26]

Lighting Spectrum

Most of us today don't think much about light and circadian rhythms. We are more likely to think of light in a pragmatic way—"I need light to read and do my work and cook dinner and not trip as I walk around."

But the old way of thinking, that all light is created equal, that "light is light," is being supplanted. Not surprisingly, this new era is being ushered in by (1) new research and (2) new technologies.

On the research front, we have learned that the intensity, spectrum (or color), and timing of the light we are exposed to all influence us. Light intensity, or illuminance, is something we are all familiar with. This is simply how bright the light is in our workspace or home. More technically, it's the amount of illuminance hitting a specified surface area, measured in lux.

Our understanding of how the light spectrum influences us is newer, and maybe less intuitive. "Light spectrum" refers to the color of the light, usually characterized by manufacturers as a single measurement of "temperature" (in Kelvin, or K). Warm light is in the range of 3,500 K, cool white light is in the range of 4,000 K, and blue-enriched light is in the range of 6,500 K.

To understand how this might influence us, consider that the sun during the day is blue-enriched (6,500 K), and it's about 2,000 K immediately after sunrise and before sunset. (For those familiar with photography, you know the phrase "the golden hour," which refers to this time period right after sunrise or before sunset, when the warm colors from the sun enhance photos and there are fewer harsh shadows.)

The research results will match your intuition—studies on students in controlled settings show that if they are exposed to blue-enriched light, they experience higher levels of alertness, better concentration, faster cognitive processing speeds, and stronger performance on tests.[27] For office workers, we see similar results—improvements in mood and concentration.[28] These effects are driven by the power of blue-enriched light to act as a stimulant (alertness effects) and as a cue to entrain our circadian rhythms (circadian effects). This is why you have seen recommendations to avoid using your cell phones at night or in bed—they emit blue-enriched light. So in addition to the never-ending stimulating content available to you, the light itself is acting as a stimulant, right at the time your body is trying to wind down and fall asleep.

New lighting technology is enabling this type of research, and it's also showing up in the market as an implementable solution in buildings. We can now control the temperature (or warmth) of our electric light. This means that we can mimic the natural world, creating warm, low-temperature light in the mornings and evenings, and blue-enriched, higher-temperature light midday. This is also changing how we go about designing our buildings. Whereas traditionally we measured illuminance in lux to capture the *photopic* response of the human eye, we can now measure *melanopic* lux to capture the full range of lighting factors that influence alertness and circadian alignment.

Views and Biophilic Design

This brings us to biophilic design, a field of research and practice that, like the body of research on light, recognizes that the historical memory encoded in our biology, shaped over millennia, is influencing us now. Acclaimed Harvard biologist E. O. Wilson's popularized the theory that we are still governed in important ways by our innate, biologically encoded connection to nature.[29] In his book *Biophilia,* he makes the case that the environment in which we evolved is very different from the environment we now live in. We evolved in the African savannah's wide-open expanses, intimate with nature and seeking protection under tree canopies. At issue is that much of our biological coding happened at a time when we were an outdoor species. In our modern world, we have sealed ourselves off from the natural world. Yet our genetic hardwiring, built over millennia, still craves that connection to nature.

Our efforts to wall ourselves off from nature have been so successful that we have recently resorted to "dosing" ourselves with nature as a practice for preventive health. In Japan they practice *shinrin-yoku* (forest bathing)— taking intentional visits to forests for restorative purposes. In the United States, the Appalachian Mountain Club (AMC) operates a program called

"Outdoors Rx," where they work with the healthcare community in Boston to give nature "prescriptions" to kids under thirteen living in vulnerable communities. (John's family has been a long-time supporter of AMC and John has served on their Board.) The National Park Service has a similar program and promotes "Park Rx"—giving prescriptions for people to visit parks and nature to get them back in contact with our natural world—as part of its Healthy Parks, Healthy People program.

The biophilia hypothesis was soon followed by the field of biophilic design—an effort to put this theory into practice *indoors*. Biophilic design is an attempt to bring some nature into our indoor life, thereby bridging the gap between our genetic disposition and the realities of our modern world. Unfortunately, it is long on theory but short on substance (so far). Relative to other fields of study, not much research has been done to evaluate the impact of biophilic design on human performance since Wilson's book first came out in 1984.

Of that limited body of research, perhaps the most widely discussed among practitioners is a study of patients on the same floor of a hospital, where half the patients had windows facing a brick wall, and the other half had views of nature out their window.[30] Everything else—the doctors, the nurses, the treatments, the medicine—was the same, and patient placement in the good and bad rooms was randomized. The results were staggering: patients with rooms facing out to nature used less medication and had quicker recoveries. It was a true blockbuster study.

But since that study was published in the mid-1980s, there really hasn't been another study like it, and no attempts have even been made to replicate it. One has to wonder why.

Fortunately, new tools, such as augmented reality and virtual reality, eye tracking, and wearable sensors, are allowing us to dig a bit deeper in this domain. Joe's Healthy Buildings team is doing just that with a series of studies as part of its BIO program (Biophilic Interventions in Offices). In his team's first study at Harvard, led by Dr. Jie Yin, they found that even brief exposure to "biophilic environments" had a direct impact on human physiology—lower blood pressure and heart rate—and also led to better performance on short-term memory tests.[31] In our second study, we added a new twist and created *virtual* biophilic environments and tested creativity. We found that people in these indoor spaces with nature performed better on three domains of creativity—fluency, flexibility, and originality.[32] In our third experiment, we wanted to test the speed at which biophilic designed spaces aid stress recovery. Here, we used a well-known stressor (a math test!) to produce a heightened anxiety state in the study participants before placing them in an office setting with or without elements of biophilic design. What we found was striking—being placed in a nature-inspired indoor space lowered the stress response within four minutes.[33]

The growing body of research on biophilic design is showing that there are real benefits to bringing nature indoors and reestablishing our lost connection to the natural world, for both our physical and mental health. Amazingly, in the first of our BIO studies, the virtual worlds generated an equivalent response to the real thing. If you've ever tried out a virtual-reality roller-coaster ride or horror experience, you know that this technology can certainly elicit strong physiological responses. There are clear applications of this research to the burgeoning metaverse, too. Will we design virtual work and gathering spaces that promote health? Or will we make the same mistakes in the virtual world that we've made with real buildings?

Now, to be clear, we're not suggesting that you throw on virtual-reality goggles instead of taking a walk in the park. But think about the many people who don't have access to nature—the very sick in hospitals, the infirm, deep urbanites. What if a brief respite in nature, even experienced virtually, could help reset us just a bit as we are hunkered down in the Great Indoors?

Our Recommendations

- Meet minimum illuminance guidelines and control flicker.
- Maximize access to daylight and windows.
- Focus on intensity, spectrum, and timing of light exposure.
- Bring some nature indoors by incorporating elements of biophilic design.

Foundation 9: Safety and Security

In Maslow's Hierarchy of Needs, finding shelter is presented as a fundamental requirement, right alongside food and water. Seeking safe shelter is at the top of our physiological priorities. This is hardwired into our DNA—humans and many other animals carry around a "wall-hugging" trait, called thigmotaxis, to keep us safe from the dangers of predators in open spaces.

When faced with fear, our tendency is to seek the comfort and relative safety of a wall at our back. (You might think of the term "wallflower," which describes a shy person at a party or a dance, or the classic mafia don who always likes to sit in the corner seat at the restaurant table so they are protected on three sides.) Our thigmotactic response is so strong that it is used to test the impact of antianxiety medicines.

The "safety and security" foundation can seem like an oddball. When thinking about Healthy Buildings, people will quickly go to things like "air quality" and "water quality," but few of us think of safety and security. We've seen the quizzical looks firsthand. At health science conferences, when we flash the 9 Foundations logo on the screen, it's inevitable that a few people will raise their hands to ask, "Why is safety and security part of healthy buildings?" The converse happens in conversations with security experts, who wonder what health has to do with their business. The reason it's an oddball is that health scientists don't typically think about security, and the security industry has no idea that it's actually in the health-care business. We're here to tell you that security and health are linked.

Fight or Flight

Safety and security have an effect on our acute and chronic health. Buildings have systems in place to protect us from obvious hazards like a fire emergency or a carbon monoxide leak—the so-called fire and life safety systems of a building. It's easy to understand how these features might impact our health.

Buildings also have other safety and security features, such as "square badge" guards at the front door and security cameras. Do these influence our health? On the acute side, the answer is yes—they are there to deter or intervene in the event of a direct threat against our safety, such as an active shooter in a building. But there are also other forces at work. It turns out that feeling safe and secure affects our stress levels and mental health and helps us to avoid chronic health conditions. Here's how it all works:

> When our sense of security is threatened, it can trigger a cascade of biological "fight or flight" responses that alter our physical and psychological functioning. Perceived threats to safety flood our bodies with stress-induced hormones like adrenaline and cortisol that elevate heart rate and increase blood pressure. While individuals vary in their response, psychological stress can

negatively affect immune function with onset of immune changes occurring in as little as five minutes. Chronically elevated stress hormones suppress immunity which can exacerbate autoimmune diseases and other inflammatory conditions, while elevated blood pressure levels can eventually lead to damaged arteries and plaque formation, putting stressed individuals at greater risk of hypertension and cardiovascular disease. Over time, these responses place wear and tear on the body that increases disease susceptibility.[34]

Most of the health evidence comes from studies of the elevated stress hormones of people living in unsafe or stressful environments. But what is the role of the building in all of this? The literature is nascent here, but what we do see is provocative: having a security guard, cameras on city streets, or enhanced locks may promote a greater feeling of safety, which can cut off the cascade of stress-related health effects.

Enterprise Security Risk Management

There are important shifts under way that are worth noting. First and foremost, the security field is moving past the notion that security is "just" square-badge security guards at the door. Our colleague Juliette Kayyem, former Assistant Secretary of Government Affairs at the US Department of Homeland Security and a faculty member at the Harvard Kennedy School, sees an important evolution away from this emphasis on physical barriers. "Security is, in many respects, the easy part," she confided. "The challenge in today's society, and a mission for the built environment, is how to promote 'secure flow,' meaning the movement of people, goods, and networks that minimizes risk but still allows for movement that is the core to our societies. Integrating technology to allow for movement through and into buildings is how we must think about twenty-first-century security. Walls may be simplistically appealing, but they are not realistic or conducive to the ease of flow."[35]

Along these same lines, a new field called Enterprise Security Risk Management (ESRM) is taking a holistic approach to security.[36] We mention it here because buildings play a central role in this changing view of the role of security in a company. ESRM gives us the security framework for managing a wider array of risks that were not traditionally thought of as pertaining to "security." We think the tie-in to buildings clear.

Hospitals are one set of buildings that have been ahead of the game on safety and security issues for a long time, and that's because they have a

TABLE 6.1   The role of buildings in Enterprise Security Risk Management [ESRM].

ESRM Focus Area	Relationship to Buildings
Cybersecurity	"Smart" buildings and Internet of Things
Business continuity	Secure flow; building or region power outages; resiliency of buildings during and following natural disaster
Physical security	Security personnel; automated locks, camera systems, and alerts; badge access
Acute event	Fire and life safety systems; training and planning for active-shooter; response to bomb threats and terrorist attacks
Situational awareness	Knowing who is in the building, when, and where; monitoring information threads (social media, police channels, official reports) in buffers around your building; "see something, say something"

framework for evaluating performance. Hospitals are reviewed by the Joint Commission, the accrediting body for health-care facilities. With annual audits and the potential for massive fines or even the shutdown of operations, hospitals spend a lot of time and resources meeting the commission's many requirements, which include things you might expect concerning patient safety, such as the use of restraints or de-escalation procedures.

If you don't work in, own, or manage a health-care facility, you might be thinking that you can gloss over this section. But there are lessons to be learned for everyone. The Joint Commission requires that every facility have a *written* security risk management plan that includes strategies for mitigating workplace violence; identifying threats and vulnerabilities; managing access controls such as key cards; operating surveillance systems and security cameras; verifying fire and life safety features, such as by ensuring that fire doors and walls aren't penetrated with cabling; negotiating active-shooter scenarios; and managing cyber and IT security.

All of this fits in with Kayyem's vision of changing security and "secure flow." The hospital needs to be operating 24 / 7, so security is not just about walls and guards; it's about maintaining security while simultaneously maintaining flow. Like the Joint Commission, ESRM is a holistic risk-management approach, where safety and security are seen as core to the business function. This is why we feel strongly that "safety and security" is one of the 9 Foundations of a Healthy Building. We hope you will come away thinking that this sounds like good practice, whatever building you are in.

Our Recommendations

- Meet all fire and life safety standards (for example, fire suppression systems, smoke detection, carbon monoxide detection, and emergency lighting).
- Focus on "secure flow."
- Develop an ESRM plan that includes a focus on the building safety and security factors (for example, fire doors and penetrations, safety lighting, physical security, surveillance and camera systems, cyber and IT security, emergency contingency planning, and the monitoring of events around your building).
- Integrate safety and security into the core management function.

Estimating the Economic Benefits of It All

There have been surprisingly few efforts to quantify the economic benefits from Healthy Building strategies. One of the most widely cited and best analyses there is was done by Bill Fisk and his colleagues at the Lawrence Berkeley National Lab. In 2011, they estimated that there would be benefits of $20 billion to the US economy if only three of these Healthy Building strategies were implemented—ventilation, thermal health, and mold and moisture control.[37]

If you are thinking these are macroeconomic numbers that don't influence your company, your building, or your investment, think again. This isn't a typical economic analysis that gets to $20 billion by including ancillary benefits to the economy like higher construction activity, or sales of better equipment, or hiring consultants. No, this analysis says there is $20 billion in benefits from employee productivity *in the building*. That's right—$20 billion of potential benefits are sitting on the sidelines, waiting to be moved from the bench into your company's bottom line.

And remember, this benefit only accounts for three of our 9 Foundations. Further, the benefit is only from employee performance. Additional gains are to be had when better buildings can be used as a recruiting tool to attract the best talent, and when they play a role in making sure that talent sticks around—not to mention reducing absenteeism and other sick building issues.

What's Next?

We've now armed you with some hard evidence of the many ways a building influences your health and your employees' health. We also sprinkled in some recommendations for each of the 9 Foundations—everything from measuring CO_2 to verifying optimal ventilation performance to measuring bacteria and pH in water to enhancing the air quality using MERV 13 or higher-rated filters or portable air purifiers. In Chapter 7 we'll get you thinking about how the products you put into these great new buildings influence the people inside them and their health.

CHAPTER SEVEN

Our Global Chemical Experiment

> If we are going to live so intimately with these chemicals—eating
> and drinking them, taking them into the very marrow of our
> bones—we had better know something about their nature and
> their power.
>
> —RACHEL CARSON

OVER 200 INDUSTRIAL CHEMICALS are now readily detectable in the blood, breast milk, or urine of Americans and of most people in industrial nations around the world.[1] Many of these chemicals come from the products we use in our buildings. Because we know so little about them, our Harvard colleague Elsie Sunderland calls this our "global chemical experiment."

The fundamental problem is that these 200 industrial chemicals are just the beginning. In the United States there are more than 80,000 chemicals in commerce. Guess how many have been thoroughly evaluated for health and safety? About 300. If that number is shocking to you, it should be. But here is an even more shocking number. Guess how many chemicals the Environmental Protection Agency (EPA) has *banned* since 1976, the year the first "toxics" law was passed? Nine. Yes, you read that right—9 chemicals out of more than 80,000 are currently banned by the EPA. That's it. And the story gets worse, because 5 of those chemicals were already banned before the law was established in 1976.[2] So in 40 years, the EPA has banned a total of 4 new toxic chemicals. Its approach is so ineffective that even something like asbestos (asbestos!) has not yet been banned. And there are many more chemicals with worrisome toxicological profiles that are not even being reviewed.

Many of these chemicals are used in everyday products—our carpets, furniture, building materials, and on and on. In many cases these chemicals can migrate out of their original product and, because of their environmental persistence or ubiquity, appear all over our homes, schools, hospitals, and the planet—in some instances up to the North Pole. And we find them in our bodies.

In this chapter we're going to focus on how the stuff we put in our buildings affects our health. This is the next frontier in Healthy Buildings—sometimes called "healthier materials," "material health," or "chemicals of concern." This movement is just starting to gain traction, with major players, from industry to environmental activists to nonprofit rating systems, all getting in the game.

Bodybuilding

In the Arnold Schwarzenegger era of bodybuilding in the 1970s, it was an open secret that anabolic steroids were commonly used. Even Arnold admits to using them, and no doubt he did plenty of hard work to sculpt a barrel chest that you could balance a glass of water on. The ultimate Mr. Universe. A picture of perfection. On the outside.

Hidden from the judges were the ravaging effects steroids can have on the body. The one that was most famously discussed (and true!)? Smaller testicles. At least one antisteroid ad campaign attempted to use this fact to scare young men, showing a bodybuilder with massive shoulders, arms, and chest . . . wearing the world's smallest jockstrap.

Steroids, and other chemicals you'll read about in this chapter, can affect our natural hormone balance. The increased testosterone throws our endogenous hormones out of whack, leading to impacts on the male testes and sperm production, as well as, for some, breast growth. Later in life, armed with additional scientific evidence, Arnold talked about his steroid use not as bodybuilding but as "body destroying."[3] He looked great on the outside, but the steroids were destroying the parts of the body we couldn't see.

To bring this back to buildings, the analogy we'll make here is that body-building is similar to what is called the "core and shell" of a building. If that term is new to you, the core and shell are what the design and construction teams deliver before the "fit-out." Meaning they deliver the skeleton and skin of the building—the concrete and steel, the windows and outside wall. The fit-out is everything else that goes into the building, based on the desires of the future occupant. Sometimes the core and shell can look really good on the outside but be wildly polluted on the inside.

Smaller Testicles from Building Materials?

Here's the connection to bodybuilding and steroids: some of the chemicals we are exposed to in buildings affect our reproductive system, just as steroids affect the reproductive system. For our male readers, let's put this another way: the chemicals in your chair could be wreaking havoc on your penis. For our female readers: don't worry, we'll get to your reproductive system shortly. We started this section by focusing on men on the advice of a female friend who, rightly fed up with action only happening when it affects men, gave us this sage advice: " Making it about MEN and THAT, you will get people's attention real fast."

Some of the chemicals used in building materials are what scientists call endocrine-disrupting chemicals. Your endocrine system is your hormone system, so this phrase "endocrine-disrupting" really just means "chemicals that interfere with your hormones."

Sounds a bit like steroids. Some of these chemicals can cause testicular cancer. Others affect sperm count. Others have been associated with failure of testes to descend in babies.

That's the story for men. The reality, of course, is that most of these chemicals are equal-opportunity offenders, affecting both men and women. For women, they can interfere with and disrupt the natural balance of the thyroid system, including the production of thyroid hormones like thyroxine (T4) and the transport protein transthyretin (TTR) that carries T4 around the body.

The assault on women's health from these chemicals also extends to their reproductive health. Some chemicals commonly found in buildings have been associated with adverse reproductive success—for example, increasing the likelihood by twofold that it will take a year or longer to become pregnant. Women in that study were also more likely to report irregular menstrual cycles.[4]

Let's now look at how we got to this state of affairs, and what you can do to tackle the problem in your buildings.

Chemicals of Concern

America's problem with "chemicals of concern" all started with a well-intentioned law in 1976, the Toxic Substances Control Act (TSCA, pronounced "tos-ka").[5] The 1970s was a time of intense recognition of the issues surrounding environmental pollution, following the publication of Rachel Carson's book *Silent Spring*, which focused on the overuse (and misuse) of pesticides like DDT and the resulting impact on the environment, birds and other wildlife, and human health.[6] This spurred a series of environmental regulations signed by President Richard Nixon and led to the creation of the EPA, the Occupational Health and Safety Administration, and TSCA.

TSCA was designed to regulate new and existing chemicals. One big problem right out of the gate was that all existing chemicals in use in 1976 were grandfathered in. The EPA was then tasked with sorting out which of these chemicals, if any, represented an "unreasonable risk to human health or the environment." It had the same goal for new chemicals introduced into the market. Seems straightforward enough, right?

While well intentioned, the EPA has clearly been overwhelmed in the enforcement of TSCA. Just look at the sheer number of chemicals currently in commerce (80,000), the number of these chemicals adequately studied for health and safety (~300), and the number that have been banned since 1976 (4). It seems unlikely that more than 79,700 of the 80,000 of the known chemicals—never mind the unknown—are fully safe for long-term ingestion, inhalation, and direct contact by humans. In fact, the scientific community has identified many dozens, if not hundreds, of chemicals since 1976 that are dangerous to human health but not on the immediate regulatory radar.

But there is a more insidious aspect of TSCA. It has led to repeated swapping out of one harmful chemical for another, in what scientists have dubbed "regrettable substitution."

Regrettable Substitution: The BPA-Free Story

Here's how regrettable substitution works. Let's take bisphenol A (BPA) as an example. We're certain most of you have seen "BPA-free" baby products or water bottles on the market. This came about as a direct result of a consumer-led campaign against BPA after word got out of its toxicity.

BPA is a compound widely used in plastics that interferes with our natural hormone systems.

To put some specifics on this, BPA binds with your body's thyroid and estrogen receptors, and a few others. We recognize that phrases like "hormone disruption" and "hormone binding" may not mean much to the average reader (and "endocrine-disrupting chemical" is understood by even fewer), so let's make this a bit more concrete. A recent review of the toxicological effects of the compound show that BPA can cause abnormalities in the female reproductive tract, decreases in fertility, impacts on the mammary glands, alterations in the function of brain neuronal synapses, and metabolic changes like altered blood glucose and insulin levels.[7] We could go on, but you get the picture. Hormones are our body's signaling system, and interfering in that system can affect our major biological systems—from our brain and reproductive systems to our metabolic and even immune systems.

All of these effects, it should be noted, were found *at low levels* of exposure to BPA (what we call low-dose effects).

We'll continue the BPA story by focusing on consumer products because that is how most people have heard about BPA, but the phenomenon applies to many building materials as well. BPA is part of polycarbonate and epoxy resins, which means it can be found in building facades and roofs, in paints and caulk, and in flooring and fiberglass binders.

Consumer concern triggered a widespread movement to shun many products, leading to the ubiquitous "BPA-free" labels showing up on baby products, toys, and water bottles on every store shelf. A public health win? Not so fast.

In many cases BPA has simply been swapped for bisphenol S (BPS), a chemical cousin with a similar toxicological profile; BPS is as hormonally active as BPA. BPS, we learned, is also estrogenic and androgenic, just like BPA. And now BPS, having gotten a bad rap, is often being swapped for bisphenol F (BPF), which, surprising no one, targets our body in the same way and has been found to have "actions and potencies similar to those of

BPA."[8] Why is this not surprising? They are chemical cousins ("structural analogs" is how it would be written in a scientific journal).

So even when the market responds with BPA-free everything, it turns out that in some cases we are simply making regrettable substitutions. This is sometimes referred to as playing a game of "chemical whack-a-mole," a reference to the carnival game where a mole pops up and the player has to quickly hit it on the head with a soft mallet. As soon as that happens, a similar, but different, mole pops its head out that the player needs to hit. Over and over. Joe wrote about this in an op-ed published in the *Washington Post* in 2016, showing how this "chemical whack-a-mole" has happened with not just BPA, but also with pesticides like DDT, plasticizers in nail polish, and even the toxic flavoring chemicals used in e-cigs.[9] There are also a few other notable examples related to building materials that we'll go into soon.

This is what the current regulatory system allows. As soon as a bad actor chemical is identified, it can quickly be swapped out for a chemical cousin, with no proof needed that the replacement is safe. Thus the cycle starts anew each time, with scientists having to prove that the chemical is harmful after it's already on the market. We "whack" one chemical only to have a similar one appear. This is how we got BPA → BPS → BPF →?. Simply put, the approach of allowing industry to police itself has not worked. Consumers are being treated as guinea pigs in a global chemical experiment.

Using a test offered by Silent Spring Institute, Joe gave himself and his team at Harvard urine tests as a holiday gift one year so they could all learn about the chemicals in their own bodies.[10] (Nerds!) Turns out, he is a perfect example of regrettable substitution. Check out his results, compared against national averages. Joe is "BPA-free," just like a baby's sippy cup. But he's loaded with BPS.

Nick Kristof, op-ed columnist for the *New York Times,* took this same test a year later. Guess what he found? Low in BPA, just like Joe. Unlike Joe, Kristof was also low in BPS. But Kristof didn't escape this saga entirely. He's an even better example of "advanced stage" regrettable substitution. It turns out he's loaded with the next substitute for BPA: BPF.[11]

So if you briefly switched to glass bottles only to have migrated back to BPA-free plastic, you may want to think twice about that decision. Here's the bad news: there are dozens of stories just like the BPA example. And it's happening in your buildings right now.

Your Results

Graph legend

- ● your chemical level
- ○ other participants' chemical levels
- ◉ participants for whom the chemical was not detected
- **ng/mL:** nanograms of the chemical per milliliter of urine from your sample

BPA (bisphenol A)

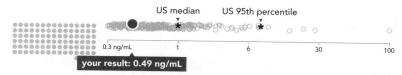

BPS (bisphenol S)

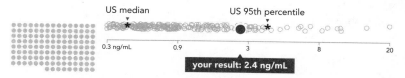

FIGURE 7.1   Test results for Joe's urinary levels of the metabolite of BPA and BPS, compared against nationally representative US data. Silent Spring Institute.

Chemical Whack-a-Mole on Steroids: Forever Chemicals

A great way to transition to focusing on buildings is to think about the highly fluorinated chemicals we use as water and stain repellents. Like BPA, most of us are familiar with these chemicals from their use in consumer products. We use them in our clothing, outdoor gear, dental floss, cosmetics, non-stick pans, and many other consumer applications. But they are also used in and on products found all over buildings—chairs, couches, curtains, carpets, and paints.

It's worth taking a look at the chemistry behind these chemicals because it's fascinating and it helps explain both why consumers like them and why they are so problematic. These stain-repellent chemicals are characterized by the carbon-fluorine bond, one of the strongest bonds in all of organic chemistry. When manufacturers string these together to create a carbon-fluorine backbone, some useful industrial properties appear. This chain of repeated carbon-fluorine links is able to resist oil, water, and grease. The ultrastrong bond is what prevents this stuff from penetrating to the underlying material. That's why we have coated our furniture, camping tents, and even our clothing with these chemicals for the past 60 years or so. It's the chemistry behind our nonstick pots and pans and waterproof rain jackets and tents, and it's a component of aqueous film–forming firefighting foam.

The problem is multifold. First, the chemicals don't always stay in the products—they escape, entering our air, food, and water. Ever wonder why your nonstick pan loses that nonstick ability after some time? Or why some stain-repellent surface treatments ask you to reapply every few months? Where do you think the chemicals are all going? The answer is that they are now found all over the globe, from the polar regions to the middle of our oceans, inside our buildings, and inside all of us. Ninety-eight percent of Americans have at least one set of these chemicals in their blood.[12]

Second, that superstrong bond comes with a dark side: the bonds are so strong that these chemicals will never fully break down in the environment. Ever. And when we say "ever" here, we mean millennia. This is why Joe dubbed them "Forever Chemicals" in an op-ed he wrote for the *Washington Post*.[13] The name is a play on the F and the C that constitute the carbon-fluorine bond, while also highlighting their most salient feature—extreme environmental persistence. (The technical name for these chemicals is "per- and polyfluorinated alkyl substances" [PFAS]—technically accurate but wholly inaccessible terminology for the general public.)

A skeptic might reasonably ask, Is there a *health concern* with these chemicals? The answer is a resounding yes. In fact, these are the very chemicals we were referring to when we first mentioned chemicals that are associated with testicular cancer in the beginning of this chapter.

Some Forever Chemicals, such as C8, are also associated with kidney cancer.[14] The public learned this only after an egregious environmental contamination issue surfaced. DuPont, the maker of many products using Forever Chemicals, was dumping them into the Ohio River for many years from its Washington Works plant in Parkersburg, West Virginia. The river supplied drinking water to tens of thousands of people downstream, who were unknowingly drinking the contaminated water. A resulting lawsuit revealed the shocking scale of this dumping activity, and the courts, seeking to understand the potential impact on those downstream, created a scientific panel (the C8 Science Panel) to investigate the spread of these chemicals in the water and throughout the environment (the plant was also emitting Forever Chemicals into the air). The C8 Science Panel was charged with determining whether there were "probable links" to human health effects.[15] Through a series of rigorous, high-profile research studies, the panel established an association between exposure to C8 and cancer. Subsequently, a class action lawsuit was filed against DuPont and the plaintiffs were awarded $671 million. (Full disclosure: Joe worked as an expert witness for the plaintiffs in this lawsuit.) This story was subsequently told in the movie *Dark Waters*.

Other studies have shown that some Forever Chemicals also elicit the most dramatic immune suppression ever observed for an environmental toxicant[16] and interfere with body weight regulation.[17] So much so that they are now being called "obesogens"—meaning that they may contribute to the obesity epidemic in America. Even if you don't use nonstick pans or spend time on office chairs whose fabric has been coated in this stuff, you still can't escape—they are in the drinking water of tens of millions Americans above the "safe" level set by the EPA, according to a study led by Elsie Sunderland and her team from the Harvard T. H. Chan School of Public Health and John A. Paulson School of Engineering and Applied Sciences.[18]

And just like the BPA → BPS → BPF example, the original Forever Chemical that grabbed our attention, C8, has now been swapped for C6 and C10 (C is the number of carbons; C8 has an 8-chain carbon-fluorine backbone, C6 has 6, and C10 has 10). C8 started to get a bad rap with major lawsuits under way in the mid-2000s. A book was even written about it called *Stain-Resistant, Nonstick, Waterproof, and Lethal: The Hidden Dangers of C8*.[19] With the rising public awareness of these hazards, C8 was phased out. But that doesn't mean the problem was solved. One C6 variant that has captured headlines is known as "GenX," having gained notoriety because DuPont (now Chemours) was dumping GenX into the Cape Fear River in Fayetteville, North Carolina—a river that supplies drinking water to people in the Wilmington, North Carolina, area.[20] Because the scientific community has only recently begun to investigate GenX, there aren't any human health studies yet. But what we know from animal toxicology studies is damning—cancer of the liver, pancreas, and testicles.

GenX is not the end of the story. We wish the story of regrettable substitution with Forever Chemicals were as simple as the linear BPA story: BPA → BPS → BPF. For Forever Chemicals, it's more like the mythical Hydra, where every snake head that is cut off returns in multiples. Sure, we wised up to the dangers of C8 and banned them from the market. But instead of just one or two substitutes, like C6 and C10, there are over 5,000 variants of these Forever Chemicals! It's chemical whack-a-mole on steroids. The game is exhausting, and dangerous.

Chemical Flame Retardants

If you thought that was a crazy story, wait until you read about this one.

This story starts in the mid-1970s, with the use of chemical flame retardants in kids' pajamas. (Do kids spontaneously combust?) One chemical flame retardant used in pajamas, which we'll call "tris" for short, was a brominated flame retardant. (Think of the far-right side of the periodic table, where the halogens reside. We've been talking about one halogen already, fluorine, and now we'll talk a bit about the halogens bromine, chlorine, and iodine.) This chemical, tris, was known to be carcinogenic and mutagenic (that is, it damages DNA), but it only really grabbed the public's attention after a simple (and elegant) study that showed that tris "escapes" from pajamas and gets into the bodies of kids.[21] In that study, they tested the urine of kids in the morning, comparing those who wore pajamas treated with tris with those who did not. They showed, definitively, that tris was being absorbed into the body overnight. As a result, tris was banned from the market. (By now in this chapter, you know this is not the end of the tris story. We'll move on chronologically, but stay tuned for more on tris.)

Also in the 1970s, another brominated flame retardant was in use, and this one was used in buildings. Polybrominated biphenyls (PBBs) are a class of flame retardants that were used in plastics found in televisions and in foam found in couches and chairs. PBBs were used in our buildings and consumer products for about a decade, but then use abruptly stopped. Why? A crazy, but true, story about how a human error at a manufacturing plant led to the poisoning of Michigan and a toxic legacy that lasts through to today.

A chemical company that sold PBBs in the 1970s, Michigan Chemical Company, also sold animal feed supplement. A shortage of preprinted bags at the packaging plant led to an accidental mislabeling, and bags of PBBs were shipped out as cattle feed supplement.[22] Want to hazard a guess as to what happened next? Farmers and ranchers reported animals with a loss of appetite (go figure . . .). Then things got bad. These PBBs are lipophilic chemicals—literally "fat loving." As the cows ate the PBBs, they stored the chemicals in their fatty tissue. It was months before the mislabeling issue was discovered, and by that time PBBs had lodged themselves into the fatty tissue of millions of animals in the food chain. Humans, at the top of that chain, were the final repository of these PBBs.

The remedy? PBBs were banned and millions of animals had to be killed (culled, in the "make us feel OK about this" parlance). But it was too late— by then, anyone consuming meat in Michigan was consuming those PBBs and, just like the animals, storing those PBBs in their own fatty tissue. But we can't cull humans (!), so the result is . . . the people of Michigan were unwilling participants in a great human toxicological experiment.

The environmental persistence of PBBs and their ability to store in our bodies meant that this was not a problem that went away quickly. The legacy persists to this day: 60 percent of people tested in Michigan in the 2000s still had levels of PBBs in their bodies that were higher than 95 percent of the rest of the US population. And it's a toxic legacy—a summary of research findings hosted at Emory School of Public Health shows that women with higher levels of PBBs in their blood had fewer days between menstrual cycles, more days of bleeding, lower estrogen levels, and higher rates of breast cancer.[23]

But that's not where things ended.

It turns out that kids born to parents from Michigan have PBBs in their blood, despite being born after the ban went into place. Their moms passed these PBBs to them through the womb and through breastfeeding. Boys born to moms with higher levels of PBBs in the body reported more genital and urinary issues. Girls born to moms with higher levels of PBBs in the body started menstruating a year earlier than their peers. When these girls became women of childbearing age, they were more likely to suffer miscarriages.

Three generations have been affected.

As shocking as these results were, they shouldn't really have been unexpected. As far back as 1978, a Harvard study reported that "these compounds *readily enter the fetus* by crossing the placental barrier and can be transferred to newborn children after extensive passage into breast milk." "Interestingly,"

the study went on, "*low doses* of PBBs exert a broad spectrum of toxicological, pharmacological, and biochemical effects despite low acute toxicity,"
causing the authors to conclude that "PBBs are *teratogenic, immunosuppres-
sive,* and potentially *carcinogenic*" (emphasis added).[24]

Knowing that PBBs are toxic to animals; knowing, based on research published in 1978, that PBBs cross the placenta and are teratogenic (that is, that
they can alter the normal development of an embryo or fetus), and possibly
carcinogenic; and seeing that the populace was rightly outraged after the
Michigan debacle, what was the industry response? Add an oxygen in the
middle of the molecule and create a "new" brominated flame retardant to
be used just like PBBs—in couches, chairs, mattresses, and plastic casings
around televisions and computers.

From the perspective of the market, and regulators, this was a new
chemical with a new name. No longer PBBs, but PBDEs—polybrominated
diphenyl ethers. The only way to really show you the insanity and the shortsightedness of this approach is to show you the chemical structures. You don't
need a degree in organic chemistry to see that the "safe replacement" for
PBBs looks an awful lot like the original.

For both PBBs and PBDEs, there are two rings (called phenyls in organic
chemistry). Depending on the number of bromines and their position on
the rings, you can have up to 209 variants (called congeners). Here we are
showing two tetrabrominated flame retardants (four bromines). The only real
difference is that, for PBDEs, there is an oxygen between the rings (this is
called an ether). That is the full deconstruction of the name "polybrominated
diphenyl ether."

PBDEs were used from the early 1980s through the mid-2000s, much of
that time escaping the notice of health scientists and the public. It wasn't
until a Swedish study was published in the early 2000s that concern started
to rise. In that study, researchers looked at breast milk samples from a biobank, which had stored samples dating back to the 1970s. These scientists

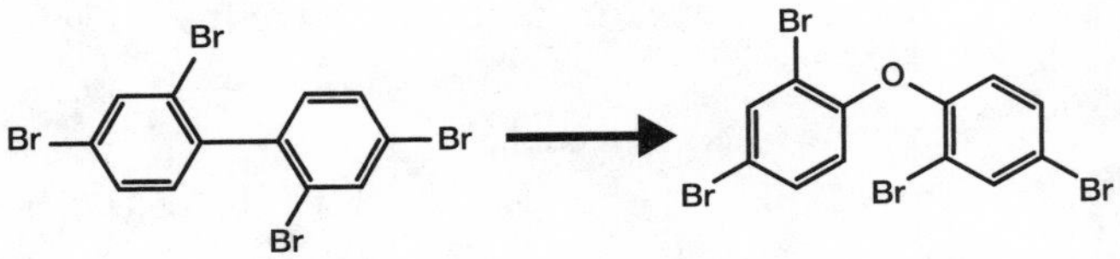

FIGURE 7.2   Chemical structures of PBBs and PBDEs.

noticed an exponential rise in the level of this "new" chemical in the breast milk.[25] (New to researchers, anyway; the industry certainly knew about it.)

This sparked intense interest from researchers—a "scientific feeding frenzy," in the words of professor Tom Webster at Boston University.[26] The scientific process followed a familiar pattern, asking and answering a series of questions.

Where were these chemicals in our environment? (Answer: in air and dust in every home, office, school, and place we looked, including in polar bears, eagles, and sea turtles.)[27]

Could they be found in humans? (Answer: yes. They are detected in the blood of nearly everyone.)[28]

Were they determined to be toxic in animal studies? (Answer: yes. PBDEs interfere with thyroid hormones and affect neurodevelopment reproductive systems.)[29]

Was that enough to ban them? (Answer: no. Claims were made that the results of animal studies do not represent human health effects.)

Were human health effects found in the subsequent human studies? (Answer: yes. Surprising no one, the human studies found what the animal toxicology studies found: impacts on the thyroid, neurological development, and re-production.[30] In one study, Joe and his collaborators found that women with higher levels of PBDEs in their body had a higher risk of developing thyroid disease—a risk that was threefold higher for women postmenopause.)[31]

What was the mechanism of action? (Answer: PBDEs look an awful lot like your endogenous thyroid hormone T4.) And here, we get to bring in that last halogen we haven't yet touched on—iodine. T4 has a phenyl ring on one end of it, just like the one we showed you for PBBs and PBDEs. But instead of bromines around it, T4 has iodine.

If you have a keen eye and were comparing T4 in Figure 7.3 with the PBBs and PBDEs in Figure 7.2, you might have noticed that the left side of T4

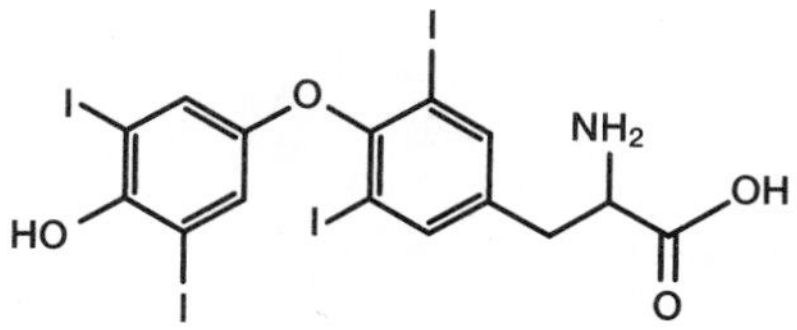

FIGURE 7.3   Chemical structure of thyroid hormone T4 showing similar ring and halogen structure as PBBs and PBDEs (left side).

here looks similar to PBBs and PBDEs. But you might have also noticed that T4 has an -OH hanging off that ring, whereas PBDEs do not, and maybe you were wondering if that difference made them dissimilar.

Well, that -OH is called a hydroxyl group, and after PBDEs (and PBBs and many other chemicals) enter our body, our metabolic system tries to make them a bit more water soluble by adding this -OH group right in between the two bromines, just like the -OH in between the two iodines. Once that happens, these "hydroxylated" PBDEs look even more like T4. In other words, PBDEs already look a lot like T4, but once PBDEs enter the body, they transform into something that looks *even more* like T4 than the original chemical. Does our body notice?

The science shows how much our bodies are confused by these chemicals. These hydroxylated PBDEs have a binding potency to thyroid transport proteins that is up to 1,600 times higher than PBDEs without the -OH.[32] They also inhibit a key enzyme that regulates estrogen with a potency up to 220 times higher than PBDEs without the -OH.[33] This may be getting slightly technical, but once you see the mechanism of action, you can understand how much PBDEs trick our body's hormone receptors, inviting them to mistake hydroxylated PBDEs for endogenous hormones. In light of this, the research showing that PBDEs interfere with thyroid hormones and are associated with thyroid disease make perfect sense.

Recall, PBDEs were introduced in the early 1980s. But research on exposure and toxicity only started in earnest in the late 1990s. This body of research on PBDEs took more than a decade to accumulate. In the end, after 30 years of use and widespread global contamination, for 20 of which they were entirely off the radar of health scientists, PBDEs were banned.

If you think the story ends here, you haven't been paying attention.

Once PBDEs were banned, a whole new set of regrettable substitutes were introduced, one of which was tris. (We warned you that we weren't done with tris from the kids pajamas just yet . . .) But how could that be? We told you tris was banned in the 1970s after the pajama fiasco. Well, it turns out that *brominated* tris was banned in the 1970s, but its chemical cousin, *chlorinated* tris, also used in kids' pajamas during the 1970s, wasn't technically banned. It was just quietly removed from the market—only to be reintroduced as a "safer" alternative to PBDEs 30 years later. Again, like PBDEs, we only discovered this when enterprising scientists like Heather Stapleton at Duke University started to investigate a "new" and curious chemical that started showing up in the data—but this time it wasn't in breast milk from a biobank. This time Stapleton and colleagues started seeing tris in baby products.[34] It was everywhere, and at high levels. It turns out that chlorinated tris was being used in kids' car seats, baby chairs, changing-table pads, nursing pillows, and mattresses. Oh, we almost forgot to tell you—tris is carcinogenic.[35]

But this is also not the end of the story.

Tris got a bad rap, again. So, with attention turning toward the halogens (bromine and chlorine), the industry deftly moved on to another set of chemical flame retardants. Next up in the "regrettable substitution" chain were halogen-free organophosphate (OP) flame retardants.

The idea that these OP flame retardants were "safer" was soon debunked. A study led by our Harvard colleague Russ Hauser, showed that OP flame retardants were associated with severe adverse reproductive issues, including a decreased likelihood of fertilization and embryo implantation and a decreased likelihood of having a clinical pregnancy.[36] It gets worse—if you were lucky enough to get pregnant, those with higher levels of OP flame retardants in their body were less likely to have a live birth. (As of the writing of this book, OP flame retardants are still widely used in buildings.)

Do we need these flame retardants? It turns out that our massive global experiment in flame retardants was thrust on us by an intense industry lobbying effort in the 1980s that aimed to take the focus off cigarettes as the core cause of an increase in the number of house fires and redirect that focus to the products that caught fire. In an outstanding six-part series called "Playing with Fire" published in 2012, the *Chicago Tribune* uncovered the work of tobacco lobbyists as they pushed to limit regulations that favored self-extinguishing cigarettes in favor of putting flame-retardant chemicals in . . . well, everything.[37] The award-winning series shows how these lobbyists relied on, and promoted, faulty science and testimony from an unscrupulous doctor who fabricated tales of children burning in fires, among other tried and true tactics intended to manufacture doubt. This led to the widespread and global use of flame-retardant chemicals in couches, chairs, curtains, televisions, remote controls, drywall, computers, pillows, and on and on.[38] Another gift from Big Tobacco.

(There are two terrific books that describe these tactics used by companies to inject doubt into the scientific debate, if you want more examples: *Doubt Is Their Product,* by David Michaels, and *Merchants of Doubt,* from our Harvard colleague Naomi Oreskes and her coauthor Erik Conway.)[39]

BPA, Forever Chemicals, and flame retardants are but three of many examples of harmful chemicals in our products and in our living and working spaces. Phthalates, pronounced "tha-lates," are another group of chemicals found all over our buildings. They are primarily used as plasticizers in polyvinyl chloride (PVC). The short list of where they can be found in our buildings includes flooring, sealants, adhesives, upholstery, and shower curtains. Why do we care about phthalates from a human health perspective? Because they have been found to interfere with our bodies' natural hormones, altering sexual development. To get a sense of what that means, consider this list: phthalates have been linked to the absence of the epididymis (testicular duct that carries sperm), failure of the testicles to descend (cryptorchidism), opening of the urethra on the underside rather than the tip of the penis (hypospadias), decreased anogential distance, and testicular lesions.[40] One study found a relationship between phthalates and premature breast development.[41] In another large study of children, higher levels of the phthalate BBzP in dust was associated with rhinitis and eczema, and another phthalate (DEPH) was linked with asthma in kids.[42]

What does this all have to do with the building? These chemicals migrate out of their products and into the air and dust in our homes, offices, and schools. Consider research from Joe's team, led by Dr. Anna Young, which found that dust is hormonally active. (Yes, you read that correctly: dust is *hormonally active*.) The study found that indoor dust imitates estrogen, testosterone, and other sex hormones. In laboratory tests, human cells exposed to the dust samples act as if they have too much estrogen, too little testosterone, or too little thyroid hormone. Every single dust sample collected from forty-six different building spaces was hormonally bioactive. The extent to which the dust mimicked hormones was significantly related to the concentrations of Forever Chemicals and flame-retardant chemicals in the dust.[43]

Stay with us through this depressing story; we will give solutions for how to break this vicious cycle at the end of this chapter. But first, let's look at the economic impacts.

The Business Impacts of Chemicals of Concern

So far we've made the case for why these chemicals matter from a health science perspective. The chemicals we are talking about are toxic, and they can be found all over our buildings: in chairs, couches, carpet and carpet backing, hard flooring, wallboard, ceiling tiles, composite wood materials, wall insulation, electronics, and even things like grout. What about the business perspective? This one is easy.

To get a sense of the scale of what's at stake, consider that 2017 brought the landmark $671 million lawsuit against DuPont.[44] Just one year later, 3M settled one for $850 million. At issue in the 3M case was the years-long dumping of Forever Chemicals (used in products like Scotchgard and Teflon) at four manufacturing sites.[45] That's $1.5 billion in legal settlements around one class of these Forever Chemicals in year—$1.5 *billion*.

We might also look at legacy pollutants and what they cost to the building industry. Anyone with a building constructed before 1976 is undoubtedly familiar with the legacy pollutants asbestos and polychlorinated biphenyls (PCBs). For those not familiar with PCBs, they are a class of chemicals that were used in transformers but also light ballasts, caulking, and exterior paint. (For those not familiar with asbestos, it is a mineral mostly used for insulation in buildings that was found to cause mesothelioma and asbestosis, a chronic lung disease characterized by shortness of breath and scarring of lung tissue.) Banned in the 1970s, these chemicals are long lasting and still an issue in older buildings.

Building owners are also undoubtedly familiar with the costs associated with dealing with asbestos and PCBs in any renovation project. By some estimates, safely removing and disposing of the PCBs in the caulking from an old building will cost you $9–$18 per square foot. That figure goes up to $24 / sq. ft. if it's the exterior paint you're dealing with, and add in an additional $6 / sq. ft. for transportation and disposal of the hazardous waste.[46] Same for asbestos, which will cost you an additional $5–$15 / sq. ft. if you find it during a renovation (and up to $150 / sq. ft., depending on the type of building and difficulty of accessing the materials). Not to mention the disruption to work and risks to brand—having a team of workers running around your building in full hazmat gear for a few weeks isn't generally considered good for business.[47]

All that to say, it's not a stretch to think about the millions of dollars in additional expenses caused by legacy pollutants, and then to realize that PCBs share some common traits with chemicals that are currently in wide use in our buildings. PCBs are just like PBBs, except with chlorine instead of bromine. That means PCBs are also very similar to PBDEs and other brominated flame retardants. And this means that they look like thyroid hormone T4, too. (Not surprisingly, studies that examine the combined effect of PCBs and PBDEs show a synergistic impact on thyroid hormones in the body.[48] To our regulatory system they are different, but to our bodies they look very similar.) The Forever Chemicals all have fluorine, another halogen. All of these chemicals are persistent, bioaccumulative, and toxic—and found all over our buildings. It doesn't take a great leap to extrapolate that future remediation of these newer chemicals, not to mention toxic torts—and settlements—is likely.

Having trouble winning this economic argument at work based on remediation and disposal costs? Then ask this: What is the cost of providing a work environment laced with chemicals that interfere with a young woman's or young man's chance of reproductive success? Mention "testicular cancer" or "decrease in live births" and see what response you get. We have seen it stop a recalcitrant architect in his tracks. But too few people know about this, and few doctors ever make a connection between problems of infertility and the flame retardant in the insulation in the walls or in your office chair.

New TSCA

TSCA has set us up with a regulatory framework that (1) has failed to address the 80,000 chemicals in commerce and keep pace with the 2,000 new ones introduced each year, (2) has failed to even catch and ban known bad actors like asbestos, (3) has succeeded in giving us a false sense of assurance that replacements are "safe" despite the problem of regrettable substitution, and (4) has set up building owners with the prospect of millions of dollars in future liabilities around what will most certainly become future legacy pollutants.

The gross failings of TSCA spurred the creation of a new TSCA in 2016—the Frank R. Lautenberg Chemical Safety for the 21st Century Act—named after Senator Lautenberg, who championed the legislation. Unfortunately, the new act is not off to a great start. Promulgated under the Obama administration, it required that the EPA start reviewing the 80,000 chemicals currently in use. But with 2,000 new chemicals coming into the market each year, what was the plan to tackle the backlog? Well, it listed 10 chemicals the EPA would start with, including trichloroethylene, perchloroethylene, and methylene chloride. Do the math—it would take hundreds of years at this speed to tackle the tens of thousands of chemicals waiting to be evaluated.

Still, the new Lautenberg Act was thought to be a big improvement on the old TSCA because at least it started to address this problem. But a few years in, we are *still* working on those same 10 chemicals. And yes, asbestos is on that list and unbelievably still has not been banned. Supporters of new act blame this lack of progress on the Trump administration, which has de-prioritized this work, but you have to wonder: Was it ever going to work? Seems like there were obvious flaws, right from the beginning.

Lack of Transparency = Lack of Awareness = Lack of Action

What is a building owner, developer, tenant, or consumer to do? Well-intentioned decisions to buy "BPA-free" products have really meant we have been buying products that should be labeled "BPA-free* (*but contains BPS)."

Imagine walking through your local grocery store and picking up a granola bar that only had a label that said, "peanut-free," but that didn't tell you that the peanuts were substituted for almonds, another common nut allergen. This is akin to what happened with "BPA-free"; they told us one potentially harmful chemical wasn't in the product, but they didn't tell us *what else* was in there that was apt to be harmful.

This is unacceptable. On our food packaging we see the claims about "peanut-free" but we can also *verify* this by looking at the fully disclosed ingredient list, and we can see *what else* might be in there that we should be aware of. We do the opposite for our buildings and the products we put in them. Ask a building owner about the chemicals that are in the building materials or products in his or her building and the owner will give you a blank stare. (Can you *imagine* if a food product manufacturer didn't know what was inside its product?)

But it's worse than this. If that same building owner asked his or her product suppliers what's in their products, the product supplier may not even know. Take this example (not from buildings, but you will get the point). Joe was at several meetings with a major airline manufacturer that at the time was working to remove the toxic flame-retardant chemical decabromo-diphenyl ether (deca for short) from its airplanes in response to new restrictions on its use as a result of the aforementioned phaseout of PBDEs. What he learned was shocking. It took them 18 months just to determine *where* in the airplane this chemical was used. This company didn't readily know. And neither did their suppliers, apparently.

The same thing is true of buildings.

The underlying issue is one of a lack of transparency, tracking, and tabulation. Transparency is what we get on a food nutrition label—a full disclosure of what we are putting into our bodies. Going forward, the absolute first step must be transparency. We simply must know what we are putting into our buildings. This seems eminently reasonable, and at some level it is sad that it even has to be written.

But it has to be *real* transparency. Take what happens with personal care products as a note of caution, because personal care products walk a fine line here. Many have ingredient labels, but that information is not completely transparent. Take a look at your shampoo bottle the next time you're in the shower. You'll see the ingredient label, but you're also very likely to see one of those ingredients listed as "fragrance." Hmmm. That seems like a disclosure of the ingredients, but at this point in the chapter you should be asking yourself, What do they mean by "fragrance"? Turns out, in many cases, "fragrance" is a code word for phthalates. (In addition to their use as a plasticizer for PVC, phthalates act as a gelling agent in consumer products, allowing the actual fragrance to last longer in the product.)

There has been some positive movement on the transparency front. Groups like the International Living Future Institute have put forth the Declare Label project, which aims to get material suppliers to disclose what's in their products. Most everyone, we think, would agree that we need to have more transparency. But it is also not sufficient to tell a customer (be it a dad at the grocery store or the owner of a multibillion-dollar building), "This product contains 2,2,4,4-tetrabromodiphenyl ether," because that doesn't mean anything to anyone. What we really need is a full reckoning of ingredients with potential health concerns. This is where groups like the Health Product Declaration (HPD) Collaborative have helped to advance the field by developing HPDs that not only list the ingredients but also list the potential health hazards. A real strength here is that the HPD Collaborative is a not-for-profit open standard with over 250 members, including architects, designers, owners, and manufacturers, and the HPDs are harmonized with the Healthy Building rating systems we discuss in Chapter 9. A key goal for these groups is increased transparency in the building and construction market. The ultimate goal, of course, is to drive solutions upstream, through green chemistry, for example.

But there is a cautionary tale to all of this. We can't just go around doing what California did with Prop 65.[49] (For those unfamiliar with this, it is the law that has led to the rise of everything—and we mean everything—being labeled as "potentially containing carcinogens.") This is a great, and sad, example of the backfiring of a well-intentioned law requiring health disclosures on products. The law has resulted in buildings in California having to post a sign to this effect:

> Please be advised this building may contain chemicals or materials known to cause cancer or reproductive harm.
> —State of California Proposition 65 Health and
> Safety Code; Chapter 6.6, Section 25249.6

Given the choice between souvenir coffee cup A, which has the Prop 65 label, and cup B, which doesn't, a consumer might be more likely to choose cup B. But for buildings, it's all but meaningless at this point. All that label is telling us is that somewhere in the building there is a chemical that may be a carcinogen. There is pretty much no chance of any consumer altering his or her choice because of that information. Very few people are in a position to switch jobs because of a diffuse warning like this; not a lot of patients would refuse to meet with their doctor in one of these buildings; and how many clients will turn away from a conference meeting after coming across that notice by the entrance of the building?

One Solution: Leveraging Demand-Side Purchasing Power for Market Transformation

With an "innocent until proven guilty" regulatory approach that is currently incapable of protecting us from chemicals of concern in consumer products and building materials, a 50-year-old supply-side approach that has delivered decades of regrettable substitution, and a Prop 65–type law that is all but meaningless for buildings, a new approach is needed. We have been working with leading companies on a market-based solution that focuses on the demand side of the equation—the buyers—to accelerate a shift to healthier building materials.

At Harvard, we started with a simple idea: we cannot ignore the science produced by our own scientists. Great research on BPA, Forever Chemicals, and many other chemicals of concern is being done at universities across the world, including our own. So we asked ourselves, How can we possibly continue to purchase products with these chemicals? The answer is, we can't. So we decided to put this research into action. We partnered with Heather Henriksen, the managing director of the Harvard Office for Sustainability, and created the Harvard Healthier Building Materials Academy. This academy has a goal of putting research into practice: to use the latest scientific evidence to inform purchasing practices at Harvard, and beyond.

We aggressively educated the purchasing community at Harvard on the science, and then, thanks to the tireless work of Henriksen, her team, and an army of purchasers, project managers, product specifiers, designers, executives, and facilities managers, we showed that we could actually purchase products with a lower overall toxic load without affecting product performance, project timelines, or costs. As of the writing of this book, there are dozens of projects under way on campus that are piloting new green building standards that specify the use of products without certain chemicals of concern like flame retardants, stain-repellent Forever Chemicals, and antimicrobials, for starters. And here's the good news—when we act, we see a difference. The building spaces with "healthier" furniture and carpet had 78 percent lower levels of Forever Chemicals in dust and 45–65 percent lower levels of two groups of flame retardant chemicals in dust compared to more conventional building spaces.[50]

As with everything we do, our goal is not simply to improve conditions at our home institution; we aim to promote solutions well beyond Harvard. So we announced a partnership with Google in 2018 and began working with other leading companies with a similar mission and vision. If the leadership team at Google wouldn't buy food without knowing the ingredients, why would they buy products for their buildings without knowing what's inside them? Amazingly, Google is a company focused on organizing the world's data, but like the rest of us, its leaders were flying blind when it came to data about the products they were putting into their own buildings. That's changing.

Along the way, we came across many other organizations, architects, and construction firms confronting these same challenges. We realized many of us were aligned on mission and vision, but not on how we were approaching suppliers. We were in fact contributing to the confusion in the market space because we were asking for similar things in slightly different ways. But this is evolving. The market is quickly coming up to speed on the potential hazards of these chemicals and developing solutions. For example, the international

---

BOX 7.1 Healthier Materials Approach

FOLLOW THE PRECAUTIONARY PRINCIPLE

- Use a "health first" mind-set and err on the side of caution (or on the side of human health).
- "Less toxic" is not "nontoxic" and "safer" is not necessarily "safe."
- Do not ignore history. (It can't be called "regrettable" if we knowingly do it over and over.)

IT'S UP TO YOU TO ACT

- Regulation has been proven ineffective; industry has not successfully policed itself.
- "Innocent until proven guilty" may be good for criminal justice, but it is disastrous chemical policy.
- Avoid future "legacy pollutants" and their associated massive costs. (What are the next PCBs?)

START WITH A FEW CLASSES OF KNOWN "BAD ACTORS"

- A class approach is warranted for some bad actors like flame retardants and stain repellents (because it's impossible to deal with these chemicals one at a time when there are over 5,000 variants).
- Persistent organic pollutants are an issue: an indoor hazard today is an outdoor hazard tomorrow.

LEVERAGE EXISTING SCIENCE

- Demand to know what's in the products you are buying and putting into your building.
- Don't ignore science simply because the regulatory apparatus has not caught up (remember, the EPA still hasn't formally regulated asbestos). Regulations trail leading science by years, or even decades.
- Don't delay decisions based on manufactured doubt. (Oftentimes we "know enough to know" that we shouldn't use some chemicals, but there are calls for more evidence and additional studies, which leads to delays.)

(continued)

BOX 7.1 *Continued*

**PRIORITIZE BASED ON THE LARGEST PRODUCT CATEGORIES
IN YOUR BUILDING**

- Consider the largest product categories by volume or mass (think about the overall "toxic load" in a building).
- Identify alternatives in most purchased products. (For many of these largest product categories, the market has products that don't have these chemicals of concern and the product performs the same and costs the same.)

THE PROCESS IS DYNAMIC

- Take this approach where feasible (alternatives for some products may not be available . . . yet).
- Do not violate code (flame retardants are still required in some instances, for example).
- Create a watch list to track what you should be thinking about next (nanomaterials, anyone?).

design firm Perkins + Will has put together Transparency, a web-based re-source on material health that brings together toxicity concerns and prac-tical information on which building products are likely to contain toxic chemicals.[51] Recognizing that industry and science are dynamic, it also has a "Watch List" to go along with its "Precautionary List" so it and others can work to avoid any future regrettable substitutions.

Our recommended approach, in broad terms, is simple: start with trans-parency; identify a few *classes* of toxic chemicals that we can all agree we don't want in our buildings; identify a few of the largest product categories in use in buildings; recognize that uncertainties exist; make decisions based on the best available science; take a precautionary approach, with eyes wide open about regrettable substitutions and legacy pollutants; and focus on op-timizing for health.

Buildings as a First Line of Defense against Covid and Other Airborne Infectious Diseases

> Cleanliness and fresh air from open windows, with unremitting attention to the patient, are the only defence a true nurse either asks or needs.
>
> —FLORENCE NIGHTINGALE

WE'VE LONG KNOWN THAT BUILDINGS can make us sick. And yes, sometimes the solution is as easy as opening a window, as Florence Nightingale told us long ago. But at some point, we lost our way. We forgot these basic lessons from centuries ago, that bringing in more fresh air is a simple—but effective—infection control measure. Since the days of mechanical ventilation, with each revision of the ventilation standard leading to less fresh air and more tightly sealed buildings, we have been steadily marching away from something the world knew back in the era of Florence Nightingale, but we seem to have forgotten since: fresh air is important.

This bumbling into the sick-building era—with our tight buildings that don't breathe and bare minimum "acceptable" ventilation rates—has largely escaped notice for the past forty years outside the specialized field of indoor air science. Until it didn't, that is—in emphatic fashion, with the arrival of SARS-CoV-2, the virus that causes Covid-19. All at once, eyes focused on this alarming new pathogen as scientists around the globe sought to unravel its mysteries. But despite the mass confusion, disruption, and death caused by Covid-19, it was not really all that mysterious a virus after all. Yes, it was novel to us, but only in an immunological sense—none of our bodies had seen it before, so we lacked sufficient defenses once it latched onto our cells and started replicating wildly in our bodies.

But that's really it in terms of the mystery. In many ways, SARS-CoV-2 acted just like many other respiratory viruses. One way it did this should have been recognized early but was missed by nearly everyone: this coronavirus, like other respiratory viruses, is airborne. Not just in the big, sometimes visible, stuff that comes out when we cough or sneeze, but in tiny respiratory particles that we all emit when we talk and breathe and that stay suspended, floating in the air.

Why did it take health authorities so long to acknowledge this? Joe and others in his field tried to warn about airborne transmission early on in the pandemic, because there were telltale signs from the beginning. First, the su-perspreading events in China and on cruise ships could not be explained by handshakes and dirty doorknobs. Nor could they be explained by coughs and sneezes—or what are known in scientific circles as large droplets. There were enough early reports of asymptomatic transmission—which, by defini-tion, meant no coughs and sneezes—to send up red flags.

There were also historical examples of airborne transmission that were seemingly being forgotten or ignored. Not even twenty years earlier the world had narrowly escaped a pandemic caused by a near cousin, SARS-CoV-1. How did we know then that the SARS virus was spread through the air? Looking back to the early days of SARS-CoV-1, there were obvious signs. In 2003, a respiratory physician from China traveled to a family wedding in Hong Kong and checked into a hotel. He didn't feel well. Within days, at least sixteen others at the hotel were sick. They traveled home to their respec-tive countries and the virus went with them. As a WHO report would later conclude, "A global outbreak was thus seeded from a single person on a single day on a single floor of a Hong Kong hotel."[1]

One man, in one hotel, infects sixteen others. Did he cough directly in the face of sixteen people? Unlikely. Did he sneeze in his hand and then touch a handrail or elevator button, only for fifteen others to touch that same spot? Unlikely.

Scientific papers on SARS-CoV-1—informed by complex modeling of air-flow patterns and disease outbreak in indoor spaces—showed that transmission was happening through the air. There were also biological studies showing that SARS-CoV-1 traveled deep into the lungs—an area that could only be reached by tiny airborne particles, not the larger droplets carried by coughs and sneezes.

In January 2020, Joe wrote an article raising the alarm: there was a very strong likelihood that this "new" virus wreaking havoc in the Wuhan province of China was also spreading through the air. Why harp on this point here? For the simple reason that, if Covid were not spreading through the air, then buildings wouldn't matter as much. But if a pathogen *is* spreading through the air, then the building does indeed matter. A lot.

We set controls for infectious disease mitigation based on how the disease spreads—and here is where the CDC and WHO got things very wrong. It took them both over a year to acknowledge that airborne transmission was a possibility. So when people were washing their groceries and leaving mail in the garage for two weeks to decontaminate, what they were doing was completely detached from the reality of how the virus spread. All of this was "hygiene theater" that honestly was not their fault. The refusal by some leaders to acknowledge the likelihood of airborne transmission was a massive, nearly incomprehensible mistake with huge consequences for human lives.

Here is why this matters to you now. All of the confusion and lack of clear guidance about surface versus airborne transmission created a spike in scientific papers that collectively prove, conclusively, that SARS-CoV-2 is airborne. One result was that scientists began to look at *other* infectious diseases and the historical record more closely. Lo and behold, the debate about modes of transmission for respiratory viruses started to tilt in favor of the proposition that *all* respiratory infectious diseases are airborne.

This is a massive paradigm shift in the medical and scientific communities—do not ignore it. What it means from a practical standpoint is that buildings are *key* when it comes to respiratory diseases like influenza and the common cold, as well as whatever respiratory pandemic hits us next. That gives us another compelling reason to invest in the tools that contribute to better indoor air quality and healthy buildings—well beyond performance and productivity.

Modes of Transmission and the Baseless "Six-Foot Rule"

Scientists have been arguing about "modes of transmission" for decades. When the Covid-19 pandemic hit, believe it or not, even for something as well studied as influenza the science on modes of transmission was not settled. Many believed that influenza and other respiratory pathogens spread by large droplets, the balls of spit we emit when we cough or sneeze.

That's how we got the magical—and baseless—"six-foot rule."

The six-foot rule comes from a misunderstanding of basic physics. When we cough or sneeze or sing, and even when we just talk and breathe, we constantly emit particles from our respiratory tracts. And if we're infected and infectious, the particles we are constantly emitting can carry a virus to its next victim. These particles, known as aerosols, come in all different sizes, from the very small to the very large. The size of the *virus* is irrelevant because it's never naked in the air—it's always hitching a ride in aerosols. Somewhat counterintuitively, larger particles don't carry the most virus. We emit way more of the smaller aerosols, and they're jam-packed with virus if someone is actively infectious.

Aerosols change once they leave our mouths, depending on things like temperature and humidity. If it's dry, they evaporate more quickly, turning into smaller aerosols. So even those large enough to be considered "droplets" evaporate, turning into "droplet nuclei"—a fancy way of saying "they shrink." This means that, in addition to ventilation and filtration, things like indoor humidity levels also play a key role in transmission. Humidity also helps keep our respiratory tract defense in top shape. When it's too dry, we produce less mucous to trap airborne particles after we breathe them in. Also, at low humidity levels, the hair-like cilia in cells in our respiratory tract beat less quickly; this is the mechanism responsible for bringing all this junk back up to our throats where we swallow it harmlessly.

You might have guessed that we're spending so much time talking about big and small aerosols because size matters. The large droplets settle out of the air rather quickly. They're too heavy to travel far, so they generally make it only a short distance—less than six feet, in fact. After they settle onto a surface—or a sneezed-into hand touches a surface—there's the potential for what is called fomite transmission. *Fomite* is simply the word used by scientists to describe any inanimate object that can harbor the virus for some time and act as a source of transference. This could be a doorknob, a countertop, or the ever-feared elevator button.

Prior to Covid-19, it was thought that most respiratory viruses were spread through large droplets. If people were contagious, it seemed to make sense that much of what came out when they coughed and sneezed would be these large particles. So if these ballistic droplets didn't hit you directly, they would settle onto surfaces, waiting there like ticking time bombs. Thus the six-foot rule and constant wiping of surfaces emerged as the leading guidance for how to stay safe as the pandemic got underway.

But there is a grave mistake embedded in this approach. To better understand what is at stake, it helps to put some numbers to these aerosol sizes. Medical textbooks assumed that a 5-micron aerosol would meet the definition of a droplet—in other words, that it would fall out of the air within six feet. When we talk, breathe, and sing, we're emitting aerosols as large as 100 microns or more, down to less than 1 micron (the submicron level). But most of what we emit is below 5 microns. What the medical textbooks got wrong is the physics of a 5-micron aerosol. These do not settle out of the air within six feet. A 100-micron particle will, but not a 5-micron one. So in no way should a 5-micron aerosol be called a "droplet"—it doesn't drop!

In fact, a 5-micron particle will travel well beyond six feet. How far can it travel? Clear across any room. It blows right past the magical and baseless six-foot line to a hundred feet or more. What's more, not only can it travel across a room, it can stay aloft for thirty minutes. And particles less than 5 microns can stay aloft for *hours*.

This is starting to sound problematic.

We constantly produce respiratory aerosols of different sizes, all of which can carry viral loads, and most of which can travel across the room and stay afloat for a long time. You might say this sounds like a recipe for a superspreading event . . .

And indeed, that is the case. If we look at outbreaks of SARS-CoV-2, we see that they all share common characteristics: time indoors in underventilated buildings. If someone is infectious indoors, and there is no way for aerosols to escape, they will fill the room over time. The nasty truth is that we're constantly breathing one another's air indoors. How much we are doing this depends on the ventilation. In a poorly ventilated space, as much as 3 percent of the air you're breathing just came out of the lungs of other people in the room. It's as if you were sharing a cup of coffee with everyone in the room— the respiratory equivalent of backwash, as Joe wrote in *The Atlantic* in 2021.[2] Another, even more startling way to think about 3 percent shared air is that it's like locking lips with the people in the room one out of every thirty breaths or so.

This concept was first introduced in 2003 in a scientific paper by Don Milton and Steven Rudnick, who coined a term for it: the "rebreathed fraction."[3] In addition to describing the phenomenon, they did the math to show that getting the rebreathed fraction below 1 percent is critical to reducing the likelihood of the spread of disease indoors.

The best way to think about respiratory aerosols is to imagine cigarette smoke, an analogy first proposed to us by Dr. Linsey Marr, one of the world's leading experts on aerosol transmission. If someone is smoking indoors in a small room and you're across that room, you'll know it. If it's underventilated, the room will fill with smoke—so much so that it will soon be hard to see across the room. If it's a very large room—like a wedding hall—and you're on the other side, you may not notice if someone is smoking (the size of the room will dilute the particles and smell) but even in that scenario, if you're next to the smoker, you'll certainly know that there's not enough space for much dilution to happen. And if you're outside? Well, it's possible to be just a few feet away from a smoker and not notice anything.

What's the difference between indoors and outdoors? Unlimited ventilation.

Take the now-infamous choir practice outbreak in Skagit Valley, Washington, where one person infected fifty-three others, and two died.[4] This was one of the earliest—and most obvious—examples that airborne spread was happening, and that the building ventilation system was playing a key role. The first clue was hidden in the early reports: the rehearsal took place in the evening. What happens to buildings in the evenings? As we saw in Chapter 6, ventilation systems are generally turned off.

Sure enough, when an expert team, led by Joe's colleague Dr. Shelly Miller, formally evaluated this outbreak and looked at the HVAC system, it found that ventilation rates were very low at the time of the choir practice. This was a critical study because it was one of the earliest formal outbreak investigations during the pandemic to show, first, that airborne transmission was happening, and second, that building ventilation (or rather, the lack thereof) was playing a key role.

Another key study was the restaurant outbreak in January 2020 in Guangzhou, China. Dr. Yuguo Li and his team modeled the airflow patterns and showed how one person infected other diners at the restaurant, including some sitting at tables far more than six feet away.[5] A review of video footage ruled out any shared surfaces or breaking of the magical six-foot rule. There was only one explanation: airborne spread. And in that case (as in others) a key contributing factor was a ventilation system that didn't bring in outdoor air. The restaurant in Guangzhou had only a recirculated air system with low-grade filters. The result was that infectious aerosols were blown across other diners over and over again.

At the same time as these studies, Joe and his team were collaborating with Dr. Brent Stephens on a forensic analysis of the *Diamond Princess* cruise ship outbreak in early February 2020.[6] That study, led by postdoctoral researcher Parham Azimi, was key because it evaluated all modes of transmission simultaneously, and showed what we now take as common knowledge, but was not acknowledged by leading authoritative bodies for a full year: that exposure was dominated by airborne transmission, and that this mattered both in the near field (within six feet) and the far field (beyond six feet), with very little contribution from surfaces.

Whether you're in church, at a restaurant, on a bus, at a gym, in a spin class, on a cruise ship, in your office, or at school, it's all the same. The location doesn't matter. It's the underlying factors of time indoors and the buildup of respiratory aerosols that make all the difference.

Evidence-based Strategies to Limit Airborne Infectious Diseases

Once we establish that the dominant mode of transmission is through the air, the control strategies quickly fall into place. How do you limit airborne spread across the room? You really have only two options: remove the aerosols through ventilation, or clean them out through filtration. These, as it turns out, are the two key tenets of the science of Healthy Buildings. For this reason, our guidance throughout the pandemic—and for controlling infectious disease spread indoors more generally—has been clear and consistent. We recommended early on that managers of all buildings and indoor spaces pursue three strategies to combat respiratory infectious diseases:

- **Bring in more outdoor air.** This is straightforward enough. It can be as easy as opening windows or outdoor air dampers to increase airflow in mechanically ventilated buildings. The challenge comes when buildings have sealed windows or outdated equipment that can't bring in more outdoor air, or don't have the capacity to condition the air during periods of high heat or low cold. If that's the case, the next point becomes even more key.
- **Increase the level of filtration.** Typically, buildings have MERV 8 filters, as discussed in Chapter 3, but they should upgrade to MERV 13.

Not only does it protect better against outdoor pollution, it actively captures respiratory particles. A MERV 8 filter captures less than 20 percent of these particles, whereas a MERV 13 filter can capture 80 percent or more, depending on the particle size. If a system isn't capable of these first two directives, or if more localized, in-room filtration is needed, there is still something that can be done. Go to point three.

- **Use portable air cleaners with HEPA filters.** These are plug-and-play devices that, when sized correctly for the room, can provide excellent reduction of airborne particles. Long proposed as a line of defense against outdoor air pollution that penetrates indoors, they are equally effective for disease mitigation. HEPA filters are the highest-grade filter we have, and they work incredibly well, so if you have a properly sized portable system, no other technology is needed.

That's it. It can be that simple. This is the playbook we used during Covid-19 for hundreds of organizations, from schools and homeless shelters to multinational corporations, entertainment companies, and performing arts centers. In some high-risk settings, another strategy is the use of germicidal UV (GUV). Upper-room GUV, in particular, can provide over twenty air changes per hour, as air at breathing level in the room gets carried to the ceiling on thermal plumes and any biological organisms are inactivated by the UV. Having the light shine only in the upper room saves the occupants of the room from harmful exposure. Advances in GUV include a promising technology called *far UV*, which uses a different wavelength of light that can be just as effective at inactivating viruses, but poses much lower risk if someone is exposed. We are both on the Lancet Covid-19 Commission as part of the Task Force for Safe Work, Safe School, and Safe Travel, and we and our colleagues on that task force set out similar guidelines in reports and peer-reviewed papers.[7]

There is one key item missing that you likely picked up on. It's one thing to say you should bring in more air, but the obvious follow-on question is: How much? And this, for Joe, has been one of the most frustrating aspects of the pandemic. Early on, ASHRAE adopted the same strategy we had been advocating for. But throughout the pandemic, they crucially failed to say *how much* fresh outdoor air was needed. Imagine being the standard-setting body for ventilation and, during a global crisis, as hundreds of millions of people were infected indoors, refusing to answer this most fundamental question. The problem continued throughout the pandemic. When, after a year or so, following a campaign by hundreds of us indoor air quality scientists, the CDC and WHO begrudgingly accepted airborne transmission, they adopted ASHRAE's language of "more outdoor air." But, because ASHRAE didn't set a target, neither did the CDC. In the end, what this meant was more confusion and no clear guidance.

Having done this type of work—translating science into practice—for over a decade, it was obvious to us that this was a problem. You can't tell a school or office owner to "bring in more air" without telling them how much. So that's what we did.

There are a few ways to do this. Earlier in this book, in Chapter 6, we recommended 30 cfm/person as the optimal target for an office building. This is a solid recommendation, based on decades of sound science, that shows benefits both in terms of infectious disease mitigation and the cognitive functions we have been emphasizing throughout this book.

In this chapter we want to introduce another approach to target-setting that is useful when thinking about infectious diseases, this one focused on "air changes per hour," or ACH. ACH is a measure of how frequently fresh air is introduced in a building, and the logic is simple: the more air changes per hour, the quicker the clearing out of contagious aerosols. ACH usually refers to *outdoor* air being brought in, but we can extend the concept to also include the other way of removing aerosols: filtration. It makes sense to do so since what we're really interested in is the amount of clean air delivered in the space (with *clean* meaning *virus-free*) and that amount can be raised through any combination of increased ventilation and increased filtration. When we consider these in combination, we talk about *equivalent* air changes per hour, or ACHe.

Let's get back to those targets. We recommend aiming for 4 to 6 ACHe. In other words, get an equivalent of the full volume of the air in the room to turn over every ten to fifteen minutes, and it doesn't really matter if it's "clean" outdoor air or "clean" air from a filtering system. Why 4 to 6 ACHe? Joe and his colleague Dr. Andrew Ibrahim argue for this in the *Journal of the American Medical Association* (JAMA) by pointing out it's the rate hospitals target in patient rooms.[8] The problem is that in homes we typically get 0.5 ACH, and in schools 1.5 ACH. (As for airplanes, the risk of spread is actually overstated—they typically get 10 to 20 equivalent air changes per hour, with all recirculated air passing through HEPA filters. The problem with airplanes can be during boarding, because crews don't always run ventilation systems at the gate. This has been a known problem—called out as early as 2013, when Joe was one of the lead authors of a National Academies report, *Infectious Disease Mitigation in Airports and on Aircraft*.[9])

There are some important caveats. This 4 to 6 ACHe target works very well in small places—rooms of an average size with typical ceiling heights. That's intuitive. Placing a small portable air cleaner in the corner of a giant atrium or open-plan office isn't going to do much good. Fortunately, however, in a high-ceiling setting like a Broadway show or movie theater or conference hall you get the benefit of all that extra volume to dilute the respiratory aerosols. (Think of the "cigarette smoke" example.) Another caveat is that, due to incomplete mixing of air in the space, 6 ACH does not actually equate to air turning over every ten minutes. Some of the air being cleaned is air that was just cleaned, so you have to account for that. Typically, 6 ACH will remove 80 percent of particles in the air in about fifteen minutes, but that varies with ventilation effectiveness and how well air is moved in the space.

Let's dive into those portable air cleaners for a second. Sizing them correctly is absolutely key, and there is a simple way to pick one that will work well. Here, we need to introduce the concept of "clean air delivery rate," or CADR, which combines the level of filtration with how much air passes through that filter. (A great filter doesn't do much good if not a lot of air is passing through it.) Most manufacturers report this CADR, which is really useful because we can tie it back to the recommendation of 4 to 6 ACHe through this easy calculation:

$$ACHe = (CADR \times 60) / \text{room volume}$$

The formula states that the number of air changes brought about by filtration depends on the clean air delivery rate times 60 minutes, divided by the size of the room in square feet. To break this down a bit, the CADR is reported in units of cubic feet per minute, so we multiply by 60 to make it cubic feet per hour (remember, we're going for air changes *per hour*). The room volume is measured in cubic feet by multiplying its length by its width by its ceiling height. That's it.

Let's look at a concrete example. A device with a CADR of 350 in a 500-square-foot room with 8-foot ceilings will give you 5.25 air changes per hour.

$$ACHe = (350 \times 60) / (500 \times 8) = 5.25$$

We can also rearrange this formula to set the target first, and then find a device that works. For example, in that same room if we wanted to hit 6 ACHe, how much CADR should we be looking for in a portable air cleaner?

$$CADR = (ACHe \times \text{room volume}) / 60$$
$$= (6 \times 500 \times 8) / 60 = 400$$

To get six air changes per hour in this 500-square-foot room, we want a device that has a reported CADR of 400.

The Hierarchy of Controls, with Healthy Buildings at the Center

To be clear, Healthy Building strategies are not the only tools we have at our disposal to protect us from infectious diseases. We have to layer defenses when facing threats—especially novel threats. We have to think about the relative efficacy and cost of each of these layers, and then weight or prioritize them accordingly. The model we put forward in early 2020 is based on a Hierarchy of Controls framework that has been used for decades in Joe's field of worker health and safety. Joe's application of it to Covid was first published in a scientific journal.[10] Shortly after that, we presented the concept to business leaders in the *Harvard Business Review*, in an article called "What Makes an Office Building 'Healthy'?"[11] As shown in the figure, the hierarchy is made up of five levels, with an "Engineering Controls" layer at its core.

To explain the contributions of each of the control layers, let's discuss them in the context of the Covid-19 response.

HIERARCHY OF CONTROLS

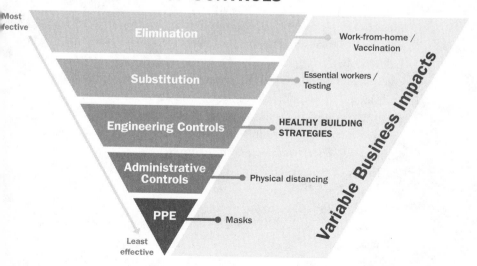

FIGURE 8.1   Hierarchy of Controls and Application to SARS-CoV-2.

Elimination. If we can, we want to eliminate the hazard. In the early days of Covid, this took the form of total lockdowns on social activities within neighborhoods, cities, or provinces. Fortunately, another way to fight the hazard itself came in late 2020 with the arrival of effective vaccines. This far less intrusive measure then became the top-line defense in the "elimination" layer, superseding isolation and quarantine. Other organizations relied on daily testing as a measure to ensure a "virus-free" workplace.

Substitution. In the early stages of Covid this was a blanket "work from home" strategy that substituted the home for the office or school. Only essential workers were excepted, and of course they were still exposed to risk. Almost every enterprise was negatively affected economically or emotionally (or both) by this substitution, although many knowledge workers found that they could work effectively at home, were spared long commutes, and gained more control over their working hours. The business impacts were highly variable.

Engineering Controls. These are the Healthy Building strategies we mentioned earlier, such as increasing ventilation rates, upgrading to better filtration, and boosting humidity. In many buildings, approaches without a solid scientific underpinning were also deployed, including wider use of Plexiglas screens, extensive (and visible) cleaning with bleaches and disinfectants, and uses of various, more exotic air-purification equipment.

Administrative Controls. These interventions, which alter the movement of people and regulate their actions, include such measures as physical distancing and temperature checks. As institutions attempted to reduce in-person contact without completely restricting entire categories of social and economic activity, we saw employers staggering work hours and days, and schools spreading students across classroom spaces and creating so-called pods and cohorts—small groups whose members interacted only with each other. Restaurants took out tables, retailers set limits on shoppers in stores, and museums admitted fewer visitors.

PPE. This is personal protective equipment. In the context of Covid-19, it meant masking. It's listed last in the hierarchy for three reasons. First, it's preferable to mitigate a hazard through the first set of approaches, rather than having to rely on an intervention that requires high end-user compliance. Second, it is often the hardest to maintain. Third, because of variable compliance, it may be least effective from a social perspective (while still providing excellent protection to the wearer, if it's a high-quality mask with a good fit).

Before vaccines, the most effective control, at the *elimination* layer of our hierarchy, was also at some level the most costly: total lockdowns could slow the spread of this disease, but they are super expensive to society in terms of lost economic activity, closed schools, and impact on mental and physical health. Partial lockdowns were and are somewhat better, but offices quickly found that the second layer, *substitution* of remote for in-person work, was less costly. *Engineering controls* and *administrative controls* were still less intrusive and economically damaging, but they required more investment from a capital or operating perspective. Organizations quickly started to balance work-from-home with work-in-a-well-ventilated-space (and similar equipment-oriented strategies) with alternating days and other administrative strategies aimed at bringing fewer people into contact without eliminating the in-person experience.

With a novel virus, there is no one control strategy that is likely to be completely effective on its own (aside from everyone staying home all of the time, indefinitely, which is not practical or realistic, and, for many essential workers, is impossible.) That is why all of the control strategies were deployed simultaneously. As the vaccine began to roll out, we saw the pull-back on some controls, like distancing and masking, because the higher order control measures were most effective, and working. But engineering controls will always remain important, for Covid and beyond.

This also happens to be the realm where building and facilities managers have the most influence and control. Good ventilation and filtration are key to reducing the amount of any virus circulating in the air, and they don't require changes in behavior (like wearing a mask) or in organizational structures (like limiting the number of people who come to work, or leaving empty chairs between people in the conference room). We'll never completely stop coronaviruses or any other airborne diseases from spreading—particularly among those working at close range—but good Healthy Building strategies make transmission across a room (what we call "far-field transmission") unlikely, essentially shrinking the number of people that any given contagious person can infect.

One last—and very important—aspect of the Hierarchy of Controls framework is that it not only clarifies what controls to put in place, but also guides how they should be rolled back as things get better. Anyone who has introduced controls to address a hazard knows that dialing them back is much harder than putting them in. It helps to have a framework that works both ways.

How Does "Bring in More Air" Work When Outdoor Pollution Is Bad?

So far, we have been talking mostly about disease transmission in offices, schools, and other work environments. But as with all things, there is a link between what's happening inside our buildings and what's going on outside. Wildfires have been raging in some regions with more frequency and ferocity, and in many industrial cities people clustered in office buildings suffer from serious problems of pollution. Research has conclusively found links between susceptibility to infectious disease and outdoor pollution. One recent study, for example, finds that as levels of smoke in the air increased in California and neighboring states in the fall of 2020 because of wildfires, so did Covid cases and Covid deaths. These effects were seen up to four weeks after the fires were extinguished.[12]

This raises an urgent question. Throughout the pandemic we encouraged people to "bring in more outdoor air." But what if the outdoor air where you live is heavily polluted? Does that take this simple, low-cost option off the table? The short answer is no, it doesn't have to. Healthy Buildings strategies help on both fronts—mitigating the effects of outdoor air pollution from wildfires (or anything else) and protecting people from Covid.

Let's look at data from the study linking air pollution to Covid deaths. We discussed the dangers of fine particulate matter ($PM_{2.5}$) earlier, and the importance of knowing the mass of it per cubic meter of air ($\mu g/m^3$). This new study found that for every 10 $\mu g/m^3$ increase in $PM_{2.5}$, Covid cases went up by 11.7 percent, and deaths went up by 8.4 percent. Considering that on wildfire days the $PM_{2.5}$ levels reached 500 $\mu g/m^3$ in some parts of California (less than 10 $\mu g/m^3$ is typical), that means risk of death from Covid in those counties rose 400 percent. And note that in some cities, like Beijing or Delhi, the levels can be over 100 $\mu g/m^3$ without wildfires.

The impacts of wildfires aren't limited to the regions where they burn. Recall that the smoke from the 2020 fire season on the US west coast could be smelled—and measured—all the way to New York and everywhere in between. In July 2021, $PM_{2.5}$ levels in New York City reached over 150 μg/m³.

Here's where the challenge comes in with regard to Covid. We know that nearly all transmission happens indoors, and that respiratory aerosols carrying the virus build up in underventilated buildings. Sealing up a building to limit infiltration of wildfire smoke would create a Covid risk—but bringing in 100 percent outdoor air would create a $PM_{2.5}$ risk. What to do?

This is not as tricky a predicament as it might seem at first glance. High-efficiency filters are great at capturing airborne particles, and they don't care whether those particles come from wildfire smoke, the lungs of the person running next to you at the gym, a coal-fired power plant down the road, or car exhaust. From a physics standpoint, these are equivalent things. And with that in mind, we know how to outline a set of controls that can protect us from any of these hazards. The steps are straightforward.

First, upgrade the filters on the *incoming* air supply to MERV 13 filters. The logic for making this recommendation is obvious—we need to filter outdoor particles at the main point of entry.

Second, increase recirculated air filters to MERV 13, too, and use portable air cleaners with HEPA filters. Both work well for outdoor air pollution. Having better filters on the recirculated air captures respiratory particles generated indoors as well as any wildfire smoke that made its way indoors. It's your backup plan for step one above.

Third, run your system! You need air passing over those fancy filters or they won't do much good. A study that Joe's team published in 2021, led by Dr. Emily Jones, found that buildings with better filtration had lower levels of $PM_{2.5}$ indoors, but the lowest levels were observed during times when the building was operating its system.[13] Breathtakingly obvious, but often ignored. In times of heightened concern over air quality degradation—be it from fires or viruses or ambient pollution—the hours of operation for ventilation systems should be extended beyond the usual set points.

In the fight against infectious disease, you can think of ventilation and filtration as two risk-reduction strategies that work in tandem. When outdoor air pollution levels are low, keep bringing in as much outdoor air as possible. We know that transmission outdoors is rare, so the goal is to make stale indoor air a bit more like the breezy outdoors. But if particulate levels are high outside, it's time to revisit your strategy and tip the balance toward filtration.

A Paradigm Shift

If some or all of this seems familiar to you, that's a good thing. The Covid-19 crisis has forced a new awareness of indoor air quality that was long overdue. And, yet, as this pandemic recedes and time moves on, we run the risk of forgetting. Humanity has made great strides in public health over the past hundred years by focusing on the basics of water quality, food safety, and sanitation—but where has indoor air been in all of this? As Joe and a group of his colleagues from around the world wrote in *Science*, "We need to establish the foundations to ensure that the air in our buildings is clean . . . just as we expect for the water coming out of our taps."[14] Notably, in a massive win for the Healthy Buildings movement, this language—and all of the recommendations we made on improving air quality in buildings from day one of the pandemic—were finally included in messaging from the White House in 2022 as part of its "Clean Air in Buildings Challenge." (The fact that its language mirrored what we had been saying was no surprise. Joe and many colleagues advised the White House on this new program focusing on the role buildings play in infectious disease transmission.)

Covid-19 might mark a turning point. The public is unlikely to forget the lost years of 2020 and 2021. This could mean that indoor air quality is no longer just an abstraction that might make us a little bit sluggish or sleepy; it's a real-world life and death problem for hundreds of millions of people. Those living in polluted cities often think of their indoor spaces as havens, but these sanctuaries very likely have problems of their own.

We expect that office workers, apartment renters, cruise ship passengers, students, teachers, factory workers, and many others will be prompted by the memory of Covid-19 to think about the air they breathe in the 90 percent of their time spent indoors. If that happens, then landlords, school administrators, managers of retirement homes, real estate developers, and condo salespeople alike will clamor to make their buildings healthier than their competitors'.

Those decision makers will want to let people know what they are doing with respect to filtration, ventilation, and cleaning. In the next chapter, we will explore how they can know that a building is healthy—and what to make of the various certification systems on the market and at their disposal. These represent objective ways to validate their improvement efforts. But which data to track, what performance to measure, and how to communicate it clearly? This is the territory of Health Performance Indicators, and the focus of Chapter 10.

CHAPTER NINE

Healthy Building Certification Systems

> Education is not a product: mark, diploma, job, money—in that order; it is a process, a never-ending one.
>
> —BEL KAUFMAN

WHEN YOU GRADUATE FROM COLLEGE, it doesn't really feel official until you have that diploma in hand—you put in the work, and now you want something to hang behind your desk to let the world know about your accomplishment. It's proof that, at least at one point in time, you were "certified" with some level of expertise in whatever you studied. This facilitates the selection of doctors, accountants, or lawyers, for example; clients can rely on the certificate without having to individually test the provider's knowledge of organic chemistry, depreciation, or patent law.

The same can be said about our buildings. Nowadays, building owners, developers, investors, and landlords want to let the world know that their building is special. They want a "diploma" on their building and appreciate the perceived value this brings.

For some in the buildings trade, it's a point of pride. For most, it's a business decision. Third-party recognition may help attract tenants who don't see the sign on a competitor's building, or it may allow you to charge a premium. Tenants are relying on the same logic and trade-off calculation we all use in everyday decisions. Faced with a choice between two health-care providers, one with a diploma from an accredited medical school and one without, who do you choose, all else being equal? It's a no-brainer. The same might be said for buildings. Some building owners and some tenants are qualified to look line by line at the performance of water systems, the disposal of construction debris, or the provenance of sustainable timber stock; but most would rather rely on outside authorities to certify that the building passes muster.

This kind of certificate of approval for green buildings has evolved among many forward-thinking tenants, landlords, and investors from a "nice-to-have" to a "baseline must-have." We expect that in the future the implementation, validation, and communication of some concept of Healthy Buildings will become an even more important differentiator for sophisticated companies.

But—crucially—decisions about Healthy Buildings go far beyond a few incremental and benign design or equipment options. Faulty systems can make people really sick. Accordingly, as Healthy Buildings get more and more scrutiny, we can expect awareness to include not just *what* the standards and measurements are but also *who* is doing the certifying—and how deeply they are evaluating the systems and results.

This chapter looks at the recent history and current status of rating and ranking systems. We also talk a bit about the factors that have historically influenced certification practices, since techniques and systems are being rapidly advanced by newer Healthy Building rating systems. Going forward, we anticipate a future that involves extensive sensors, analytics, and real-time reporting. New rating systems will evolve, and we will share some thoughts about the direction things are going.

Our hope is that by the end of this chapter we will have convinced you of the following:

1. The green building movement and green building certification offer important insights into the burgeoning Healthy Building movement, but certifying something as "healthy" is very different from certifying something as "green."

2. The first Healthy Building certification systems are a good start for promoting a "people-centric" approach to rating buildings but each have different strengths and weaknesses.

3. The capital expenditures and certification costs for Healthy Buildings, while at first glance cost prohibitive, are less so once human performance and health are factored in.

4. *Who* is doing the certifying is as important as *what* is being certified.

5. Expertise (and available tools) will evolve rapidly, and the systems and standards can be expected to be fluid.

Lessons from the Green Building movement

Pioneering efforts in the early 1990s involving architects, designers, equipment manufacturers, and standard-setting organizations started the first conversations about creating *green* buildings—ones that use materials thoughtfully, are environmentally sensitive, and conserve energy. The concept of a green building is important in its own right, certainly. But it also pioneered a competitive way of benchmarking buildings against some design standards and against each other, an essential innovation that really got the movement to take off. This quickly led others to identify the need to *recognize and certify* green buildings. Some sort of a "diploma" for buildings was in order.

One of the first major players in the green buildings space was the U.S. Green Building Council (USGBC), which, under the leadership of its founder and first CEO, Rick Fedrizzi, established the most influential green building certification standard, Leadership in Energy and Environmental Design (LEED).[1] Soon after the idea of the green building plaque displayed on a wall in the building entryway was born. And just as we have graduation ceremonies for new grads, there are now plaque ceremonies for new buildings.

The LEED concept was highly influential. The early green building acolytes really had no formal standing in the design and construction community, no direct influence on building codes or equipment standards or inspections, and no financial influence. How could they get the things they cared so passionately about onto the radar of the broader community? Most of the industry was cautious and not paying much attention to "going green" at that time. By conceiving, establishing, codifying, and relentlessly promoting a clear, understandable, compelling, and universally applicable rating system, the USGBC eventually influenced the language of local and national building codes; the standards promulgated by bodies like the American

Society of Heating, Refrigerating and Air-Conditioning Engineers; zoning and permitting processes in many cities and towns; leasing standards for huge national tenants; and even investment and underwriting decisions by important financial players.

Since the rise of LEED and USGBC, over 100 green building councils have emerged around the world and dozens of green building certification systems have been developed, nearly all of which administer plaques to display on buildings that meet specified criteria—an incredible testament to the success and vision of the movement's leaders. Green building certification codes all share many common elements, and since LEED paved the way and is still the predominant standard in most places, we'll talk about LEED here to give you a sense of what these green building rating systems look for and how they work. Much of what we write applies to other green building certification systems too, though the specifics may vary. There are important parallels, as you will soon see—and a few notable differences—with the Healthy Building movement.

Green building ratings are all based on a scoring system. A building team gets "credits" for different strategies that they pursue. For example, LEED will rate your building based on the scores you get for things like water efficiency, energy efficiency, design, and the sustainability of the site. Depending on your total score, the building will then be classified at one of three different levels—LEED Silver, LEED Gold, and LEED Platinum.

One of the major benefits of a certification system is that it offers a common benchmark for consumers and investors. LEED likens its green building points or credits to the information on a food product's nutrition label, an analogy that we've also found very effective.

Much as a nutrition label allows us to compare food products and tells us what's inside, a good building certification system lets us compare buildings. A LEED Platinum building in New York shouldn't be too different from a LEED Platinum building in Dubai. (This not 100 percent true, as there are prerequisites that every building has to hit, local parameters and environmental challenges, and optional credits allowing for different pathways to certification.)

This ability to compare buildings across wide geographical locations has had dramatic economic consequences. One key reason for this is that many of the "customers" of these buildings are institutional investors, who typically allocate 5–10 percent of their portfolios to real estate through

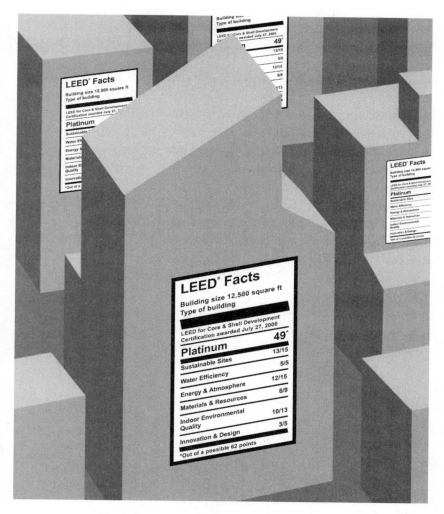

FIGURE 9.1   Example of a building "nutrition label" from the USGBC's LEED program. U.S. Green Building Council.

direct investments or managed funds like limited partnerships or real estate investment trusts. In the last several years, many investors have indicated their preference for green buildings, too. The Global Real Estate Sustainability Benchmark (GRESB) reports that over $7 trillion of global real estate investment is managed by entities who track their green building performance.[2]

One of the main critiques of green building certification systems is that they largely represent the design and performance of a building at one particular point in time. Does the LEED Platinum plaque in an office from 2007 really tell us anything about the performance of that building today, more than a decade later? The answer is largely no. (And we expect this would hold true if any of us were to be tested *today* on the things we knew at the time we received a college diploma, too.)

Fortunately, just as there has been a movement in education toward "lifelong learning," there is a corollary in buildings as we seek to move from static determinations to dynamic assessments, where building performance is measured and verified continually. Under the direction of Fedrizzi's successor at USGBC, Mahesh Ramanujam, the company attempted to move to more dynamic scoring of buildings. (More on the details of measuring and tracking building performance in Chapter 10.)

LEED has had remarkable influence on the market. As of 2019, there were over 8 billion square feet of LEED-certified space globally.[3] One of the drivers of this success is the promised financial return on investment through energy savings. LEED buildings save around 20 to 40 percent of energy use intensity when compared with their noncertified counterparts.[4] This translates into bottom-line operating savings for the business—savings, as we illustrated in the pro forma tables in Chapter 4, that have the really nice feature of being very easy to estimate, measure, and verify. Energy savings are a line item in the operating budget that everyone can understand. Some building owners and users have the internal capability to do sophisticated cost-benefit analyses of engineering investments, particularly in energy efficiency. Some of those bristle at the relative simplicity and lack of financial analysis in LEED-certified building. But for the most part, the points system has been remarkably effective at moving the industry in a green direction.

Today in some markets, such as New York City and San Francisco, green building is now business as usual. If your new commercial building is not LEED certified, this will often raise red flags. Part of this comes from market forces ("If my competitor is doing it, I had better do it, too"). Part of it is a new set of expectations (tenants now look for the LEED plaque and investors want to see it, too). And partly it is driven by local government. (New York announced in 2019, as part of its Climate Mobilization Act, that it was mandating that buildings reduce carbon emissions by 40 percent by 2030 and 80 percent by 2050.)

LEED is not in itself a building code or ANSI-approved national standard. It's not a measure of realized performance, nor does it come with a detailed cost-benefit analysis. Even so, USGBC and LEED have driven designers to design more creatively, builders to build better, manufacturers to innovate, and developers to develop more sustainable buildings by almost any measure. What might be next, now that the public and the market have both grown accustomed to certifications and awareness of the human and financial cost of sick buildings is growing?

Healthy Building Certifications

It probably won't come as a surprise to you to hear that with the rise of the Healthy Building movement, there has been a corresponding push for Healthy Building certification systems to replace, compete with, or complement green building certifications. (The distinction depends on whom you talk to, and how they view these new certifications.) Several certification systems have an early lead to fill this gap. Let's briefly review these early contenders, not so much to endorse or criticize them but rather to give you an understanding of how this is playing out in the market, and how we think it *should* be playing out. Broadly, we think things are changing fast in terms of current market awareness, with some key participants shifting from viewing such certifications as a nice-to-have to viewing them as a must-have. Some key participants are also reporting "certification fatigue." They want to do what's best for their building and the people in it, but don't want to go through a certification process or pay the certification fees. We are confident that there are substantial high-impact benefits to be unlocked by new technologies and enhanced "smart building" capabilities and this shift to Healthy Buildings, with or without certification.

Early Days: Good Science, Poorly Disseminated

The Healthy Buildings movement has existed for decades, really, but it was first led by scientists who largely mobilized around the theme of "indoor air." Early research on indoor air quality spawned scientific organizations like the International Society of Indoor Air Quality and the academic journal

Indoor Air (for which Joe is an associate editor). Most scientists are not businesspeople, few are skilled communicators, and even fewer have access to decision makers in the real estate industry. The result is that much of this compelling evidence on healthy indoor air remained bottled up, so to speak, in academic journals and conferences that failed to penetrate the market that these scientists were ultimately trying to influence—the people who design, operate, maintain, and certify buildings.

Joe was struck by the depth of this problem at a meeting of the Real Estate Roundtable in 2016, when he said, "We're overcomplicating what it means to have a Healthy Building. There are only a handful of things we need to control, and everyone knows what they are." At which point the entire room leaned in and began asking questions that would be considered basic by the "indoor air" crowd. This drove home the fact that the body of rich scientific evidence had yet to be leveraged by practitioners.

Three things were becoming very clear: (1) there was a gap between research scientists and practitioners, (2) there was a demand for Healthy Building knowledge and services being voiced by the market, and (3) someone was going to fill that demand. Thus, the rise of Healthy Building certifications.

The WELL Building Standard

The WELL Building Standard was created by Paul and Pete Scialla, two brothers with experience in the finance world, who recognized the immense potential of combining two of the largest sectors in the US economy—real estate and health care. What the Scialla brothers lacked in formal training in health they made up for in experience in the business world. They saw a market opening up and launched Delos, a health and wellness company, and founded the International Well Building Institute (IWBI), the arm of their company that created WELL.

On the marketing front, the Scialla brothers and their team were quickly able to achieve impressive results. Rather than compete outright with existing green building certification standards, they teamed up with USGBC and began sponsoring the main conference on green buildings, Greenbuild, which is attended by between 10,000 and 20,000 people each year. This created a seemingly seamless connection between LEED and their rating system, WELL.

WELL was first released in 2014 and within a matter of months, the entire global real estate market seemed to be talking about it. Wherever we have traveled around the world, someone has inevitably asked us about the WELL Building Standard—a credit to both the rise of the Healthy Buildings movement and the communication and marketing skills of the team at IWBI.

WELL's splashy launch helped socialize the different elements of a Healthy Building. Suddenly people in the green building world began to understand that they should be looking beyond the green building's indoor air quality standard—or what we consider "IAQ 101"—by putting quantifiable targets on new things like lighting, noise, and ventilation. In short, WELL got people in the green building certification world to start thinking about *prioritizing* health.

Like all measurement and incentive systems, WELL was susceptible to efforts to game the rating system. This mirrored the experience of LEED, where skeptics will point to the oft-maligned "bike rack credit"—a meaningful addition for some buildings but a "check the box" credit for the many suburban office parks surrounded by giant parking lots and road networks that don't support biking. So the building gets a LEED credit for encouraging energy-reducing behaviors like biking, but in reality it would have been better off focusing on actual energy-conserving measures.

For WELL, this "gaming" could be seen with visible category signaling, as artifacts and devices were placed in a prominent space as part of a hunt for less expensive points. This led to no end of grousing as some scoffed that the next thing you know, you'd see companies placing a bowl of nuts next to a treadmill in the main lobby area of a WELL Platinum building so the company could get credits for both nutrition and movement.

But WELL continued to evolve. In 2017 IWBI recruited the principal architect of the green building movement, Rick Fedrizzi, to become CEO. Rick quickly brought on several key players from USGBC, including the former director of USGBC's Center for Green Schools, Rachel Gutter, who is now the CEO at WELL. This further strengthened WELL's ties to the established green building movement and brought in an experienced team to deliver the second version of WELL. (For several years, a few of these executives were on the advisory board of a center at Harvard that Joe was a part of, and Joe was on the advisory board for the Center for Green Schools at USGBC. Joe has not formally worked with them since they moved over to WELL.)

WELL v2, released in 2018, addressed many of the issues that had impeded the success of the initial launch. For starters, the certification price came down by a factor of 10. Many features were now less confusing and more streamlined. The company also introduced pricing strategies and discounts that supported the adoption of WELL in developing countries, and a portfolio option so large companies wouldn't have to certify their buildings one by one. IWBI installed an advisory board with a few top-notch scientists and hired several scientists with master's degrees in public health and other related health fields. All solid moves in our view.

In many ways, v2 is a public health win. Its "features" cover many of the factors of the 9 Foundations of a Healthy Building that we discussed in Chapter 6, but WELL went with these 10: air, water, light, movement, thermal comfort, sound, materials, mind, community, and nourishment. The entry of executives, business leaders, and investors from the green building certification world into the Healthy Building world was a good signal for those who wanted to see the Healthy Buildings profile raised. These green building and business leaders had the skills necessary to bring Healthy Buildings to the masses, and they had the wherewithal, as all good leaders do, to bring in experts in areas where they did not have expertise, leveraging the science and bridging the gap to drive research into practice.

Fitwel

Fitwel, another certification system that is gaining prominence, was created as a joint initiative between the leading institutions in the US federal government that focus on health and on buildings: the Centers for Disease Control and Prevention and the General Services Administration, the federal agency responsible for managing all government buildings. They eventually spun out the Fitwel program and it is now being administered and managed by a nonprofit, the Center for Active Design. And Fitwel is getting traction: Tishman Speyer, a leading company in the commercial real estate space, announced in 2017 that it was going to deploy the Fitwel certification across its global portfolio.[5] In 2019, Boston Properties rolled it out across 11 million square feet of class A office space.

Like WELL, Fitwel aims to promote healthier indoor environments. But the two certification systems differ in important ways. First and foremost, Fitwel is a self-administered checklist. Essentially, the building representative surveys a new or existing building and looks for things that satisfy Fitwel's list of health-promoting items.

Some of these things are uncontroversial common sense, such as verifying that every building has an automatic defibrillator and ensuring that asbestos is managed properly. Some are potentially open to gaming ("Adopt and implement an indoor air quality policy" and "Provide access to sufficient active workstations"). Some are dictated by code ("Provide at least one ADA compliant water supply on relevant floors"). Some of it isn't really tied to health, per se ("Provide at least one publicly accessible use on the ground floor").

Perhaps the most important difference between WELL and Fitwel (certainly the one most noticed by the market) is that Fitwel only costs a few thousand dollars per building to administer, while WELL can run up to hundreds of thousands of dollars for a large project. This makes it attractive to the market, and this aspect allows someone like Tishman Speyer to consider rolling it out to over 2,000 tenants in over 400 real estate assets covering 167 million square feet across four continents.

But an important question remains. The few thousand dollars required for Fitwel makes it an attractive alternative because it's enough to get a building owner a plaque out front signaling that this is a "Healthy Building." But does this self-administered checklist really mean that Fitwel buildings are demonstrably healthier buildings? This remains an open question. Some of the points or credits in the Fitwel rating system are quite subjective, opening up different interpretations for everyone involved. For example, if a building has a Fitwel credit for having an indoor air quality plan, the devil is in the details. Such a plan could be a one-page "plan" that says something basic like "monitor carbon dioxide on each floor," or it could be an exhaustive blueprint for monitoring all of the 9 Foundations of a Healthy Building.[6] And for the market, how do you compare these two buildings, both of which might have received Fitwel certification?

The counterargument, naturally, is that Fitwel is a good first step. It signals that the owner is thinking about health. That's an important start.

RESET and LEED

There is certainly good news here. It is undeniable that the market is migrating toward a desire for truly Healthy Buildings, and that it is looking for solutions, including some means of ascertaining that the asset in question is objectively healthy. This suggests that designers and building owners will also be seeking more comprehensive information to support their decisions.

As of this writing, many other players are jumping into the certification or rating-system game. RESET, a standard first developed in China, falls somewhere between Fitwel and WELL in terms of cost and rigor (closer to WELL).[7] RESET is interesting to us because it approaches the assessment of Healthy Buildings from a technology and performance standpoint. The method avoids checklists and prescribed paths, opting instead to focus on results: if your building meets some performance standard with regard to indoor air quality, they don't care what path you took to get there. The RESET certification relies on the rise of new technologies that allow for the continuous measurement of indicators of indoor air quality, such as CO_2, particles, and temperature and humidity. The downside to RESET is that it does not currently cover any of the other 9 Foundations of a Healthy Building, or any of the other air-quality factors that cannot be measured with real-time monitors (we will discuss those in Chapter 10). Still, RESET is clearly positioned for a smart building future where more and more of the 9 Foundations will be able to be measured reliably in real time. One can predict that other Healthy Building certification systems will have a similar focus on real-time performance verification in the near future.

LEED, the original green building standard-bearer (primarily focused on energy, waste, and water for many years) is also expanding its reach into the Healthy Building space, spending a lot more time talking about "health and human performance"—up until now a second-tier consideration. The latest version of LEED dedicates approximately 15 percent of its credits to indoor environmental quality, which may not seem like a high percentage at first glance, but when you explore the specifics under this category, you see that

LEED is looking at a lot of the same factors as the other rating systems: acoustics, lighting, controlling tobacco smoke, and taking into account certain factors like controlling emissions of volatile organic compounds from products and testing the indoor air quality for those compounds, $PM_{2.5}$, and formaldehyde.

All three systems have their benefits and drawbacks. We're less interested in who will become the dominant player in this space (we actually think there is room and a need for all of them, and more), and more interested in understanding how this Healthy Building movement can scale. This brings us to the perceived barriers to adoption, most notably, cost.

The Cost of Certifying a Healthy Building

Let's look more closely at the costs of certification. Securing a WELL v2 certification involves several layers of costs. These include registration, certification, and on-site performance verification; substantial capital costs (called CapEx, for capital expenditures) may also be needed to meet the certification standards.

To put some numbers to this, we took the pricing structure on the WELL website as accessed in 2019 and applied it to two different building types: a 100,000-square-foot (sq. ft.) and a 1,000,000 sq. ft. building. We concluded that the costs to obtain this certification would be in the tens of thousands to several hundreds of thousands of dollars, respectively.[8] (Pricing rates and structures for WELL and other certifications can change rapidly, and may vary based on the unique characteristics of each building).

Costs for any additional CapEx and the required "on-site performance verification" are not included in the WELL certification costs, so we used a few different sources to estimate these values. For the additional capital cost estimates, we relied on a report by the Urban Land Institute that examined lessons from early adopters of the WELL Building standard.[9] ULI conducted interviews with several owners and developers of WELL projects, who pointed to the "hidden" capital costs necessary to improve the building in order to achieve the certification, which ULI reports as $1–$4 per square foot. They also cite one example, the WELL-certified CBRE Headquarters in Los Angeles, where additional capital costs were reported as a 5 percent

TABLE 9.1   Example costs to receive WELL certification for two differently sized buildings.

	EXAMPLE 1: 100,000 SQ. FT. BUILDING		EXAMPLE 2: 1,000,000 SQ. FT. BUILDING	
	Price per square foot	*Total price*	*Price per square foot*	*Total price*
Precertification (optional)	$0.02/sq. ft.	$2,000	$0.02/sq. ft.	$20,000
Registration Fee	$0.028/sq. ft.*	$2,800	$0.0042/sq. ft.*	$4,200
Certification	$0.175/sq. ft.	$17,500	$0.145/sq. ft.	$145,000
On-site Performance Verification†	$0.08/sq. ft.– $0.48/sq. ft.	$8,000– $48,000	$0.08/sq. ft.– $0.48/sq. ft.	$80,000– $480,000
Estimated Process Subtotal	**$0.30/sq. ft.– $0.70/sq. ft.**	**$30,300– $70,300**	**$0.25/sq. ft.– $0.65/sq. ft.**	**$249,200– $649,000**
Estimated additional capital costs to meet certification	$1/sq. ft.– $4/sq. ft.	$100,000– $400,000	$1/sq. ft.– $4/sq. ft.	$1,000,000– $4,000,000
TOTAL		**$130,300– $470,300**		**$1,249,200– $4,649,200**

*The registration fee is a flat rate of $2,800 for buildings between 50,000 and 249,999 sq. ft. and $4,200 for buildings between 500,000 and 1,000,000 sq. ft. We normalized this to a cost per square foot for this hypothetical 100,000 or 1,000,000 sq. ft. building.

†On-site performance verification is required to achieve certification but is administered by third parties; fees for this testing are not listed in the WELL certification pricing. Our cost estimates are derived from: 1) the ULI report referenced in this section, which reported a combined certification + performance verification costs of $0.18–$0.58/sq. ft., and 2) our own research in compiling an equivalent test protocol using consultants, monitoring equipment, and outside laboratories.

increase in overall price. (Another WELL-certified building, in Toronto, lists its increase in capital costs for this purpose at 15 percent.)

Are Healthy Building Certifications Cost Prohibitive?

You are probably thinking this seems expensive. As with many "health" up-grades to a building, the costs often represent a barrier to adoption—in our view this is a shortsighted barrier. In our interviews with real estate leaders, cost was one of the main concerns. But health insurance can chew up to 25 percent of annual payroll expenditures if you consider the "fully loaded" cost including taxes and benefits. And think of the money we spend on nutrition, exercise, or vitamins—or the premium many of us pay for "healthy" food every day. If we are personally willing to spend so much of our hard-earned cash on a whole host of things that will make us healthier, why, when it comes to buildings, are we so afraid to spend on health?

The answer is that the known costs are deemed too great for what are perceived to be uncertain benefits (that and the issue of split incentives, which we will get back to shortly). These expenditures are shunted aside as a boring cost center without any perceived operational, revenue, performance, or reputational gain. That common assessment is what we are trying to challenge with this book.

It's not the case that a building has to be certified in order to be a Healthy Building; but for our purposes here, let's add in the cost of a Healthy Building certification to the cost-benefit analysis in our pro forma from Chapter 4.

It's worth noting at this point that we are entering the realm of forward-looking real estate finance projections and departing the domain of empirical measurement of science experiments. For all but the most routine infrastructure and real estate projects, financial projections are relied on to organize assumptions and understand possible future outcomes. Developers must make numerous decisions under conditions of high uncertainty. Generally, they examine ranges of possible long-term results in order to make both the primary "go or no go" building decision and hundreds of incremental choices about individual components of the building that will never have directly traceable revenue or cost linkages. For example: How much should be spent on windows, on carpets, on kitchen counters and cabinets, on the pool or the gym, or on the parking—or the ventilation system? For many developers, this is an art that comes down to experience and intuition around the aggregate appeal of all aspects of the product, and what the market might pay.

The classic example is a new apartment building that might range from $150 to $200 per square foot to build, where the rental rates upon completion and stabilization might be $1,500–$2,500 per month for a two-bedroom unit, and interest costs might range from 4 percent to 6 percent per year. At the time of the initial commitment to the project, all of these are unknown and most of them will be revealed many years in the future. Here's how this plays out, in very round numbers: If a two-bedroom unit is 1,000 sq. ft., then at $150 / sq. ft. it costs $150,000 to build. If the rent is $2,000 per month, then that's $24,000 per year; $24,000 / $150,000 = 6.67 percent cash-on-cost yield. If the developer can borrow at 5 percent (an interest rate that is less than the yield), then the project "pencils in" favorably on a back-of-envelope basis; the annual cash flow will work and the developer will make money. But at $200 / sq. ft. cost, that becomes $200,000 to build. If the building doesn't perform as well as expected and is only able to command rent of $1,500 / month when the building opens three years from the start of construction, that's $18,000 per year, or only 3.6 percent cash-on-cost yield. If interest rates at completion and permanent financing have jumped to 6 percent, then the promoters will lose money—the cash flow won't even cover the interest cost—and the developers should not have started the apartment building project.

Real estate people focus on two aspects of analysis. First, how closely can our assumptions be based on comparables in the market today? Current rental rates and historic construction costs can be approximated if there is good access to information from other firms. Then the questions become, "Is the number truly comparable to the number for this other design?" and "What changes do we think will happen in the market during construction?" The second aspect involves sensitivity testing (for banks, stress testing). A typical sensitivity test would be something like this for a developer: "All else being equal, how low can occupancy rates fall for us to still realize positive cash flow?" Or for a bank, "How far can market yields rise for us to still have complying loan-to-value ratios?"

Both parties are trying to find the boundaries of a successful deal. This degree of uncertainty is unsettling for empiricists, since the data is really not out there at decision time. But it's second nature for project developers ranging from dam builders to tract housing promoters to big-city office building developers. The following sections use "what if" examples to determine the boundaries of what has to unfold for these decisions to make sense. We explain our rationale for the figures, and readers are encouraged to consider impacts and draw their own conclusions if their underlying assumptions or market expectations are different from the ones modeled here.

With that understanding about how cost-benefit calculations work in real estate, let's get back to our opening question in this section: Are Healthy Building certifications cost prohibitive in the big picture? For discussion purposes, let's assume that an office building design calls for about 250 sq. ft. per employee. (Your office probably isn't 16×16 feet; that figure also includes an allocation for common areas like lobbies, conference rooms, and washrooms.) We'll assume that this building's construction cost is $400/sq. ft. for the base building and the tenant fit-out work, a number that would be in the ballpark for a suburban office building but low for New York City or San Francisco. If the capital cost upcharge to include all of the incremental labor and materials that result in a certifiably Healthy Building is taken to be 3 percent (a middle figure from the costs just discussed), that's about an additional $12 per square foot, or $3,000 per person for each person's allocated 250 sq. ft. of space.

Let's now return to our financial model for Healthy Buildings Inc. (HB) and factor in the new anticipated CapEx for building a Healthy Building and getting the building certified. On the capital expenditure side, the $3,000 per person cost we just estimated sounds like a lot—until you consider that it's a one-time cost. Assuming a typical office lease of 10 years, and assuming that 100 percent of the cost is absorbed by the tenant company, that works out to $300 per person per year. With respect to the 40 employees of HB, it's a cost to the company of $12,000 per year in total. On the benefits side, as a reminder, in Chapter 4 we showed how improving ventilation could lead to a 3 percent productivity boost from health and a 1 percent payroll effect. You'll see those numbers in the same spot here on the left-hand side of the model. Now, let's factor in an estimate of all of the *other* benefits of the 9 Foundations of a Healthy Building, which also show up in Healthy Building certification systems (for example, light, noise, allergens in dust, and water quality). These benefits are *in addition* to the ventilation and filtration discussed in Chapter 3. Let's assume, conservatively, that collectively they improve the company's revenue and payroll performance by half of one percent each. We feel comfortable making this assumption based on the science we presented in Chapter 6—findings like higher throughput at optimal temperatures, how lighting conditions affect mood and concentration, and real-world examples of poor building maintenance shutting down work altogether. The numbers follow.

With all of these assumptions, using the same figures we have been carrying throughout the book, this company's projected bottom line (net income after taxes) improves from the original $1,169,000 to $1,305,313 here—a nearly 12 percent improvement.

Is this plausible, or just fantasy? We maintain that impacts on this order of magnitude are real and should be considered. From a decision-making point of view, there is a significant financial improvement, *plus* people are

TABLE 9.2   Pro forma income statement for H&W with full productivity and health boosts proposed from all 9 Foundations of a Healthy Building.

BASELINE COMPANY ASSUMPTIONS

Number of Employees	40
Average Salary	$75,000
Payroll as % of Revenue	50%

BASELINE BUILDING ASSUMPTIONS

Square Footage of the Building	10,000
Square Footage per Employee (gross including common areas)	250
Construction Cost per Square Foot (base building and tenant)	400
Lease Term (years)	10

(X) WHAT IF?

	IMPACT
OpEx Cost (energy)	$40/person/yr.
Payroll Effect: Health	−1%
Payroll Effect: All Other Strategies*	**−0.5%**
Productivity Boost: Ventilation	3%
Productivity Boost: All Other Strategies	**0.5%**
Rent Increase*	**15%**
Healthy Building Certification: Amortize over 10 years	**$12,000**
Healthy Building Certification: Annual Fees	**$1,667**

Bolded items are new in this model

(X) ITEMIZED IMPACTS OF HEALTHY BUILDING DECISIONS

	Baseline	Rent/Opex Impacts		Payroll Effect: Health		Productivity Boost: Health		Healthy Building Certification	Base Heal Build
Revenue	$6,000,000					3.5%	$210,000		$6,
Payroll	$(3,000,000)			−1.5%	$45,000				$(2,9
Rent	$(300,000)	15%	$(45,000)						$(3
Utilities	$(30,000)		$(1,600)						$(
Healthy Building Certification (Amortize CapEx)								$(12,000)	$(
Healthy Building Certification (Annual Fees)								$(1,667)	$
Other Expenses	$(1,000,000)								$(1,0
Net Income before Taxes	$1,670,000								$1,
Taxes (30%)	$501,000								$
Net Income after Taxes	$1,169,000								$1,
Change									

healthier, happier, and more creative. And remember, this model includes the CapEx that often give owners pause when they start considering building to a Healthy Building standard, as well as the associated costs.

Even with this broad brush, you can see that the costs of the certification process are trivial in the context of the whole project. When a number of less than $12 per square foot is considered in the context of $400 per square foot of construction costs, it can be absorbed quickly. If one amortizes the $12 per square foot over the ten-year cycle, and think about it on a per-employee basis, that's $300 per year per employee. This is about the price of one cup of fancy coffee each week!

Split Incentives?

You may be thinking this is a naïve analysis for the simple reason that, with the exception of owner-occupied buildings, the costs and benefits are not incurred by and going to the same company. The building owner and developer pay the additional CapEx and certification costs, while the tenant gets the benefit in employee productivity and health. The cost-benefit incentives are not aligned.

If you were thinking along those lines, take another look at the pro forma. You'll see that the rent premium is now modeled at 15 percent—and the company is *still* better off than the baseline. The landlord may not be able to capture all of this benefit in additional rent—the tenant might be a better negotiator and could retain more of the marginal value for itself (or share it with employees)—but the numbers show that there is a lot of value to be created that can then be shared. We chose a 15 percent rent premium to highlight the magnitude of value created, not to suggest that the lease agreement might contain this sort of language. Everyone can win. The landlord gets a rent premium, the tenant gets a productivity boost, and the employees are healthier.

A Tower for the People: 425 Park Avenue

Moving beyond this hypothetical, let's explore the financial implications of decision-making around Healthy Buildings certification in an actual building, We did this recently for our joint Harvard Business School / Harvard T. H. Chan School of Public Health case study about 425 Park Avenue in New York City ("A Tower for the People," written with Joe's former doctoral student Emily Jones).[10]

In the words of David Levinson, chairman and CEO of L&L Holding, the project's developer, 425 Park Avenue is "the first new office building on Park Ave in New York City in 50 years."[11] Levinson selected none other than Norman Foster of Foster + Partners to design the new building to replace a building constructed in the 1950s. They shared a grand vision for the new space. In Foster's words, "Our aim is to create an exceptional building, both of its time and timeless, as well as being respectful of its context and celebrated Modernist neighbors—a tower that is for the City and for the people that will work in it, setting a new standard for office design and providing an enduring landmark that befits its world-famous location."[12]

Levinson has a long history of acting ahead of the curve with respect to design innovation. He told us that he makes decisions based on his intuition from decades of experience in the industry (and, no doubt, plenty of sophisticated research).[13] His intuition on 425 Park Avenue? That health will be the differentiator for his tower, which will be the first WELL-certified commercial office building in Manhattan.

Perhaps the most interesting take-home from our conversations was this: Levinson is not just thinking about what his tenants will want this year or next. He is thinking about the tenants 5, 10, and 20 years from now. His major concern is that if he doesn't take these steps toward health now, his building will be outdated in a few short years, surpassed by the next "latest and greatest" building. In some ways, it's a risk-management decision. He is future-proofing his building.

In our case study we look at decisions in the design phase, before the building was built. (Since this is the first commercial building pursuing WELL certification in New York City and these are the early days of landlord awareness, at this writing there are no finished, rented, stabilized examples of this degree of attention to occupant health and indoor air quality.) During the design phase, the financial projections are just that—projections. We walked through many of the decisions made by Levinson and his team, including decisions about ventilation, filtration, and whether to pursue WELL certification. For our purposes, here we are just going to cover the economics of pursuing a Healthy Building certification.

The building at 425 Park Avenue has approximately 675,000 square feet of gross leasable area across 47 floors. The average asking rent is $150 per square foot per year on a triple net lease basis. (This is a common office lease arrangement where the tenant is responsible for its own operating expenses and an allocation of property taxes and building expenses; effectively, the gross rent for the building is in excess of $200 / sq. ft.) The $150 / sq. ft. / year is an average for the building, but as you would expect, the rent on the top floor is higher than for lower floors, so we built multipliers into the model to account for that. The cost to construct this building in the heart of Midtown Manhattan is about $750 / sq. ft., not including land.

We combined all of this in order to estimate net operating income over development cost, a standard ratio for evaluating the expected economic performance of a new real estate development. We then repeated the analysis but added in a 3 percent construction cost premium for achieving the WELL certification as estimated by the L&L team, and a 2 percent rent multiplier to illustrate the general impacts.

In baseline projections, the development cost is about $1.2 billion and the annual net operating income is anticipated to be about $72 million, penciling out to a yield of about 6 percent as a percentage of original project cost, year after year. (This is in range for new office developments in New York City.) Many other factors go into assessing returns on building projects, with key aspects being bank loans, any partnerships in the equity portion of the project, and assumptions about value at refinancing or sale; we don't go into this here, but they are the foundation of John's real estate courses at Harvard Business School.

In this model, Levinson and L&L receive an extra $1.5 million per year in net operating income (that is, cash flow from operations) and the cash-on-cost yield improves by about 25 basis points. The upcharge in initial costs is clearly worth it if the achievable rent also increases along these lines. The market, investment, and cost strategy approach includes three aspects to consider from the point of view of the developer and architect planning the project: (1) Does a Healthy Building strategy increase the likelihood of a fully occupied building? (2) Will the landlord be able to realize a material rent premium today for a certifiably Healthy Building? and (3) Will trends in the market mean that rents rise faster in a building with these characteristics than they will in other, less healthy buildings?

Levinson believes he needs to have this Healthy Building differentiator if he is to attract tenants and command the $150 / sq. ft. per year net rent. What if the added construction costs for a Healthy Building are the difference between a fully occupied building and one that is not? The financial implications are stark—if 425 Park Avenue falls to 95 percent occupied, the yield drops below 6 percent, with about a $3 million revenue hit. It could be that the Healthy Building investment defends the building against vacancy in the event of a downturn.

For questions 2 and 3, there are opportunities for Levinson and L&L to charge a greater rental premium for this building. Now, what if Levinson were able to realize a 5 percent rent premium instead of 2 percent, based on the health benefits to tenant employees? This would amount to an additional $3 million per year in revenue. That's a big deal. And remember, in the earlier portions of this book we argue that tenants are making a better business decision if they are willing to pay a little more for a space that demonstrably gives people a chance to be more productive and effective. The incentive structures are in place for Levinson to charge a premium, and a shrewd tenant should be willing to pay it.

Levinson recognizes the significance of these three strategic aspects. In fact, it's an explicit part of L&L's billion-dollar bet. In his words, "In an up market, I get the premium. In a down market, I get the tenant."[14]

What If You Get It Wrong? The Case for Expertise

One major concern with the burgeoning Healthy Building movement is this: if a LEED professional screws up the water or energy analysis for a green building certification, it's bad, but no one dies. If a WELL professional screws up, he or she is potentially jeopardizing the health of everyone in the building. Putting the world "health" in a business equation draws positive attention, but it also comes with great responsibility. A short aside here is worthwhile because it highlights the potential moral and legal perils of unconstrained enthusiasm about representing what's in a Healthy Building.

The aside: Elizabeth Holmes was the self-made billionaire founder and CEO of Theranos, a company that promised to replace the venous-draw approach to human blood testing with a simple pinprick test. This would be truly revolutionary, had it worked. But it didn't. The entire company was a fraud that was ultimately exposed by the *Wall Street Journal* reporter John Carreyrou and immortalized in his book, *Bad Blood*.[15]

As detailed by Carreyrou, Theranos knowingly rolled out a faulty blood-testing service in the drugstore chain Walgreens and began reporting incorrect lab results to patients. One woman, who is now suing Theranos, was incorrectly diagnosed with a thyroid disorder that resulted in her being put on medication she didn't need. Another was a heart surgery patient who received faulty results from Theranos and then switched his medication and underwent what he claims were unnecessary follow-up procedures. These are not two isolated incidents, either; over 1 million lab tests from Theranos had to be voided or corrected.

Here's the relevance to buildings. Holmes was simply doing what others in Silicon Valley had done before—she initially delivered imperfect products, confident that her company would eventually iterate and ultimately get it right. The problem is that, unlike a software company, which can deliver imperfect first-launch software supplemented by periodic fixes or patches, Theranos was playing with people's lives. It wasn't selling software; it was selling health. So when the firm got it wrong, people's lives were at stake. As of the writing of this book, Holmes has been convicted on fraud charges, because her "getting it wrong" was not an accident; it was willful misconduct, as alleged and documented in the indictment.

The same cautionary tale should be heeded with Healthy Building rating systems. With Healthy Buildings, a mistake here, or a promise of a Healthy Building not based on sound science, is ultimately about health and people's lives. In the end, perhaps our biggest concern with the current Healthy Building rating systems is not just *what* the standard is but also *who* is doing the certifying. And what the implications are if they get it wrong.

When you need your building designed, you hire an architect. When you need a building permit, you hire a professional engineer to sign off on the plans. When you sign a contract, you hire a lawyer to review it. All of these professions have intense qualification protocols. When it comes to certifying the health of your building, it stands to reason that you should hire someone qualified with expertise on indoor health.

Following the lead of LEED, which uses accredited professionals (APs) to evaluate and certify buildings, current Healthy Building systems are also using APs. APs are critical to the success of these certification systems. They offer guidance and strategic support on how to navigate the various rating systems, and they often interface with the architects and design teams to ensure buildings attain their desired status (for example, LEED Silver, Gold, or Platinum).

WELL has the WELL AP, RESET has the RESET AP, and Fitwel does the same thing but calls them Fitwel Ambassadors. This approach—training and accrediting to a common standard—has been crucial in changing the industry, and the world, by engaging hundreds of thousands of people in the building sector and giving them ownership, and opportunities, around certifications. There are already hundreds of thousands of APs who essentially act as brand ambassadors for LEED, WELL, Fitwel, and others.

Yet as much as these APs are essential, another type of expert is also needed—people with deep knowledge of how to measure, monitor, and interpret environmental data in buildings. WELL has started to move in this direction by outsourcing the performance verification of WELL buildings to "WELL Performance Testing Agents" in an approved "WELL Performance Testing Organization." The requirement to become a testing agent is different from that to become an AP—two days of training hosted by WELL.

That's a good start, but here we make a strong recommendation: that the Healthy Building movement engage with the community of Certified Industrial Hygienists (CIHs). The CIH certification, now 40 years old, is administered by the American Industrial Hygiene Association. The term "industrial hygiene" is still widely used in the trade, but Joe hates it. Who wants to be an industrial hygienist? It sounds like a dental assistant who works on an oil rig. So we prefer to use the shorthand CIH, and we like to think of it as "Certified Indoor Health," because that's *actually* what a CIH does.

Why CIHs? These are experts at anticipating, evaluating, managing, and controlling hazards for workers. In addition to *four years* of coursework in the sciences (and oftentimes another two in a master's program), the classroom training must be followed by *five years* of work experience under the mentorship of a seasoned professional. Industrial hygiene does not have to be confined to food processing, factories, refineries, and hospitals. These skills matter in every occupied space, including commercial office space.

Now take a look at the type of skill sets they are required to have—and the intensity of the certification exam—and you'll quickly see that this is the exact type of expertise needed if you really want to understand what's happening in buildings.

BOX 9.1   Certified Industrial Hygienists

Required Education: bachelor's degree in biology, chemistry, engineering, or physics

Required Experience: five years plus professional references

Examination Rubrics:

- Air Sampling and Instrumentation
- Analytical Chemistry
- Basic Science
- Biohazards
- Biostatistics and Epidemiology
- Community Exposure
- Engineering Controls and Ventilation
- Health Risk Analysis and Hazard Communication

- Industrial Hygiene Program Management
- Noise
- Nonengineering Controls
- Radiation / Nonionizing
- Thermal Stressors
- Toxicology
- Work Environments and Industrial Processes

Sample Examination Questions:

- **Air Sampling.** The limit of quantitation for a particular sampling method is 9.3 µg/sample. An industrial hygienist wants to conduct a personal exposure monitoring study with a target concentration of ≥ An of the TLV. The TLV of the substance at issue is 0.1 ppm and the gram molecular weight of the substance is 30.031 g/mol. The proscribed flow-rate for sample collection on an adsorbent tube is 0.050 LPM. How many minutes of sample collection at the proscribed flow rate are required to collect a quantifiable sample result, assuming the concentration is at least 10% of the TLV?

- **Analytical Chemistry.** An air sampling procedure is accurate within ±16%, and the analytical procedure is accurate within ±9%. What is the accuracy of the total analysis? 16.7%, 17.6%, 14.8%, or 18.4%.

- **Basic Science.** A mixture contains: 50 mL benzene (m.w. = 78; v.p. = 75mmHG; sp. gr. = 0.879), 25 mL carbon tetrachloride (m.w. = 154; v.p. = 91mmHG; sp. gr. = 1.595), and 25 mL trichloroethylene (m.w. = 131.5; v.p. = 58mmHG; sp. Gr. = 1.45g). Assuming Raoult's Law is obeyed, what will be the concentration of benzene in air at 760 mmHG saturated with vapor of the above mixture?

(*continued*)

BOX 9.1 *Continued*

- **Biohazards.** Which fungal type is inappropriate for detection with spore traps and microscopy? Alternaria spp., Stachybotrys chartarum, Aspergillus fumigatus, or Basidiospores.

- **Biostatistics and Epidemiology.** An industrial hygienist has the following exposure data from a similarly exposed group of employees. The occupational exposure limit for the substance is 100 ppm. The IH wants to ensure the average exposure is less than 10% of the exposure limit. What is the 95% upper confidence limit of the average exposure from this group?

- **Risk Assessment.** Which of the following would be considered an acceptable cancer risk in the workplace by OSHA? 10^{-3}, 10^{-4}, 10^{-5}, or 10^{-6}.

- **Radiation.** The human body is best at absorbing nonionizing radiation within which range of frequencies? 3 KHz to 30 MHz; 30 MHz to 300 MHz; 3 GHz to 6 GHz; >6 GHz.

- **Thermal Stress.** Calculate the estimated radiant heat load from surrounding objects with radiant temperature of 101°F using the formula $R = 15(t_w - 95)$, where: R = radiant heat load (BTU / hour), and t_w = radiant temperature of surrounding objects (F).

- **Toxicology.** What is the major mechanism of toxicity for carbon monoxide?

- **Ventilation.** Calculate the airflow in cfm when the velocity pressure is 1.1 inches water and the circumference of the duct is 56.25 inches.

Sources: Example questions compiled from: American Industrial Hygiene Association, "Sample Exam Questions," http://www.abih.org/become-certified/prepare-exam /sample-exam-questions; and courtesy of Bowen EHS CIH exam prep, https://www .bowenehs.com/exam-prep/cih-exam-prep/.

When you look at the required education, required experience, and sample questions from the certification exam, you will quickly recognize that their expertise is in the science of a Healthy Building. If something is found to be "off," this group has the skill set to identify what that is and come up with a solution. We don't know about you, but we would feel better sitting in our Healthy Building if we knew a CIH was determining how healthy it was.

Naturally, there are business challenges with the cost and availability of CIHs as Healthy Buildings increasingly come into the mainstream. We believe that the certification protocols and standards that will be most influential in the long run will include CIH knowledge at a scale and degree of accessibility that are both rigorous and objective, while also being widely propagated.

What Makes a Great Healthy Building Certification?

Overall, the appearance of these Healthy Building certifications is a positive sign. It proves that awareness is growing and shows that the market wants a solution. We are hopeful. First offerings always need fine-tuning, and we pointed out a few of those in this chapter. Because the demand is so high, we are confident that the market will continue to iterate until it gets this right.

Here is what "getting it right" for a Healthy Building certification protocol looks like to us:

1. Evidence based and supported by peer-reviewed science
2. Flexible and can incorporate evolving research and new advancements in technology
3. Standardized, consistently defined, and verifiable
4. Cost effective (and with a cost-benefit analysis that includes human health and performance)
5. Not defined solely at one single point in time
6. Administered and verified with on-site testing by experts trained in how to anticipate, evaluate, manage, and control hazards
7. Entails performance verification that includes monitoring Health Performance Indicators (covered in Chapter 10), such as real-time indicators of indoor environmental quality, in areas that are representative of where people are spending their time
8. Developed in close coordination with end users (for example, designers, architects, owners, investors, and tenants) and building health experts (for example, engineers, health scientists, and medical professionals)

9. Recognized by the market and investors as providing commercial value

10. Incentivizes shared value across stakeholders (for example, investors, owners, and tenants)

We don't know yet what system will eventually be considered the "gold standard" for Healthy Building certifications. This section of our book will become dated very quickly. That's a good thing: we look forward to seeing how the system evolves, and to seeing this new certification gain the same level of influence as LEED and other green building rating systems.

CHAPTER TEN

Moving from KPIs to HPIs

> Employees are a company's greatest asset—they're your competitive advantage.
>
> —ANNE M. MULCAHY

WE SPENT CHAPTERS 6, 7, 8, AND 9 DEFINING *what* a Healthy Building is. Now we'll look at examples of *how to measure* the health impact of a building because, as the influential management guru Peter Drucker famously put it, "If you can't measure it, you can't improve it." To date, no one is really measuring building performance effectively. But you can—and you should. In this chapter, we want to show you how. We'll do it in two parts, first by showing you how it's done badly, and then by showing you how to do it right.

Felix Barber and Rainer Strack wrote an article in the *Harvard Business Review* called "The Surprising Economics of a 'People Business,'" in which they argued that the performance of employees drives the bottom line.[1] We agree. And though it's not exactly a revelation that in jobs calling for human labor, or wisdom, or creativity, or analytics, the performance of employees will affect the company's performance, their key insight was captured in this sentence: "Business performance measures and management practices don't reflect the particular economics of people-driven businesses." In short, there is a disconnect—we know human performance drives company performance, but we're terrible at measuring it.

In fact, we're not just terrible at measuring it; oftentimes we are measuring the wrong thing. Take the work of leading Silicon Valley investor John Doerr and the insights he offers in his book *Measure What Matters*.[2] Doerr is chairman of Kleiner Perkins and was an early backer of Amazon, Google, Uber, and other companies. His work on what he calls "OKRs"—Objectives and Key Results—extends Drucker's ideas into the startup and innovation world, charting the path from hope to execution. Doerr has helped move companies from measuring Key Performance Indicators (KPIs) that don't matter to measuring those that do. The most well-known, and most important, of his interventions were his conversations with the cofounders of Google, Larry Page and Sergey Brin, back in the days when Google was still being run out of a garage in Menlo Park. He convinced them to use his OKR system, which was expressly designed to measure and track success.

We want to marry Barber and Strack's insight and Doerr's rigor to extend the "what gets measured" line of thinking to include the health performance of buildings—and to advance the toolkit for measuring the right things. Our central thesis in this book is not only that employee performance drives the bottom line but also that *the building* (or indoor environment) plays a vital role in optimizing that human performance, and that this *building performance* has been mismeasured to date. We are putting far too much faith in self-reported employee surveys, which, as you will see (and as any epidemiologist would tell you), have a tendency to be wildly misrepresentative.

Doing It Wrong: The Mismeasurement of "People Businesses"

One of the most commonly used tools to measure building-related productivity and performance is the "Post-occupancy Survey" (also commonly known as a "Post-occupancy Evaluation"; we are going to stick with "survey," for reasons you'll soon see). As people have begun to appreciate the value of Healthy Buildings, there are now all sorts of claims being bandied about regarding the health of a building and the productivity of employees. Since some of these claims are based on surveys, they require some scrutiny. We will look at five real-world examples of Post-occupancy Survey data and consider how the data is being used to describe the impact of a workspace on productivity and health. Our goal here is not to say that surveys cannot be used at all but rather that if they are going to be used, they must be used very carefully. For each fatal flaw, we'll also give you the solution for how to avoid it, because as Joe's brother Brian always says, if you point out problems without offering a solution, that's just complaining.

Warning: what follows will be an equal-opportunity critique.

Here are five claims made by companies about a new office space they've designed or moved into after conducting a Post-occupancy Survey. We've picked a few especially notable examples, but the reality is that everyone is doing this.

- Company A reported that 91.6 percent of employees say they feel healthier because of indoor air quality improvement, 56 percent of occupants report an overall improvement in visual comfort, and 42 percent report an improvement in acoustics.
- Company B reported that 80 percent of employees believed their new office enabled them to be more productive.
- Company C reported 95 percent satisfaction with its new space.
- Company D reported that high-performance buildings save energy and water, cost less to operate, produce less waste, and have more satisfied occupants than typical buildings.
- Company E reported that occupants report 30 percent fewer sick-building symptoms in green-certified buildings.

Well, to any untrained eye with even a slight bit of healthy skepticism, much of this reads just as it should: like B.S. That's why we like calling these "Post-occupancy Surveys," so we can use the acronym POS (use your imagination).

To keep this more highbrow, we'll couch our critique about why POSs are problematic using two epidemiological concepts: selection bias and dependent measurement error. If this sounds like it might get too technical, rest assured, every time you read a word or phrase that belongs in an epidemiology textbook, you can simply swap in the phrase "common sense."

Fatal Flaw 1: Selection Bias

At its most basic, selection bias happens when the people who take the survey don't represent the underlying population that could, and should, be queried. When looking at any of these bold conclusions from Companies A–E, we should immediately be asking ourselves a few questions about sample size, representativeness, and loss to follow-up:

- Sample size: Was it a survey of the entire company or a small subset?
- Representativeness: Was only one type of worker or group in the company surveyed?
- Loss to follow-up: Is anyone missing from the survey?

We don't know any of the specifics that underpin the results from Company A, and we don't mean to imply it did anything wrong, but let's put some hypothetical numbers to this to see how these four aspects of selection bias could potentially influence our interpretation of the headline finding that "91.6 percent of employees say they feel healthier because of indoor air quality improvement."

Sample Size

There are a few ways to get to that 91.6 percent number. Let's suppose that Company A is a 600-person company, the company sent the survey to all 600 employees, and 500 ended up responding and taking the survey—a pretty good sample size and response rate (83 percent). If this were the case, we would know that 458 employees reported feeling better because of indoor air quality (458 / 500 = 91.6 percent).

But what if, in that same 600-person company, only 83 people took the survey? That would mean that 76 people responded positively about the building, giving us the same reported percentage of people satisfied with the air quality (76 / 83 = 91.6 percent). Under either scenario, the company would be technically correct to report that 91.6 percent of people report feeling good about the air quality, but the implications are vastly different. The claim that 91.6 percent reported positive feelings about indoor air quality would mean something different if the survey sample size represents less than 15 percent of the company.

Representativeness

Let's assume that 500 of the 600 people in the company did take the survey and the sample size is not the issue. But what if the 500 people who were given the survey were all executives and knowledge workers who had offices on the exterior of the floor plan in a traditional office setup—you know, the window offices—and the 100 who weren't given the survey were the administrative staff located on the interior in the cubicle farm? We'll take it to the extreme in our hypothetical—if the 100 people in the cubicle farm all did not like the air quality, the "true" resulting percentage of people who liked the air quality could be as low as 76.3 percent if the survey had included the 100 people in the cubicle farms $(458 / 600 = 76.3$ percent). Quite different from the 91.6 percent that was reported.

Now let's assume the company sent the survey to all 600 people in its company, thereby avoiding any intentional selection bias. What if the people who decided to complete the survey were somehow different from those who opted not to complete the survey? The people who decided to take the survey are what we call "self-selected"; they willingly raised their hand and asked to participate. The difference between responders and nonresponders becomes critically important to understand because we know from the epidemiological literature that self-selectors are very different from others. (You might think of the Yelp effect—the people who post on Yelp are usually either extremely satisfied or extremely dissatisfied, and they have time to post a review on a website.)

For Company A, we would want to know who the self-selected responders are. Are they all of the marketing department, executives, and building managers responsible for air quality—the people who most certainly know that Company A just invested millions of dollars into this new buildings and also know that the company is going to use these results to market its products? Despite this company's best attempts at a representative survey, did the administrators in the cubicle farm all decline to answer the survey, so in the end the survey really just sampled those in the private offices again?

Understanding and evaluating selection bias, in all its forms, is so important that in nearly every single peer-reviewed epidemiological study, the very first table in the paper is one that shows the sample size and examines, side by side, any potential differences between responders and nonresponders. Epidemiologists do this to show that there was no selection bias introduced as a result of who ended up taking the survey. In our hypothetical, if the results are to be believed, the headline finding would have to include a similar table showing that the 500 who took the survey were similar to the 100 who did not across things like age, gender, title, salary, education, office type, and office location.

This problem can be avoided, even with a smaller sample size, through a random selection process.

Loss to Follow-Up (and the Healthy Worker Effect)

Now, even if Company A addressed the small sample size and representativeness issue, there is still another potential for selection bias: it only surveyed the people who were in the office that day. In epidemiological terms, this is a type of selection bias that can arise from what is called loss to follow-up (and a kind of corollary, "the Healthy Worker Effect").

This type of bias arises because, on average, people who are at work are different from those who are not. Those not at work may be absent because they are sick or otherwise unable to work, or because they have moved on to another job and can no longer be contacted. They are "lost to follow-up."

Let's say Company A did manage to survey 500 of its 600 total employees with a representative and random survey with no self-selection bias. Are the 500 people who were *in the office* that day the true denominator? In other words, do they represent the entire population potentially "at risk"? In addition to employees out for client meetings or conferences or vacation, what if someone else was out sick that day? Then he or she wouldn't be included in the survey. And what if the building was the *reason* that employee was out sick? That is, what if you were only surveying "healthy workers." What if a few people in the company absolutely hated the new workplace, so much so that they just quit and no longer worked there when the survey was administered? All of these employees would be lost to follow-up and wouldn't be included in the survey either. (Instead of just calling this the "Healthy Worker Effect," we might call this the "Happy Worker Effect," where the only people left in the company are those who actually like the company; the disgruntled or unsatisfied having moved on.)

This problem can be avoided by ensuring that the survey captures all of those "at risk," not just the healthy and satisfied.

This is just a hypothetical, so we could explore these issues in Fatal Flaw 1—we don't actually know the sampling details for Company A that underpin the claim that "91.6 percent of employees say they feel healthier because of indoor air quality improvement." And therein lies the problem.

Fatal Flaw 2: Dependent Measurement Error

With the basics of selection bias behind us, we want to get to another major problem with these POSs: their use to find causal associations between design features and outcomes. Those conclusions can be erroneous as a result of the potential for these POSs to create what is called dependent measurement error.[3]

To show you how this can be a problem, we'll start with a hypothetical and then show you an actual example. Suppose we ask you, a happy person, how you like the room you're in right now. You say, "It's great. I love the air quality and lighting in here." Then suppose we also ask you how you're feeling. You answer: "Great." Any headaches? "No." Any fatigue? "No."

Now, we turn to your colleague. You know the one. We ask him, How are you feeling today? "Terrible." Any headaches? "All day, every day." Any fatigue? "I'm exhausted." Then we ask him, How do you like the building and room you're in right now? "I hate it." How is the air quality? "It's terrible." And so on. You get the picture.

This POS is really testing whether people are stoics or complainers. The stoic is likely to answer all questioners similarly—in a positive manner. And the complainer will likely do what complainers do—answer everything negatively. This is the dependent measurement error and here's why it is so insidious. What researchers, survey analysts, or companies typically do next is put the responses of the stoics and complainers together, along with those of everyone else who makes up the middle ground and took the same survey, then they plot it out and draw a nice regression line.

Voila! You have yourself a *very* strong, but misleading, relationship between an "exposure" and an "outcome," with complainers anchoring the bottom left and stoics driving the top right. This is usually backed up by fancy-sounding but meaningless phrases like "statistically significant" results that give the study some imprimatur of being robust. However, if you took the stoics and complainers out of the survey and only focused on those in the middle (the gray open circles in our figure), the figure would no longer show any relationship between the two variables.

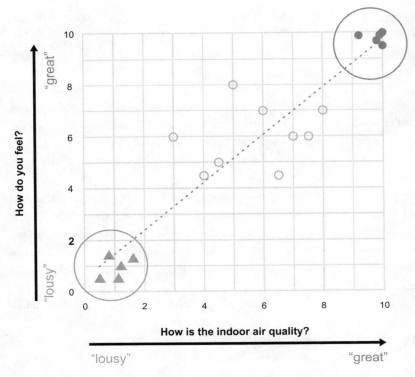

FIGURE 10.1   Illustration of dependent measurement error and "stoics versus complainers."

This is called dependent measurement error; the measurements of exposure and outcome are dependent on each other. The assessments of exposure and outcome are not disentangled. That is, they are not independently assessed.

The issue? The ensuing analysis purports to show a relationship between two factors when actually what has been "discovered" is that this company, like all companies, has some stoics and some complainers. The implication? Companies then report these spurious "findings" and executives may make decisions about their company and buildings based on them.

This problem can be avoided by using an objective measure of exposure (for example, measuring air quality in the environment), an objective measure of an outcome (for example, cognitive function tests), or objective measures of both.

Doing It Right: Health Performance Indicators

The higher-order, fundamental flaw we just examined is that POSs are subjective and only rely on human perceptions. This makes them prone to bias and dependent error. The solution is to track *independent, objective* measures of performance across an array of indicators. Businesses have been doing exactly this for decades. Now we just need to apply these measurement techniques to buildings.

Businesses track KPIs every second, every day, every week, every month. They track things like revenue and return on equity; earnings before interest, taxes, depreciation, and amortization (EBITDA) and net profit margin; and operating cash flow. But if we want to capitalize on the 90 percent cost of our buildings—the people inside them—are traditional KPIs the right way to go about it? The short answer is no. Using traditional KPIs has led to the mismeasurement of "people businesses," as shown by Barber and Strack.

"Measuring what matters," to our mind, means measuring health performance. The rationale is straightforward—if *people* constitute the vast majority of your business expense and productivity, and *their health* is a key determinant of their ability to be productive, then the most "key" KPI is health. So, as Joe and his colleagues argue in a recent article, companies need to start being intentional about how they measure the health and well-being of their employees. This means measuring Health Performance Indicators (HPIs),[4] and it goes way beyond using POSs.

The HPI concept is all about tracking the factors that can be leveraged to optimize the building for health and performance. In this book we focus on how the HPI concept can be applied to the building, but it can be extended to the entire business enterprise. (You might think of other factors in a company that influence worker health and the bottom line but aren't building related: company culture, maternity and paternity leave, autonomy, salary, purpose, and other health-promoting activities not linked squarely to the building. A "toxic" or adversarial work culture can have a significant negative impact on health, as can poor sleep, stress, and long hours.)

For now, we will stay focused on buildings and will populate our framework with new HPIs that we think all companies should consider tracking that relate to their building. Because really, after you have spent so much time, effort, and money sorting through candidates to find the best and the brightest—the internally motivated and highly skilled—wouldn't you want to create the optimal working environment to maximize the performance of your investment?

The HPI Framework

In creating this HPI framework, we adopted, or rather co-opted, the language of KPIs so that we could use terms and concepts that would be very familiar to the business community and therefore easy to implement. As with KPIs, there are leading HPIs ("before impact") and lagging HPIs ("after impact"); some are direct indicators of health (that is, they measure the people) and some are indirect (that is, they measure the building). A nice way to visualize this is to split the HPIs into quadrants.

In their original research paper that briefly touched on HPIs, Joe and his colleagues populated this framework with some examples. For this book, we have relied on our presentations, workshops, and conversations over the past two years with executives across various industries (for example, commercial real estate, tech, and pharma) and across various functions in their companies

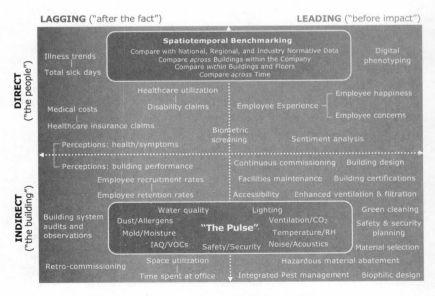

FIGURE 10.2   Health Performance Indicators (HPIs) for buildings.

(for example, Human Resources, C-Suite, and facilities) to populate the framework with some new HPI ideas. (HPIs will necessarily be different for each company, particularly the direct indicators on the top half of the framework, but the ones on the bottom related to buildings are universal.)

Let's start with the top left quadrant and work our way around counterclockwise.

Direct and Lagging HPIs: Measuring Worker Health after the Fact

At the end of the year, businesses can track several metrics to understand how health performance *as a result of the building* may have been affected that year. This includes tracking gross-level trends on things like total employee sick days, health-care utilization, and specific illness trends, such as an uptick in asthma attacks or influenza cases. Importantly, the key to determining whether these represent potential building-related issues is what's written in the box at the top center—you have to analyze and benchmark results against normative spatial and temporal data (this is known as spatio-temporal benchmarking). What the heck does that mean? Put more straightforwardly, companies should track these indicators by looking for differences over *space* and *time*, both within and outside their organization.

For an example of how analyzing these types of HPIs can lead to actionable information, take the recent investigation led by research associate Jose Guillermo Cedeno Laurent on Joe's Healthy Buildings team.[5] He analyzed health record data from university students living in different buildings and, simply by stratifying the results by building on the campus, found that students who lived in one upperclassmen building on campus had strikingly lower rates of allergies, year after year, over a five-year period. The health data was a clue that something was different in this building. But what was it? The value of analyzing the HPIs in this upper left quadrant was that it tipped us off that there might be something interesting in this one building. Because of what we saw in the health data, we did a follow-up investigation. It turned out that this building was the one in the study with mechanical ventilation, supplying filtered air at higher ventilation rates. (Surprise, surprise.)

Just as one KPI does not tell you everything you need to know about a company, the same holds true for HPIs. But this group of HPIs, taken together, can provide a strong indicator, using data most businesses already collect, of direct impacts of the building on health.

Real-World Example: Using Illness Trends to Catch a Cancer Cluster

A 300-person services firm operating out of a newly renovated space on the outskirts of a major US city had a process for formally monitoring employee illness trends. The building was originally part of an old industrial complex that had been newly renovated and rehabbed as office space, with beautiful high ceilings, tall windows, and an open floor plan in some areas with interesting second-story office and meeting spaces that looked out over the main hall. After reviewing the illness trends in one year (lagging and direct HPIs), the company noticed something unusual—two of its longtime employees who worked on the same floor had been diagnosed with Bell's palsy, a weakening in your facial muscles that only occurs on one side, causing half of your face to droop. The etiology of Bell's palsy is unknown, but there are several hypotheses, including viral infection. There is also some evidence that environmental factors are a risk factor, including exposure to volatile organic compounds (VOCs).

Concerned, the company opened a formal inquiry to dig deeper into the potential problem and, in the process, learned of two more Bell's palsy cases in its workforce in the same time period. It hired an occupational physician and epidemiologist who, as we suggest in the top middle box in our HPI framework, compared the incidence rate within the building, across buildings, and even with the general population using national disease incidence data (that is, spatiotemporal benchmarking). The epidemiologist confirmed that this rate of Bell's palsy in a workforce that size was outside the bounds of what could be expected as a result of chance alone. Based on this finding, the firm initiated an environmental investigation led by Certified Industrial Hygienists, who discovered that there was a plume of VOCs in the groundwater below the building. Solvents had been dumped onto the land many years earlier at an adjacent building, contaminating the water below, which spread into a plume that now reached under this newly renovated building. Testing of the indoor spaced confirmed that VOCs from the groundwater under the building were permeating up into the new building. (This is not that uncommon, and it is called vapor intrusion.) The fix? Several tweaks were made to the mechanical system to help keep the building positively pressurized (a negatively pressurized space acts like a vacuum and sucks the VOCs into the building), and a sub-slab vapor intrusion remediation system was put in place.

Indirect and Lagging HPIs: *Proxies* for Worker Health Performance after the Fact

Moving down to the lower left quadrant, we get into the realm of indirect measures of health. (You can ignore the box labeled "The Pulse" for now. It's so important that we'll dive deeply into that after we work our way around the HPI quadrants.) In this quadrant you'll see a few indicators that businesses may also track at the end of the year or end of the month—indirect measures of health performance, such as tracking employee perceptions (done right!) of the building and air quality, or after-the-fact observations about the building or unusual events (unusual odors, systems failing unexpectedly).

Consider two related HPIs here: space utilization and time spent at office. As Covid-19 upends the utilization of office, school, and retail space—perhaps permanently—these trailing indicators become increasingly relevant and useful in measuring effectiveness of healthy-building choices. We can imagine this in three scenarios. First, for workers and others who must be present at the workplace, obvious markers like days lost to Covid isolation or to other illness are easy to quantify and vitally important to organizations. Second, for workers who can elect to work from home (thanks to a fortunate combination of their tasks and their living situations), employers will need to show that the formal work environment is as safe as the home and that the statistical health outcomes of being in the office (or in the school) are acceptable. Third, it's not automatic that any of the nine foundations—including ventilation and filtration, but also noise, security and more—are in place at home, either. Lagging HPIs will show whether organizations need to help upgrade worker's home environments, too, based on results—just as they need to upgrade formal office and school settings.

What does this have to do with utilization of HPIs? If your goal is like that of IBM (or other companies that want people in the office, such as Google, Apple, Aetna, and Yahoo), then you definitely want to be sure that the building you're making your employees move back into is one they'll be happy to be in; otherwise, you run the risk of losing them. How might you find out how effective your enhanced building is at bringing workers together to collaborate? Track and measure an HPI like how much time people actually spend in the building, and see whether this varies across different buildings or before or after a Healthy Building intervention. If you like your office, or feel more productive there, chances are that the amount of time you spend there will go up. (If you're thinking, sarcastically, "Yeah, people love being tracked this way," you might consider that this is already happening, just not so overtly. Every time you log into your computer, the company knows where you are, just as it does every time you send an email. More than knowing when you are there, it even knows *where* you are in the building; as you move throughout your building during the day, the phone in your pocket is constantly pinging the Wi-Fi, so you are being tracked every minute of the day.) This type of data can be used to understand what spaces are working for your employees and what spaces aren't, letting you prioritize your next renovation.

Real-World Example: Building Performance Observations and Perceptions

In late 2008, the US Consumer Product Safety Commission began receiving reports from homeowners and builders about something unusual going on in Florida. People were noticing that air conditioners and other appliances in newly built homes stopped working after a few short months. Replacement appliances failed just as quickly. Upon inspection, they noticed a dark coating on the cooling coils of the failing air conditioners and a similar dark coating on other metal surfaces—even on their jewelry. The issue with the appliances was accompanied by a rotten-egg smell in the home.

Within four years, the Consumer Product Safety Commission had logged nearly 4,000 reports across 43 states, the vast majority of which occurred in Florida. Early signs pointed to defective drywall as the culprit. (The problematic building product, it turned out, had all been sourced from vendors in China. Thus, the problem product and resulting issue in homes came to be known colloquially as "Chinese Drywall.") The commission launched its biggest and most expensive investigation ever to identify the root cause of the problem and find remediation solutions. A 51-home investigation, led by Joe, Jack McCarthy, and the team of consultants at Environmental Health & Engineering, used a combination of air-sampling techniques and the placement of "corrosion classification coupons" in the houses. We determined that the drywall used in this new construction was emitting hydrogen sulfide into the homes.[6] Hydrogen sulfide is highly corrosive to copper and silver—thus the dark coating on copper and silver surfaces (technically copper sulfide and silver sulfide)—and it's known for a rotten-egg smell and very low odor detection threshold (in the parts per trillion).

Additional work by Lawrence Berkeley National Laboratory, using small-scale chambers to test emission rates of chemicals from the defective drywall, confirmed what was found in the homes—hydrogen sulfide and other reduced sulfur compounds coming off the drywall.[7] They also found that these emission rates increased with temperature and humidity.[8] Once the problem was identified, the main challenge in remediation was, How do you determine *where* it was used in each home? (Painted drywall looks the same whether it is problematic Chinese drywall or nonproblematic drywall.) Our subsequent study led to a way to "see through the wall" and identify markers of Chinese drywall using a slick real-time forensic fingerprinting technique (portable X-ray fluorescence and Fourier-transfer infrared spectrometry, in case you were curious). A follow-up health investigation by the US Department of Health and Human Services concluded that the people in houses with problematic drywall could have experienced adverse health effects from the hydrogen sulfide, most notably exacerbation of preexisting respiratory conditions, eye and nasal irritation, and nasal tract lesions.[9]

The takeaway from this case is that oftentimes the first indication that something is potentially wrong in your office, home, or school is a noticeable change in building performance (for example, failing systems, corrosion, or damaged walls). In the Chinese Drywall case, the forensic investigation was aided by a unique feature—the failing systems and appliances were caused by a chemical that was pungent. If it happened to be caused by a chemical with no odor, the mystery of the failing appliances would have taken longer to uncover, while people would be breathing in whatever was in the air.

Indirect and Leading HPIs: Ahead of the Curve

The lower right quadrant is the most critical quadrant when we are talking about HPIs related to buildings. This is where a company, building owner, or manager can have the greatest impact on the health and productivity of employees, and therefore on the business. And because these are leading indicators, the business can be sure that it is getting the benefits from the building immediately, rather than waiting for a problem to arise and only addressing it after negative impacts have started accruing.

Let's start with the most important first step in a Healthy Building life cycle: building design. Many of the 9 Foundations of a Healthy Building can be built into the DNA of a building right at the beginning in the design stage. Want higher ventilation rates? Design for it. Want healthier building materials? Spec them. Want higher-efficiency filters? Buy them. In short, if you want a Healthy Building and the economic benefits that come with it, the best thing is to design for it.

Then, after you design the building for health, make sure you are getting what you paid for by commissioning the building. Designing a building, building it, and then not testing it is akin to buying an airplane and putting it in service without first giving it a test flight. No one would want to get on that first flight, and no one should want to be the first one in a new building that hasn't been fully tested either. Commissioning is a "test flight" for your building. (Fine, the analogy isn't perfect because an untested building doesn't run the risk of immediately killing its occupants. But notice we used the word "immediately" . . .)

To extend this imperfect analogy, you also probably wouldn't want to get on an airplane that had a test flight but then was never checked again. That's why ongoing commissioning of your building is recommended, not just one-time commissioning. Ever wonder why flying is the safest form of transportation? It's because health and safety have been built into the heart of the industry. Airplanes get an "A Check" every 200–300 flights. It's reasonable that your building should get similar checkups. By this point in the book, we hope you are motivated by the health performance benefits, but just in case, commissioning also comes with considerable energy savings—a study from Lawrence Berkeley National Lab found that commissioning can yield energy savings between 13 and 16 percent.[10]

Additional HPIs in this quadrant focus on ensuring that the building is meeting preset conditions, like building certification prerequisites, a safety and security plan, following green cleaning procedures, and using integrated pest management techniques. By tracking and measuring these, the business is controlling nearly everything it can with regard to building performance. Health is built into its DNA.

Real-World Example: How Material Selection Can Reduce the Toxic Load

Kaiser Permanente, a US-based health-care company with over 200,000 employees, pays a lot of attention to the health of its patients and of its staff. It also pays a lot of attention to what goes into its buildings, of which it has many—over three dozen hospitals and over 600 medical offices. In 2006 it started examining the evidence supporting the use of antimicrobials in its building materials (that is, it was interested in healthier material selection). Conceptually the use of these chemicals might appear to makes sense; it seems logical on first glance that a hospital would want its walls and flooring to have antimicrobial properties.

But it turns out that what might on the face of it seem logical—the desire to have antimicrobials embedded in finishes, fabrics, and just about every high-touch surface in a health-care facility—was simply not supported by the science. A number of studies had shown that it was just as effective to use soap to wash hands as it was to use an antimicrobial soap, that there was no evidence that using these chemicals in surfaces and finishes made patients healthier, that their overuse came with the unwanted effect of promoting antibiotic resistance, and that many of these chemicals, most notably triclosan, were actually harmful to human health. (Triclosan, like a few of the chemicals we discussed in Chapter 7, is a halogenated chemical with two phenyl rings that interferes with thyroid hormone function and reproductive success.)[11]

What did Kaiser Permanente do? First, it issued a recommendation that these chemicals not be used in its buildings. Then it banned triclosan outright because of its known human toxicity. And finally, most recently, it banned a whole host of other chemicals widely used in other buildings and hospitals from use in surfaces in its facilities.[12] The result? Healthier buildings, because of a reduced toxic load from unnecessary antimicrobial chemicals. It raises the question, If Kaiser Permanente, one of the largest health-care providers in the country, has deemed it unnecessary and even harmful to use these chemicals in its facilities, why do you have them all over your office building and home?

Direct and Leading HPIs: Real-Time Measures of Employee Health and Performance

The bottom right quadrant is where every business should spend its energy and focus to ensure that its building is being leveraged for the health and performance of its employees, but we recognize that the top right quadrant is where everyone *thinks* they should focus their attention. In an ideal world, wouldn't we all want clear, leading indicators of employee health and performance? We could get there, sure enough, by requiring employees to take periodic cognitive function tests and participating in measuring real-time biometric data to track their personal health. But we'll let you in on a secret: that's what academics do so you don't have to. We have already done the studies, wiring everyone up to collect biometric and cognitive function data and then assessing how indoor environmental factors influence human physiological performance. That's how we know that everything in that bottom right quadrant is important to measure and track.

That said, there are some things in the top right quadrant that are worth exploring. The most important of them is "employee experience," which can be summed up as, "Listen to your employees—are they happy or upset?" Ask your building manager about the temperature complaints he or she gets every day and you're likely to get an eye roll and a snide comment about how some complainer-type employees are always unhappy with this or that. But dismissing these complaints is an economic mistake, as we showed in Chapter 6. A better approach is to empower your facilities manager to think as if he or she were in the health-care business and to treat these complaints and reports as vital to the company's success.

Last, as we move into the world of personalized health, sometimes called mHealth for "mobile health," we will be able to track, monitor, and support employee health performance in real time through the use of smart phones and wearable technologies. Researchers can now use moment-by-moment data from the sensors in phones to understand behaviors, social interactions, speech patterns, physical activity, and more, in what our Harvard colleague J. P. Onnela has coined as "digital phenotyping."[13] But we dare you to tell your employees that you're going to digitally phenotype them and analyze the tone of their social interactions! Our guess is you would see a sharp decline in positive sentiment correlated with the timing of the announcement. That said, keep an eye on this quadrant as new AI-enabled analytical approaches and smart building sensors and technology start being adopted in the building community. Our guess is that digital phenotyping and sentiment analysis at scale is not far off.

Real-World Example: Tracking Real-Time Employee Absence to Identify Problems Early

The top engineer at a large multinational told us a story about something that happened on a floor in one of its buildings. That particular floor had about 30 employees, each of whom earned a six-figure salary. Several workers in the space started reporting sick building symptoms, such as headaches, fatigue, and difficulty concentrating. At first it was dismissed by managers who thought these were "complainer-type" employees. Then the problem escalated, as more and more employees on that floor joined in the chorus and many began calling in sick and refusing to work in the building. Executives in the firm noticed this uptick in absenteeism. When the top engineer was summoned to determine whether the building was the potential cause, he inspected the mechanical system and found that the motor for the outdoor air damper for the building had failed, causing the damper to be stuck in the closed position. In other words, no outdoor air was coming into the building. The motor for the damper was quickly fixed after this discovery, and the negative reports immediately stopped. Problem solved.

The downside was that some of the damage was already done: 30 employees with a combined salary of well over $3 million annually ($250,000 for that month) had been distracted and disabled for an entire month, and several had refused to show up for work. The upside is that the firm caught the problem before it went on for multiple months or years—or someone got seriously sick.

It turns out that the real-time monitoring of the employee experience, when combined with what we'll talk about in the next section—real-time air-quality monitoring—would likely have caught this issue even earlier.

Taking the Pulse of the Building

So far we've conveniently ignored that big box in the middle of our bottom two quadrants. That's because we wanted to save the best, and most important, for last. Buildings, like the human body, change every minute. So it's absolutely critical to have a mechanism in place to constantly check the pulse of the building.

If you want to take the pulse of the building, and (indirectly) of your employees, you need to do environmental monitoring; it's your first line of defense if you want to be certain that your building is operating as it should. Without a monitoring program in place, you're flying blind and it's highly unlikely that you are tapping into the full potential of your employees.

Think about how we typically take the "pulse" of our buildings today. Most buildings get a one-time stamp of approval at the opening. A great example of this is the LEED plaque on the wall at the Landmark Center building at the Harvard T. H. Chan School of Public Health where Joe works. Yes, it may very well signal the performance of that building when it was first opened, but is it realistic to assume that this building, certified 16 years ago, still performs that way today? Of course not. Yet that plaque remains on the wall, purporting to tell all who enter about the credentials of our space. Would you assume that your car, or your laptop, or your furnace at home continues to perform like new for years (or decades)? No way. You should have the same skepticism when it comes to buildings. A commercial or institutional building is a very complex machine, and it needs attention in ways that are not always obvious: you can't really tell that something is wrong in the way you can with a leaky radiator or flat tire.

Fortunately, a key market shift is under way. Thanks to advances in sensor and Internet of Things technology, we can now keep the pulse of a building as never before. We are quickly shifting from static to dynamic: indoor environments that we can monitor and track continuously, and buildings that can react in real time, too. Make no mistake, there is massive potential here, because for the first time ever we will be able to monitor and influence indirect HPIs: all of those factors that help determine how the 90 percent costs of our buildings, its people, can best perform.

Here are two quick examples to show you why monitoring environmental performance is so important, and to rebut the argument that "buildings are set in stone."

Example 1: Invisible Hazards

Take this recent example, where we monitored environmental performance of a newly renovated office space housing a group of (expensive) knowledge workers as part of our global study of workers in office buildings. For background: By all accounts, when you walk into the space, it is clean, welcoming, neatly designed, and managed by a top-notch facilities team at a high-profile organization. Nothing would suggest anything is "off" in this space. In short, it's a place where you'd want to work, or you'd want your son or daughter to work. Well, we started monitoring this space. Take a look at the data for airborne dust ($PM_{2.5}$).

The first thing that should jump out at you is the difference in concentrations between work hours and nonwork hours. Between the hours of

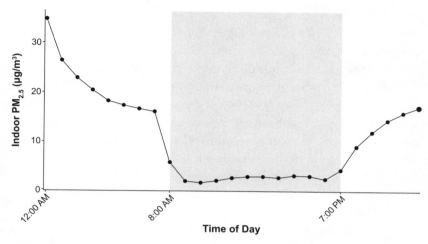

FIGURE 10.3   Indoor particle concentrations in a newly renovated office.

8:00 a.m. and 7:00 p.m., the indoor particle concentrations are much lower than the early morning, evening, and overnight. The second thing that you might have noticed is that the levels indoors are frequently quite high. (For reference, the acceptable level for outdoor air, codified in the US National Ambient Air Quality Standards, is 12 ug/m³.)

Taking the pulse of this space with real-time monitors shows that something is amiss—the level of indoor airborne dust in this newly renovated office is very frequently above 12 ug/m³, and there are significant changes occurring throughout a 24-hour period. Because these particle levels are not visible to the naked eye, the only way we knew about this issue was because the monitoring tipped us off. So, what is happening here?

This is a building in Chengdu, China, where the outdoor PM$_{2.5}$ concentration on the day of our sampling was about 40 ug/m³. Why, then, are indoor concentrations in this building so low during the day? We explored this, and lo and behold, we found that the filters used in this building were MERV 14, which has a very high capture efficiency against PM$_{2.5}$. (You may recall our discussion of MERV efficiency in Chapter 6 that showed a MERV 8 filter has a PM$_{2.5}$ capture efficiency of approximately 50 percent. A MERV 14 has a capture efficiency around 90 percent.) The cost differential of upgrading the filter? Twenty dollars. The cost of the "energy penalty" for the pressure drop because the fans work a little harder to push air through a tighter filter? A few bucks a year. Compare that to the cost of the potentially acute health effects for $PM_{2.5}$ for the ten employees in this space, breathing the air day in and day out, at levels above the National Ambient Air Quality Standards, in a building owned by a high-profile organization.

Now what about that other interesting part of this figure: the differences over the course of the day? By this point in the book you likely guessed why the pollution levels are high outside of working hours. The building mechanical ventilation system starts at exactly 8:00 a.m. and shuts off at 7:00 p.m. Measuring the pulse of the building with real-time sensors made the invisible visible, revealing just how much the building system was protecting the health of workers in this company during the day. And when that system is off, or if employees work into the evening, the indoor air starts to look a lot like outdoor air. This is a great example of an avoidable risk, made possible by measuring the pulse of a building and implementing a simple, cost-effective filter intervention.

Now, if you are reading this in the United States or Europe and think this example doesn't apply to you because "our outdoor air pollution isn't that bad," think again. Yes, air pollution levels may be lower in these place, but still, in California there are close to three thousand premature deaths per year attributed to $PM_{2.5}$ alone. And in Europe nearly half a million premature deaths are attributed to outdoor air pollution each year. Is your building protecting you? The only way to know is to take its pulse.

Example 2: Day-to-Day Fluctuations

Buildings change day to day, and hour to hour. Take, for example, this real-world data from a building in Los Angeles, overlaid on the classic psychrometric chart we mentioned in Chapter 4.

The details of psychrometry go far beyond the scope of this book, but for our purposes, what you need to know is that it essentially defines the relationships among temperature, humidity, and moisture, which then allows us to figure out the "sweet spot" of thermal health. In the figure here, we show the psychrometric chart and that sweet spot, as defined by Standard 55.1 of the American Society of Heating, Refrigerating and Air-Conditioning Engineers; this is the zone where 80 percent of people report being "comfortable."

Here's why we introduce this. This is real data from one commercial office building, where each blue dot represents the conditions at a worker's desk.

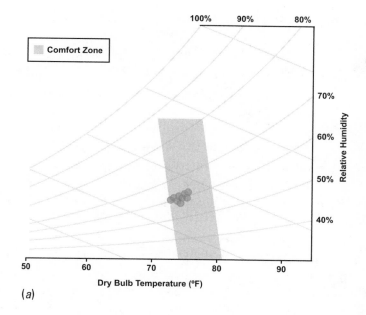

(a)

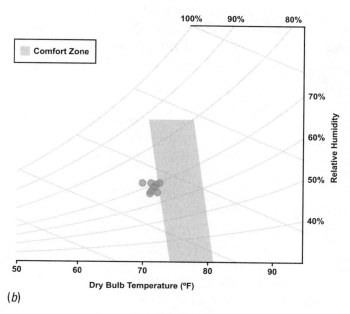

(b)

FIGURE 10.4 Psychrometric chart showing office workers falling out of temperature "comfort" ranges on consecutive days.

You can quickly see that in the figure on the left, everyone is in that sweet spot, but in the figure on the right, things have changed and nearly everyone has migrated out of that sweet spot. The temperature has dropped down below the point at which it is comfortable. This may be what is happening in office buildings where employees regularly complain about the cold.

Now consider this—the two graphs map out data points that are one day apart! That's right, even in this high-performing, Class A office building, with *no discernible changes* to how the building was operated day to day, there were big differences in temperature and humidity. This figure represents a day of diminished productivity: all of those blue dots out of the sweet spot on day 2 represent top-line revenue and bottom-line profits walking out your door.

Showing this figure also serves another purpose. The only way to "see" this happening in your building is by monitoring for these factors in real time. Active monitoring reveals that people are frequently working in impaired conditions that diminish their potential to be productive. Very often they don't even perceive it—and if they do say something, their comments are generally discounted.

If you're not constantly keeping the pulse of the building and proactively responding, then the way you will find out about these issues is when some of the blue dots place a call to your facilities team, or email their manager. And that's if you're lucky. What if it takes three or four days for these complaints to roll in? That's three or four days of low throughput, as we showed in the section on thermal health in Chapter 6.

Let's go back to Health & Wealth Inc. to explore the economic implications here. Recall that this 40-person hypothetical company had a fully loaded average salary of $75,000 per year. Assuming employees at this company work a typical 250 days per year, the company is spending $12,000 per day on payroll. In Chapter 6 we presented data from a study showing that there was a 1 percent loss of productivity per 2°F temperature change outside typical "comfort" ranges. The figure in this chapter conveniently shows about a 4°F change (2°C), on average, which would correspond to that 2 percent decrease in productivity.

Putting that all together, this slight change in temperature could be costing the company an estimated $240 per day in productivity (2 percent of $12,000). You might be thinking $240 isn't much. Even $240 multiplied by those three or four days may not seem like much. But what if we now told you that this temperature issue lasted for the entire month? Now it's

$240 times 20 working days, which costs the company $4,800 that month. And if the problem continues for a full year? The total grows to $57,600. Worse yet, what if instead of your company being 40 people, you had a company of 400 people, or 4,000 people? This slight change in indoor temperature can become a multimillion-dollar hit to your bottom line.

Now, imagine you deployed real-time monitors. You would capture this change immediately. Your team would respond *before* employees started complaining. You'd then save a day's worth of lost productivity capacity.

Big Picture

In each of the six real-world cases we have given you, there was no initial indication that anything was wrong in the building. These were successful companies in beautifully designed office spaces that, to the naked eye, seemed like ideal environments to work in. Without tracking HPIs, in each case, the company would have been blind to important building-related issues affecting its employees.

What's next? The goal of Part II is to help you define and operationalize a Healthy Buildings strategy. In Chapter 6 we introduced the 9 Foundations of a Healthy Building. We also gave you some practical guidance for things you can do in your building right now that will put the building to work for you and affect your bottom line. All of this is supported by hard scientific data and is evidence based.

In Chapter 7 we looked at how the *products* we put into our buildings can influence our health. In Chapter 8 we explored how buildings protect us from infectious disease. And in Chapter 9 we discussed the current Healthy Building certification systems available on the market. In this chapter, we looked at how (and how not) to measure and track the health performance of your building. In other words, how do we go about verifying that our spaces are continually optimized for health and wealth?

In the closing chapters, we will consider Healthy Buildings in the context of energy, air pollution, climate change, and public health (Chapter 11), and then we will look at the future of the Healthy Buildings movement (Chapter 12). We urge you to stay with us here for this reason: we will explore critical topics like how new technologies will impact market performance, how buildings impact society and the environment, and how this all impacts you and your business.

CHAPTER ELEVEN

Beyond the Four Walls

Architecture must not do violence to space or its neighbors.

—I. M. PEI

UP UNTIL THIS POINT in the book we have largely looked inside buildings. We've explored the physical configurations and mechanical systems that drive performance, and we have demonstrated the ways in which a Healthy Building is a sound investment for owner, tenant, and employees alike. To wit, we've focused on two primary objectives: enhancing *human performance* and enhancing *business performance*. We are confident that we have shown this to be a winning endeavor. But there is a wider and equally important objective: to serve another key stakeholder in the Healthy Buildings movement—the general public.

The now famous BlackRock letter and other responsible capital trends have forced an expanded conversation about environmental, social, and governance (ESG) measures and the broader purpose of business. For those in the building industry, this has set up a challenging question (and one they must now answer): "What is the *social performance* of your real estate asset?" If the evidence allows a landlord to answer well, we can open a door to new investment opportunities: investments and investors that are focused on "doing well by doing good."

In this chapter we will extend our analytical tools beyond a building or two and a handful of large tenants out into the broader world. We will look at the energy efficiency–Healthy Building equation; the contribution of buildings to greenhouse gases; calculation of health benefits at the portfolio or city level; and opportunities in resilience finance.

The Nexus of Buildings, Energy, Health, Climate, and Resilience

We opened the book by talking about some of the mega-changes shaping our world, our buildings, and all of us. Perhaps the most important of these mega-changes are the four major forces of population growth, rapid urbanization, resource depletion, and a changing climate. These are altering our natural landscape and creating both challenges and opportunities for people and for fixed assets. With regard to climate change, it's a straightforward, five-part story:

Buildings: Buildings consume 40 percent of the energy produced globally.[1]

Energy: Of that global energy, 80 percent is produced by fossil fuels.[2]

Health: Burning fossil fuels emits air pollutants that create an immediate health burden for the population.

Climate: Burning fossil fuels also emits greenhouse gases, which leads to climate change and a cascade of effects that affect human health, ecosystems, and property.

Resilience: Buildings are affected by air pollution and the changing climate, and this is having an impact on real estate valuations and decision-making as a result of pollution, flooding, drought, wildfire, and more.

Buildings are clearly part of the air pollution and climate problem, but Healthy Building strategies can ensure that they are part of the solution, too. Here's how: Healthy Buildings that incorporate energy-efficiency approaches can offset some of the emissions of air pollutants, thereby providing what is called a health "co-benefit." To understand how this works, and how it can be quantified in terms of ESG, we need to quickly dive into the science behind air pollution and health.

Health Impacts from Burning Fossil Fuels

The famous Harvard Six Cities Study begun in the 1970s and concluded in the 1980s put air pollution on the map, literally and figuratively.[3] The study recorded the health status of 10,000 adults and 10,000 children who lived in six different cities across the United States, each with varying levels of $PM_{2.5}$. Steubenville, Ohio, in the heart of industrial America, had the worst air pollution in the study, and Portage, Wisconsin, 100 miles from the nearest major US city, had the best, with four other cities having levels that fell somewhere in between. This study was the first to show that being exposed to higher levels of $PM_{2.5}$ was associated with a greater risk of premature mortality. The blockbuster findings became the basis for air pollution limits in the United States, called the National Ambient Air Quality Standards, and for air pollution standards globally.

Since then, the findings of the Harvard Six Cities Study have been replicated many dozens of times. Most recently there was a "600 cities" study, which confirmed, once again, a strong link between $PM_{2.5}$ and premature mortality, but this time across multiple countries.[4] The findings have held over time and across regions of the world. Even more important, perhaps, is research published in 2018 showing that there are still health risks from outdoor air pollution even when the levels are *below* the most stringent air pollution limits set today.[5] Further, in addition to premature mortality risks, along the way we also have learned that $PM_{2.5}$ is associated with increased risk of hospitalizations,[6] asthma attacks,[7] chronic absenteeism in schools,[8] and hospital admissions for dementia, Alzheimer's disease, and Parkinson's disease.[9] One study even showed that higher exposure during the third trimester of pregnancy was associated with a higher risk of autism.[10]

Climate Impacts from Burning Fossil Fuels

Burning fossil fuels for energy not only releases air pollutants that have an immediate health impact, it also releases air pollutants, such as carbon dioxide, that are causing climate change. We are already seeing the impacts of a changing climate in the United States in the increased frequency and severity of hurricanes, like those that recently devastated Puerto Rico and Houston. We also see this manifested in unprecedented wildfires, like those occurring in

California and across the Northwest United States, as well as sea rise flooding in Miami, Norfolk, and Oakland. The risks from climate change also include things we don't always see directly or so overtly but that we know are happening or are predicted to happen based on scientific research: increases in infectious and waterborne disease; sea-level rise; ecosystem disruption; and impacts on forestry, fisheries, and agriculture . . . affecting our food security. Buildings, as major consumers of energy globally, are contributing to these health and climate impacts in their construction and in their operations. How can they be better contributors to a solution?

Exploring the Health Co-benefits of Energy-Efficient Buildings

When energy-efficient buildings reduce demand on the energy grid, this leads to a concomitant reduction in emissions of air pollutants since less power is demanded and less fuel needs to be transported and burned. Those averted emissions can be thought of as a health co-benefit of the energy-efficient buildings. This is not just a theoretical exercise; these co-benefits can be quantified. Analysis of co-benefits (sometimes called "multiple benefits") of energy efficiency upgrades has been used to evaluate policy decisions around power generation. Perhaps most notably, this type of analysis was used to evaluate the co-benefits of the Obama Administration's Clean Power Plan (a study showed the plan was slated to generate $29 billion in health co-benefits when enacted).[11] Joe and his team have now applied this methodology to buildings with a tool they call CoBE, for "co-benefits of the built environment."[12] There are three major outputs of the co-benefits analysis: money saved, emissions averted, and health gained.

Output 1: Money Saved

The first output of this CoBE tool is hard cash earned through energy savings. This type of economic cost-benefit analysis is easy, has been done for decades, and has been the primary driver of the green building movement and energy efficiency upgrades in buildings. The analysis is straightforward because buildings can be metered and monitored for energy use, the costs of energy are well understood, and the variations from expectations are small. The US Energy Information Administration, for example, reports on the distribution of energy use and production, and the costs for each source, with regional factor variations across the United States. (Individual companies have their own information on historic and projected energy use and cost, of course.) Most building managers and businesses have done this type of energy cost analysis already. For example, your company may have decided to implement a green building strategy that would save energy, such as by super-insulating to minimize air infiltration, installing energy-recovery ventilation systems, or deploying more efficient lighting or dynamic glass. Engineers can calculate the energy savings from those interventions and a payback period or even estimate a return on investment using the first cost and the projected savings.

Output 2: Emissions Averted

The CoBE tool's second output is the air pollutant emissions averted as a result of that reduction in fuel burned. Typically, energy savings can be translated into metrics like "kilotons of CO_2 averted," an important metric in our battle against a changing climate, but one that is largely uninterpretable to all but a handful of sustainability and climate experts. How many of us can quickly interpret what 30,600 kilotons of averted CO_2 means to us or the planet? Still, the sustainability movement over the past 20 years or so has demanded that companies report these numbers. So companies dutifully do this and typically report the number in the sustainability or ESG section of their annual report (if they even have such a section). But that's where the analysis usually stops. The measure of carbon averted addresses greenhouse gas and climate change concerns . . . but stops short of making this directly relatable to the general public.

Output 3: Health Gained

The third output of CoBE is the key, because it gets directly to the "What does this mean for health?" question. Going beyond the typical analysis that stops with Output 1 (money saved) and Output 2 (carbon averted), Output 3 is where those measures of averted emissions—the kilotons of CO_2—can be combined with public health research to estimate the health benefit of those reductions in air pollution. This results in a set of quantifiable, objective metrics that actually mean something perceptible and tangible to real people: number of lives saved, number of missed work days and school days averted, number of asthma attacks avoided.

How do we do this in public health? The big idea is elegant and easy to understand conceptually (in practice, it can be harder). Consider a portfolio of buildings in a country where the decision makers have taken actions and made investments that lead to a reduction of 30 percent in year-over-year energy use compared with a baseline. We use publicly available data from agencies like the aforementioned US Energy Information Administration to discern the fuel mix for each region of the country—be it energy from coal, nuclear, or natural gas power plants in that region. Thanks to required reporting and other scientific studies, we also know how much air pollution each of these different types of power plants emits per unit of energy created and delivered. Scientists then take the emission rate of air pollutants from those sources and put them in atmospheric models that let us estimate the concentration of air pollution that people breathe near, and downwind from, those power plants. With knowledge of weather patterns and how long the chemicals and particles stay in the air, we can even track impact across state lines (and national borders). Last, thanks to great research like the Harvard Six Cities Study and the many hundreds since, we have what are called "exposure-response" functions that allow us to estimate the health risk per unit increase in the concentration of a number of specific air pollutants. For example, some of the newest research on the health impacts of $PM_{2.5}$ found a 7.3 percent increased risk in mortality rates for every 10 $\mu g / m^3$ increase in $PM_{2.5}$.[13] This is an exposure-response function.

Combining all of this—energy use and savings in buildings, pollutant emission rates from various power plants, atmospheric modeling, population demographics, and epidemiologic exposure-response functions—is how we can estimate things like the number of lives saved and economic metrics like missed work days *attributable to energy savings from a group of buildings*. Any health co-benefits accruing outside the four walls of the subject building can then be converted back into monetary savings to round out an economic argument.

An Example: The Health Co-benefits of the
Green Building Movement

To show how this works in practice, we'll quickly walk you through a study we did about the health co-benefits of the green building movement globally. We ran the global energy savings of green buildings in six countries through the CoBE calculator and found that, in the United States, engineering modifications and building management changes spurred by the 20-year-old green building movement saved $6.7 billion in energy (Output 1). Then we estimated the averted emissions from all of that saved energy (Output 2). We are going to give you the important, but boring and uninterpretable, numbers to drive home the point that this output doesn't mean much to most people. Those buildings saved 30,600 kilotons of CO_2, 1.62 kilotons of methane, 0.32 kilotons of N_2O, 36.6 kilotons of SO_2, 28.2 kilotons of NO_x and 0.39 kilotons of $PM_{2.5}$. As we said—largely uninterpretable to most people outside a handful of sustainability experts.

Now for Output 3, which we promised was the interesting part. In the United States, adoption of key green buildings methods, as compared with the nongreen baseline, *prevented* the following:

- 54,000 respiratory symptoms
- 21,000 lost days of work
- 16,000 lost days of school
- 11,000 asthma exacerbations
- up to 405 premature deaths
- 256 hospital admissions

When converted to economic values, these health co-benefits amount to another $4 billion in health and climate co-benefits, on top of the $6.7 billion in energy savings, for a total benefit of $10.7 billion. On a dollar-for-dollar basis, for every $1 saved in energy in the United States, there was a very significant $0.59 in health and climate co-benefits that were previously unaccounted for (since they don't inure directly to the building owners and occupants). The impact is even greater in places like India and China, where the dominant fossil fuel source is coal. There, the health and climate co-benefits are more like $10 for every $1 saved in energy—a stunning ratio.[14]

Think about what that means for a second. The entire 20-year-old green building movement has been based on energy savings, and it turns out that there is *a nearly equal social benefit* . . . and as much as a tenfold social benefit savings in developing countries. This additional health co-benefit had never been quantified until our paper was published. Yet now, for the first time, the owners of energy-efficient buildings can *quantify* the social benefits of the energy choices they've made in their buildings; they finally have a way to quantify the social part of ESG.

Co-benefits Extended to the Portfolios and Individual Buildings

This research on the effectiveness of the green building movement showcased how a co-benefits analysis could yield a new, and important, metric on Healthy Buildings—their *social performance* across wide regions. Importantly, the approach can be applied to individual portfolios and individual buildings, too.

We'll give you two examples so you can see how this could work on a more regional and local scale. Piers MacNaughton, former postdoctoral fellow on the Harvard Healthy Buildings research team and now director of health strategy at View, took our CoBE tool and applied it to Harvard's portfolio of buildings (about the same square footage as those occupied by Google). Then we also applied this analytical approach to Carrier's new Center for Intelligent Buildings in Florida.

First, let's look at Harvard's data. Harvard undertook an aggressive 10-year energy reduction initiative beginning in 2006. But like everyone else, Harvard fell into the usual format of reporting energy savings (Output 1) and an impressive 30 percent reduction in greenhouse gas emissions (Output 2), without reporting what this means to health (Output 3). To address this, we took Harvard's energy savings and ran it through the CoBE calculator. Here's what we found: all of that energy savings led to an additional $12.3 million in savings through health and climate benefits that Harvard had yet to formally capture or quantify. That is, it hadn't fully explored the benefits of its aggressive energy-conservation efforts to the health of people who live and work in the surrounding community. This is a story worth telling.

This analysis isn't only suited for a university—we did it at Harvard first because we had easy access to the data. The broader point is that this type of approach can be applied to any portfolio—health-care systems, commercial real estate, government complexes, and cities.

Now let's look at how this type of health co-benefits analysis can be done with an individual building. Carrier's new global headquarters, which opened in 2018, was designed, as one would expect, to showcase all of the company's advanced building component technologies. Perhaps unsurprisingly for one of the global leaders in air-conditioning and building technology, it featured high-efficiency chillers and air-conditioning, building automation systems, and access controls. It was also designed to highlight how the use of Carrier's high-end products can lead to energy-efficiency gains when compared with other choices. It turns out that the building accomplishes this well, as it is designed to save an estimated $172,000 per year in energy costs over its conventional rivals. As a reminder, that's a cost savings that goes directly to the bottom line. Now for the health co-benefits part. Our analysis using CoBE revealed that all of that energy savings yielded an additional $83,000 in health and climate benefits, for a combined benefit of $255,000 per year. The big picture here is this: Carrier is doing well for itself with the energy savings while at the same time doing good for the community it joined with the opening of its new building. That's good business—and a powerful message about being a good community partner.

Are the Goals of "Green" and "Healthy" in Conflict? Debunking a Myth

In Chapter 4 we talked about the supposed energy-versus-health tradeoff. We discussed the need to find the sweet spot between reducing operating costs and spending a little more to enhance ventilation and health. We argued, quite convincingly we hope, that the benefits of higher ventilation rates to both people and the business amply justify the added cost required to increase the amount of fresh air a building brings in. But does this somehow conflict with what we've now presented in this chapter? In other words, throughout the book we argue that higher ventilation rates come with an energy cost, yet in this chapter we are talking about the benefits that come from *decreasing* energy consumption in buildings. Are these positions destined to be in conflict?

The answer is no, they don't have to be in conflict at all. A Healthy Building can have both higher ventilation rates and lower energy usage than a standard design. We get challenged on this frequently during presentations, so let's now debunk the myth that having healthier indoor air with higher ventilation rates is somehow incompatible with energy efficiency. Here's how the system can, and should, work.

The first thing we need to do is stop thinking about individual factors in the building and start thinking about this "problem" holistically. In other words, consider both energy and ventilation at the same time. An example: We previously mentioned an economic analysis Joe and his team performed where they estimated that the high-end cost for doubling ventilation rates was $40 per person per year.[15] What if that increase in ventilation were coupled with a holistic strategy to decrease energy?

When you think of these together, some opportunities appear. In that same paper, Joe and his team estimated what would happen if a building simultaneously doubled ventilation and adopted just one energy-saving feature: energy-recovery ventilation (ERV). (This is usually a form of heat exchanger that captures some of the temperature and humidity of exhaust air to warm or cool new intake air.) When buildings employ an energy-saving feature like this, the costs for higher ventilation drop from $40 per person per year to a few dollars per person per year. Essentially, adding the ERV mitigates most of the higher energy requirement for higher ventilation rates. It gets even more impressive if all you are doing is trying to hit a 30 percent increase in outdoor air above the minimum specified ventilation rate. In that case, adding an ERV leads to so much money in energy savings that, even with this 30 percent higher ventilation rate, there is an *overall net savings*. In other words, using energy-efficient technologies frees you up to make better choices regarding ventilation. It's one way you can have higher ventilation rates while decreasing overall energy use.

This works even if you're not building new buildings and can't retrofit your existing systems to include something like an ERV. Think of the analysis by Lawrence Berkeley National Laboratory that we introduced in Chapter 10 showing that properly commissioning your existing building systems can provide an energy savings of up to 16 percent.[16]

What if you paired that commissioning work with an effort to enhance ventilation rates? We can go back to our model in Table 4.5 to see what the holistic impacts are on the company. For that example, we have shown energy costs of $30,000 per year. If the company saves 16 percent of costs based on the commissioning, then its energy costs that year will go down to approximately $25,000. If it then doubles the ventilation rate and we take the high-end $40 per person per year cost, the incremental energy cost for this 40-person company is $1,600. So the net effect of this holistic Healthy Building approach with higher energy efficiency and higher ventilation rates is that the company's energy costs are now $26,600 per year, still a net savings of $3,400. And don't forget that the higher ventilation rate had the effect of adding nearly 9 percent to the bottom line. This business can have its cake and eat it, too, when it comes to higher ventilation rates, energy savings, and health and climate co-benefits. We just have to tackle the problem holistically.

As we look to where buildings are headed, there will be even more ways to disentangle the false energy-versus-health tradeoff. When we become smarter about when and where we pump in more fresh air—providing air in rooms only when people are there, as opposed to dumping loads of fresh outdoor air into empty conference rooms—then we can keep ventilation rates high even while controlling energy costs. We can also be smarter by using under-floor ventilation, which provides air closer to the breathing zone of occupants than overhead ductwork, and with innovations like demand-control ventilation, which reacts to real-time measurements of rising CO_2 concentrations in a room to tell the system precisely when it needs to deliver more air. The solution here is to be smarter about how we ventilate our buildings. (It is formally called ventilation effectiveness.) Essentially, this approach is about using technology to eliminate waste.

Refuge, Resilience, Exposure, Uncertainty, and Opportunity

Now that we have shown you how buildings are part of the problem (and solution) of air pollution and greenhouse gas emissions, let's look at the other end of the cycle—the part where buildings can be negatively affected by these factors. We are already seeing that pollution and climate change are having a real impact on real estate. In many parts of the world, outdoor air pollution is so bad that people are warned not to spend time outside because of the severe health risks. Take events in China in December 2018 as but one example. During that time, public health "stay indoors" warnings were issued for 79 Chinese cities that were blanketed with a thick and dangerous layer of air pollution.[17] The affected area was wide, covering Beijing and several provinces (Shanxi, Shaanxi, Henan, and Jiangsu). This isn't an abstraction—it is about deadly, disease-causing, cognition-damaging pollutants that are in the air, affecting health right now.

Now pause and reflect on what that "stay indoors" warning is really saying. It's saying that the building is a place of refuge from the outdoor air pollution. In many cases, this is true. Think back to our discussion in Chapter 6, where we talked about different filtration levels. The amount of dense outdoor air pollution that penetrates indoors can be significantly reduced with the right level of filtration and proper operation of a building's mechanical system. In such a scenario, buildings can adapt and effectively respond to changing levels of outdoor air pollution. In other words, they are resilient and responsive. In these situations, the recommendation to stay indoors is a sound one. However, many buildings around the world are not resilient. They do not have these types of filter systems in place, so staying indoors offers some reduction in exposure, but it does not offer the protection that it could. The recommendation to stay indoors is good relative to remaining outdoors, but it isn't always really good in the absolute sense, and it may give a false sense that the building is more protective than it actually is.

Exposure and Uncertainty

In addition to thinking about how buildings can protect us from the immediate and direct health impacts of air pollution, consider resiliency in the face of threats from a changing climate. The 2018 Intergovernmental Panel on Climate Change report predicts dire consequences under our current energy use trends.[18] The investment community is taking note. In 2018 an analysis by Ali Ayoub and Nils Kok at GeoPhy, a company that integrates geographic variables to evaluate investments, looked at the climate risk of buildings in the portfolios of 133 real estate investment trusts (REITs) in the United States—over 36,000 buildings and several billion square feet of real estate.[19] They combined historic Federal Emergency Management Agency flood risk data with projected flood risk data to evaluate how much of each

REIT's portfolio was at high risk. What they found is quite interesting—only 2 REITs out of 133 are *not* exposed to "high" flood risk by the GeoPhy measure. For some REITs, nearly 10 percent of the properties in their portfolios are rated by GeoPhy as high risk. This type of blending of geography, climate, and finance might be new to you and me, but you can bet there are smart, well-informed investors—armed with much more data than we have—making bets on properties today. There is a good chance that health risk will join flood risk on their radar in the near future.

Investment Opportunity

Much of John's work is about financing resilience in real estate and infrastructure. The type of macro analysis of REIT risk done by GeoPhy is also percolating down to decisions on an individual basis. As an illustration of the concepts, take the example of Mary the business owner and Nancy the bank manager, drawn from one of John's Harvard Business School teaching cases. Nancy and Mary are fictitious characters, but their dilemma is real.

Consider a simple situation: Mary, the owner of a small shop in Norfolk, Virginia, or Miami Beach or Brownsville, Texas, whose building is self-insured; and Nancy, the manager of a community bank that keeps mortgages on its balance sheet. Mary thinks her building is worth $600,000. Her mortgage is written with the assumption that there is a 1 percent probability of a flood that would destroy the property (a 100-year flood).

Then, a redrawn base flood elevation map in her town indicates that her store has a much higher risk of destruction from flood than was previously believed. The probability of flood risk is reset at 5 percent (a 1-in-20 flood risk). The bank also receives this information. Now, on an expected value (EV) and net present value (NPV) basis, including risk of destruction, Mary is in violation of the loan-to-value clause in her mortgage. At this level of exposure, the market won't even offer flood insurance.

Should Mary sell, invest to "harden" the building, or just sit tight and hope that the bank doesn't act and the weather doesn't harm her property? As far as she can perceive on a day to day basis, nothing has changed.

Nancy holds the mortgage on the building housing Mary's store. Mary is now in violation of the loan-to-value covenant—and also in violation of the base flood elevation (BFE) rider that was part of her loan approval. Should

Nancy foreclose? If not, when Mary's note comes due, should Nancy refinance? With what terms?

Or should Nancy's bank offer a financial product that loans to Mary's business the $50,000 needed to perform resilience and "hardening" work on the building—which would bring the new probability of destruction back closer to 1 percent, as the building would then be able to resist most events that would have crippled it before?

John's recent Harvard Business Review article, "Climate Change will Transform How and Where We Build,"[20] proposes that for properties (and municipalities) facing climate-related weather perils—whether sea rise, river flooding, wildfire, or drought—there are basically five courses of action. These are: reinforce, retreat, rebound, restrict, or rebuild. (The sixth, of course, is "do nothing.") In Nancy and Mary's circumstances, a loan to finance reinforcement makes sense. For many other asset owners and even cities, restricting where development happens or retreating from some areas may be the prudent course of action.

This simple example underscores many of the issues being faced today by homeowners, property owners, businesses, banks, and insurance companies in the low coastal cities of the United States. There is near certainty that seas will rise or storms will worsen if we continue down our current carbon path. There will be many more Marys and Nancys. How should the two of them even think about what to do? Will there be an industry to help you invest in making your building demonstrably more resilient in the face of building stresses? We expect there will be a large one.

Healthy Buildings and the Clean Energy Future

With all of our focus in this chapter on how buildings contribute to air pollution and climate change through their energy use, and how we need to consider adaptation and resiliency strategies in light of significant potential health and financial risk, we want to be sure that we do not lose sight of the bigger issue upstream. If the fuels used to generate power are cleaned up, then the actual energy consumption becomes less of an issue and the downstream effects of climate change will be significantly reduced.

How will we get to a clean energy future? In our opinion it's mostly going to depend on the improving economics of renewable energy and the adoption of new technologies. In the United States, the lifetime levelized cost of energy from new-generation facilities running on wind and solar is now lower than the levelized cost of energy from a new power plant that burns coal. On top of this favorable trend, advances in battery and energy storage capacity are mitigating one of the primary weaknesses of wind and solar, and microgrids are letting us have more nimble energy systems that are responsive to local demand conditions. To complement these new sources, the rise of blockchain technology is making it possible to verify that energy purchases are in fact traceable back to renewable sources. This can then be securitized and traded, thus creating and advancing new energy markets.

We are optimistic that the world will decrease its reliance on fossil fuels, so let's be a bit provocative: if we design buildings to last for 100 years or more, and much of our design constraints focus on energy, what will a Healthy Building look like when our energy grid is clean? That is, when energy consumption has zero external environmental costs? Designing for health without energy constraints opens the door to a whole host of new possibilities. If this energy-penalty-free future doesn't seem like a reality, consider what then New York Governor Andrew Cuomo announced in late 2018: 100 percent carbon-free electricity across the entire state by 2040.[21] We're not that far off from a future of designing places to live, work, shop, and play where we can think of health first, second, and third, and energy a distant fourth or fifth.

Further, if we move to a future with a clean energy grid, does that mean buildings will be off the hook in terms of their contribution to air pollution? It turns out that the answer is *no*—on two fronts and for surprising reasons.

First, many buildings still have on-site combustion of fossil fuels. And it accounts for a larger share of greenhouse gas emissions and health damages than you might think. The Environmental Protection Agency estimates that nearly 30 percent of greenhouse gas emissions from residential and commercial buildings come from fossil fuels burned on-site.[22] Research on the ten-year energy transition away from coal in the United States by Joe and collaborators Dr. Jonathan Buonocore and Dr. Parichehr Salimifard found something surprising and very important for building owners and operators: health impacts of energy use are no longer dominated by either the electricity sector or by coal. Industrial boilers and buildings have higher health impacts than electricity.[23]

Here's what we need to do right now. We need an all-out effort to electrify our buildings: gas stoves, hot water heaters, and boilers and burners used for space heating. Everything in our buildings that relies on fossil fuels. Why? If we don't, the energy grid of the near future that is based on renewables will deliver clean electricity, but we'll be left burning fossil fuels on a hyperlocal scale—in our buildings.

Second, in addition to air pollution generated from energy use, there is something new happening. It's what we call the dirty secret of *indoor* air pollution. (The corollary to the dirty secret of outdoor air pollution we introduced in Chapter 3.)

It turns out that in places doing a good job of ramping down traditional sources of air pollution—like that from coal-fired power plants—the dominant source of outdoor air pollution is now chemicals coming from *indoors.* In a landmark paper published in 2018, researchers found that emissions of volatile organic compounds (VOCs) from building materials, cleaning materials, air fresheners, and personal care products are migrating outdoors.[24] The VOCs then react with traditional outdoor air pollutants, such as nitrogen oxides from automobile exhaust, to generate ozone and particulates. In the 33 industrialized cities studied, these VOCs that started indoors were found to account for the *majority of outdoor air pollution.*

This is a shocking finding. And it speaks to the continued importance of buildings and building systems to public health outdoors. As we transition from fossil fuels to renewable sources of energy and we electrify our buildings, emissions of VOCs from buildings may become the dominant source of outdoor air pollution. Building owners, managers, tenants, and investors should be prepared for this future—one where emissions of VOCs from buildings will be measured, managed, and perhaps even regulated.

Beyond the Four Walls

We focused much of our discussion in this chapter on the building-energy-health-climate-resilience nexus as it impacts and takes place in the built environment. Thankfully, there are important efforts under way to make buildings "carbon neutral." This burgeoning movement, sometimes called net-zero buildings, and with a renewed emphasis on embodied carbon in construction materials, is just getting going.

But beyond energy there is so much more to talk about in looking at the intersection of buildings and health. Buildings influence our health through where they are sited, through their water and resource consumption, and through their waste generation, just to name a few additional factors that impact both the provision of a healthy environment, and the lowering of energy cost. The profound impact of our buildings and development on the natural systems that sustain life on Earth cannot be overstated. As we mentioned in Chapter 2, the situation has become so dire—with human activity causing what has been called the sixth major extinction, which threatens millions of species—that E. O. Wilson, in his book *Half-Earth,* has declared that we need to immediately dedicate 50 percent of the planet to nature.[25]

These topics are critically important, but they go beyond the scope of this book. Our aim in this chapter is to make two key points. First, a true Healthy Buildings strategy must consider external impacts. Second, when we do account for these external impacts, we can further expand the circle of those involved in, and invested in, the Healthy Buildings movement.

The now visible impact of the first four mega-changes of population growth, urbanization, resource depletion, and climate change has forced a rapid shift in attention to how we must think about the impact that we, and our businesses, have on the planet. (Recall our tenth mega-change in Chapter 2, changing values.) This attention must be balanced against the reality that we are now an indoor species. We cannot sacrifice our indoor world for the natural world; the two worlds must coexist. With Healthy Buildings as an organizing principle, they can. The big question then becomes, What forces are in play and what levers need to be pushed to ensure that this Healthy Building movement scales beyond a few niche markets?

CHAPTER TWELVE

What's Now and What's Next?

> The future is already here–it's just not evenly distributed yet.
>
> —WILLIAM GIBSON

THE GLOBAL REAL ESTATE and building industry is large and fragmented, and its levels of sophistication are not consistent. The quality of indoor—and outdoor—air also varies quite a bit around the world. The rise of cheap, ubiquitous, connected sensors; the ability of those sensors to talk to each other and share historical and predictive data; and growing individual attention to the details of health augur significant adjustments in who has knowledge about indoor air quality, and what they will choose to do with that knowledge.

Ultimately, we are interested in how to accelerate an industry transformation that is already under way. In this chapter we will present a vision for how to hasten the spread of these ideas and suggest how they might manifest next. We will, in other words, consider "what's now" and "what's next."

What's Now? Adoption Curves, Industry Composition, and Clockspeed

The current Healthy Building movement may feel like a race that's only open to elite companies and well-heeled landlords. In some ways, that's the present state of play. Much of the leading action takes place in cities like Paris, New York, Hong Kong, London, San Francisco, Shanghai, and Singapore. There, best-in-class participants in the real estate industry are thinking hard about how to further differentiate their businesses and their spaces, and how to address the apparent future concerns of occupants who will have plenty of access to information.

We are professionally engaged with some of the leading companies in the Healthy Buildings movement, but when we tell people that we are collaborating with leading real estate developers in Manhattan, or that we worked with Google on a healthier materials strategy for buildings and consulted with Salesforce or Amazon on Healthy Building strategies, we can feel the proverbial eye roll. These companies are unusual; they have the vision and ambition to pursue endeavors like these—and they have the resources to pull it off. So when we talk about their success, others don't necessarily see themselves or their companies in those stories.

We hope we've shown you that the benefits of Healthy Buildings aren't limited to the elite. This is why we intentionally made our hypothetical Health & Wealth Inc. a small, 40-person company in a 10,000 sq. ft. building. It was intended to reflect the vast majority of companies and buildings, which don't have the purchasing power and research capabilities of a Pfizer or a Google.

Interestingly, this first group to enter the Healthy Buildings movement is doing so in cities that are not experiencing fast demographic growth. The total number of buildings in New York, Paris, and San Francisco increases so slowly that each new crane on the horizon is a big deal. The Healthy Building movement in places like these will have some limited focus on new construction, but the biggest opportunity is in the existing building space. Here we need to look beyond the initial category of first-mover participants in the building industry who already pursue investments and actions leading to certifications from LEED and WELL.

In other places in the world, demographic growth is rapid and the focus is on new development. In much of the developing world, housing, offices, government buildings, schools, and hospitals are going up quickly and in large quantities. The installed base is small, so there are not a lot of older buildings worth renovating. Buildings in many fast-growth locations may also be in poorer countries, with less wealthy landlords, where one can see that the outside air is palpably bad before even using instruments to measure anything. This might be Mumbai or Mexico City or Lagos or Chongqing.

Both settings—cities with established building stock and cities where new construction will dominate—feature connected people, largely young, who are well informed and who care a lot about their health and that of their children. There is opportunity everywhere to deliver cleaner air and healthier buildings, regardless of the starting conditions. Moving the needle may require a shift in how we think about these issues. Much as it is now accepted that "outdoor air" is a public good, a status that has helped raise attention to this issue globally, the World Health Organization has declared "healthy indoor air" a fundamental human right. This signaling is important.

What will it take for the means and methods in this book to propagate throughout the industry? Our research indicates that there are three factors to consider: diffusion of innovation, characteristics of real estate and construction, and life span of the assets. We express these as the Healthy Building adoption curve, industry composition, and clockspeed.

Healthy Building Adoption Curve: Knowledge Generators, Early Adopters, and Leading Markets

The Rogers Adoption Curve is a theory that was developed at Iowa State University in the 1950s to map out how farmers took up new ideas and techniques in agriculture.[1] The concept has been used again and again, notably by Geoffrey Moore of the Chasm Group at the birth of the internet era in his seminal marketing guide *Crossing the Chasm* and by Clayton Christensen as one of the foundations of his enormously influential strategy book *The Innovator's Dilemma*.[2] The basic idea is that the uptake of innovations flows from innovators, to early adopters, to an early majority of users, to a late majority, and finally to laggards. Together these customers represent 100 percent of the market.

To use this concept to predict (and influence) the adoption of innovations in the broader building industry, we have developed a Healthy Building adoption curve. To see how progress can be made from a race for the elites (the early adopters) to "all buildings everywhere" (the broad majority), it's worth considering where we are on this curve. The good news is that we're making progress, with Healthy Building strategies being adopted in leading

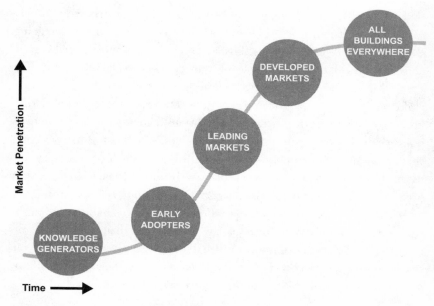

FIGURE 12.1   Healthy Building Adoption Curve.

markets, and the COVID-19 crisis accelerating awareness and adoption of Healthy Building strategies. Before we go into what will be needed to get us to the top, let's take a look at the first part of this adoption curve.

Knowledge Generators

Movements usually start with knowledge generators, mostly from business or academia, who invent new tools or come up with new techniques. Moving from the lab to practice, a handful of inquisitive early adopters seek out, test, and deploy new knowledge or equipment.

Readers new to the topic might suppose that the key knowledge generators are the relatively new building certification systems that we mentioned in Chapter 9; the Healthy Buildings movement is relatively young, so for many people their first introduction to this topic might have come from thoughtful promoters like WELL and Fitwel. But the history is much deeper, and we think it's important to recognize the true early pioneers—the initial knowledge generators—in the Healthy Building space. These were the early "healthy worker" researchers of the early 1900s, who were then succeeded by researchers who started the field of "indoor air" beginning in the 1960s and 1970s.

Today's Healthy Building researchers stand on the shoulders of giants who came before. These are not the high-profile science giants who are household names like Isaac Newton or Marie Curie, but their names should be immortalized just the same. The giant of giants was "Harvard's first lady," Alice Hamilton. Hamilton was the first woman from any field appointed to the faculty of Harvard University, and she advanced the field of worker health (then called "industrial medicine"), memorialized in her book *Exploring the Dangerous Trades*, first published in 1943.[3] Hamilton studied the work environment of the Industrial Revolution, but her focus, methods, and findings still hold sway today, 100 years after her appointment.

The field of worker health was largely constrained to clinical medicine and industrial sites for much of the twentieth century, until the birth of the environmental movement in the 1970s. This spurred the creation of the Environmental Protection Agency and the Occupational Safety and Health Administration, the latter of which was the first major effort in the United States to codify and enforce worker protections. And while many Occupational Safety and Health Administration exposure limits were focused on industrial and manufacturing environments, this attention paved the way for other worker-health-focused research and entities.

Also at about this time, some scientific researchers began peeling away from the study of outdoor pollutants to focus on the indoor environment. Ole Fanger was a venerated researcher who gave us our first thermal health targets for offices and other environments. (They are still in use today.) Others, like Joe's mentor Jack Spengler and a handful of additional researchers across the globe, including Jan Sundell at the Karolinska Institute in Sweden and the Danish Technical University, Lance Wallace at the Environmental Protection Agency, and Bill Fisk at Lawrence Berkeley National Laboratory, started turning their queries toward indoor environments, too. They were some of the first to tell us about the potential harms of secondhand smoke, volatile organic compounds (VOCs) off-gassing from products in homes, low-level lead exposure and its impacts on kids' IQ, and the hidden hazards of mold, radon, and unvented combustion sources in homes. This era also produced early research not just on the hazards of bad air and sick buildings but also on the benefits of better building strategies, notably how bringing in more fresh air can reduce sick building symptoms and how air purifiers can be an effective tool for controlling indoor particle levels.

These "indoor air" giants then opened the door for another cohort of scientists studying indoor air. Contemporary researchers like Heather Stapleton at Duke University are moving us past "Indoor Air Quality 101" and telling us about the less obvious chemicals in our indoor environment—those that seep quietly out of building materials and out of our rugs, curtains, chairs, and mattresses and stealthily begin wreaking havoc on our hormones and other bodily systems in ways we can't immediately see. Others, such as Frederica Perera at Columbia University and Tracey Woodruff at the University of California, San Francisco, focus on children's and women's health indoors. Others in academia and industry are using new tools to expand our understanding of the reactions that take place on surfaces in our buildings (and on the skin of people in those buildings)—the field of study called indoor chemistry.[4] Recently, more researchers are using new metagenomics tools to explore the role of biological organisms in and around us—a new field of study called the microbiome of the built environment.

On the nanoscale side of things, our colleague Philip Demokritou studies engineered nanomaterials currently in and on products throughout our buildings. They are hard to track because disclosures are not required. We don't currently know very much about these nanoparticles when it comes to potential human health impacts, but research in Demokritou's lab led by Dilpreet Singh showed that when certain nano-enabled products are disposed of and incinerated, they catalyze the formation of toxic polycyclic aromatic hydrocarbons.[5] A collaboration between researchers in France and China found that photocatalytic paints in buildings that use titanium dioxide nanoparticles may also generate and release formaldehyde indoors.[6] Nanotechnology also holds the potential for benefit, and Demokritou is working on a "nature-inspired antimicrobial" using engineered water nanostructures.[7] These fields are moving quickly, and these are just some of the knowledge generators whose contributions will be incorporated into Healthy Building strategies in the next 5 to 10 years.

During this period of increasing attention to public health, the business world was similarly advancing thinking on the power of people to drive business profits. Harvard Business School's James Heskett, Earl Sasser, and Leonard Schlesinger shared the concept of the "service profit chain." This management work established substantial links between employee satisfaction and customer satisfaction, between employee loyalty and customer loyalty, and of course between customer loyalty and profit in service businesses.[8] This has taken us a long way from the manufacturing and process experiments of Frederick Winslow Taylor, who saw humans more as manipulable cogs in a machine, and it paved the way for the works by Felix Barber, Rainer Strack, and John Doerr that explored the economics of "people businesses" and "measuring what matters."

Early Adopters

These early pioneers of health and business science raised awareness of the problem and created the beginning of a new scientific base of information. As this scientific evidence accumulated, some early adopters started to implement Healthy Building strategies, well ahead of the advent of formal Healthy Building rating systems. Buildings like the Adam Joseph Lewis Center for Environmental Studies at Oberlin College, by David W. Orr, adopted green building strategies in the mid-1990s, at a time when most builders had not even heard of the idea of a green building. These early adopters in the green building spaced opened up pathways for the first "green + healthy" buildings that followed about a decade later. The Bank of America Tower at 1 Bryant Park in New York, owned by the Durst Organization and designed by COOKFOX Architects, is a great example of early leadership in the Healthy Buildings space. The design focused on increasing fresh air, increasing access to daylight, and, perhaps most notably, formally incorporating biophilic design into the building. Crucially, the team also went beyond just designing a building that claimed to focus on health at the ribbon cutting: they actually sought to measure and verify that they were achieving their targets over time. The tower at 1 Bryant Park does things like tracking and monitoring real-time Health Performance Indicators such as CO_2 levels on each floor. (They don't call them HPIs yet . . . but we think they will!)

This early adoption of Healthy Buildings is happening in Europe, too. Norman Foster continued to advance his early work on breathing buildings with the SwissRe building in London (affectionately known as The Gherkin). Completed in 2004, it has an atria that serves as the building's lungs, bringing in fresh air through panels in the façade and distributing it around the building. He continues to invoke his buildings as living, breathing creatures;

with his most recent work on the Bloomberg Headquarters in London, he talks about using "fins as gills" that not only enable the building to breathe (through a vortex starting at the ground floor), but also act as filters that attenuate sound. Here he also incorporates a living ceiling; 2.5 million petals with chilled and warm water pulsing through to modulate acoustics and temperature.

Another recent innovative building that highlights how technology is being incorporated into this movement is the Edge building in Amsterdam, which opened in 2015 and which Bloomberg dubbed "the Smartest Building in the World."[9] The developer, OVG Real Estate, created a "digital ceiling" embedded with thousands of sensors that let the building track and respond to light, temperature, and other factors at a hyperlocal level. The Edge, designed by PLP Architects, represents an early marriage of smart buildings and Healthy Buildings.

For early adopters of healthier materials, we need look no farther than our own campus. The revitalized Harvard Smith Campus Center by Hopkins Architects and Bruner / Cott and the brand new Klarman Hall at Harvard Business School by Willam Rawn Associates, both unveiled in 2018, and Harvard's new Science and Engineering Complex, opened in 2021, feature products and building materials that carefully avoided several classes of toxic chemicals mentioned in Chapter 7, such as flame retardants, Forever Chemicals, and antimicrobials. Led by Heather Henriksen, the managing director at Harvard's Office for Sustainability, Harvard worked with (that is, forced) suppliers to revisit their supply chains and deliver products without toxic chemicals. Some of these suppliers initially said they couldn't, or wouldn't, do this—but then ultimately found a way. The most important takeaway from these projects was that the sourcing of healthier materials had no impact on the budget, project schedule, or product performance. We repeat: a healthier indoor environment *with no impact on budget, project schedule, or product performance.* So why aren't we doing this more often?

As is typical for this phase of the curve, all of these players acted on the science well before their peers acknowledged that this was a winning strategy. Foster + Associates (Norman Foster's firm), Oberlin, COOKFOX Architects, OVG Real Estate, and Harvard were acting as early adopters, pushing themselves, and the market, toward healthier buildings. These are elite organizations, but their pushing of boundaries, investment in resources, and establishment of best practices make it easier for others to follow.

Seeking Competitive Advantage: The Industry Anticipates
User Preferences

Where are we today? The early adopters have set the stage for *Fortune* 500 companies, with their global portfolios, to get in the game. This phase of the adoption curve is happening in leading markets from Singapore to San Francisco, but we'll start with the New York City commercial real estate market and expand our discussion from there.

New York City seems to be in a contest for who can have the healthiest building. We've discussed our case study on the health aspects of 425 Park Avenue, where we explored the decisions made by David Levinson and L&L Holding about health.[10] Just a few blocks away, JPMorgan Chase is building a new headquarters and they have a bold vision, as one would expect. In the words of Alec Saltikoff, an executive director at the bank and a point person for the project, "Employees are our most important asset. We have the best talent and best technology, now we want the best building."[11]

Saltikoff told us that he and his team examined the science and then applied their own analysis and came away with the conclusion that current building standards are not designed to optimize human performance. Ultimately, he sees pursuing excellence in JPMorgan Chase's new headquarters as good business, and as consistent with their company philosophy. "By virtue of enabling our people to perform their best, we are also serving our clients and simultaneously serving our shareholders," he said. "Creating an environment that maximizes these three factors becomes a competitive advantage. We don't see the building and people as one-time investments—they are part of a systemic and philosophical approach consistent with the vision of our founder, John Pierpont Morgan, who set the goal of 'first-class business in a first-class way.' We are now creating a first-class building."

Pfizer is moving its New York headquarters to Hudson Yards in New York and adopting Healthy Building certifications. Boston Properties announced that its entire portfolio would be certified under the Fitwel system. And several more major companies that we can't name are making similar moves. The race is on. It's a race because these savvy real estate players are asking the same questions that David Levinson shared about 425 Park Avenue: What would happen to tenancy and rents if he didn't design his building for health, but all of his competitors did?

This is not just a contest going on in New York City. Look at what Apple is doing with its new headquarters in Cupertino, California. The new headquarters, designed, like 425 Park Avenue, by Norman Foster, will feature real-time air-quality monitoring using technology from a company that runs tubing into each room to draw air into centralized monitoring locations, "sniffing" the air every few seconds. They will be measuring CO_2 in real time throughout the building.

If you look at what the major service providers in the facilities management and user experience space are doing, you will find more evidence of the seismic shifts under way. JLL has its "Healthy and Productive Workplace" offering and its 3-30-300 analysis discussed in Chapter 3. CBRE has a healthy office research arm and has certified its headquarters in Los Angeles as a WELL building. The list of leading companies continues, from Boston Properties to Beacon Capital Partners and many others.

It's not just the owner-operators and facilities management companies that are in the arena, either. Once a critical mass of leading companies with massive global portfolios started to design with Healthy Buildings in mind, building suppliers and technology companies began moving in this direction with them. Take Carrier, a major supplier of building technology to real estate developers best known for its air-conditioning business unit. We mentioned in Chapter 11 that Carrier recently designed, built, and moved into a new building of its own called the Center for Intelligent Buildings. This was designed specifically as a space where prospective buyers could walk through the building to discover the often hidden aspects of how building systems work. Importantly, this living showroom is not just about how chillers and mechanical systems operate—it showcases how these building technologies *promote health and human performance*. What's motivating all of this? Carrier's Chairman and CEO David Gitlin sums it up: Healthy buildings "have gone from nice-to-have conveniences to must-have protections."[12]

View is another building product company focused on health. View makes dynamic glass—windows that that can automatically change their tint to adjust the glare coming in based on the time, day, and season. This comes with significant energy savings (20 percent reduction in operating expenses). But take a look at how its leaders are positioning the company: the first thing its website talks about is how the company's glass affects *health and productivity*. They even created a new position, director of health strategy, and quickly filled it with a public health expert, Piers MacNaughton. Why the health focus? MacNaughton says, "At View we've come to realize that in the built environment, health is the primary motivator."[13] Taken in isolation, these examples from JLL, Carrier, and View may not seem like much, but this turn toward health in the built environment represents nothing short of a seismic shift in the market.

New technologies are transforming possibilities for monitoring and conforming with every one of the 9 Foundations of a Healthy Building. New healthy lighting offerings no longer talk about light levels and lux—they address how their products affect circadian rhythm and health. There are sensor startups that sell monitoring systems to track real-time air quality in offices and homes, and the big players are getting involved, too. Carrier announced a new platform called Abound that can integrate real-time monitoring with the building management system for constant tracking of HPIs and autonomous—and immediate—response by the building to optimize air quality conditions continously. And there are some big building product manufacturers, like Velux and View, that are leading the charge toward "smart" building technology by incorporating sensors right into their skylights and dynamic glass windows. In the building safety and security startup space are companies like Evolv, which is deploying rapid screening technologies combined with employee-recognition systems to improve the security checkpoint process—increasing speed and effectiveness ("secure flow"), while decreasing the burden and associated stress of this function.

Add to this landscape the many companies innovating in energy. This list includes established global players like Schneider Electric, with its strong focus on energy efficiency, microgrid solutions, digital buildings, monitoring, and optimization. (Schneider Electric, long known for its energy services, is now also moving into the Healthy Building space with digital services for smart buildings, like its Workplace Advisor, which monitors and reports real-time space utilization and indoor environmental quality.) The energy innovation movement also includes startups like Phase Change Energy Solutions, which uses the natural heat-absorbing and heat-releasing properties of so-called phase change materials as a super energy-efficient insulator. Products like this come with an energy benefit, but they come with a health benefit, too. The demand for these types of energy-saving and health-promoting products is set to grow rapidly.

Then there are companies working on better ways to clean the air. This includes the big incumbents and recognized brands in the portable air purification space, like the *health-care company* Dyson (we're going to convince you yet . . .), and startups like EnVerid, which can install a system within your existing ductwork to capture and purge VOCs, CO_2, and other chemicals.

Investors are getting in the game, too. In 2018, JLL introduced a $100 million fund to invest in Healthy Building technologies. SoftBank created its $100 billion Vision Fund, which has a heavy focus on "PropTech"—technology and companies that focus on real estate buying, selling, and management. And recently, colleagues of ours at Harvard have been engaged with PGGM, a multibillion-dollar pension fund, which is exploring how to invest in "healthy companies." Healthy Buildings are part of that conversation.

We've introduced a few specific companies at this point not to promote them but because they provide good examples for how the market is advancing, and how much innovation and rapid adoption are now taking place. We chose to single out these particular companies because we've gotten to know them well. We've met with dozens of executives from different organizations, and there is a reason these companies show up in our book: we think they are doing it right, or are on the path to doing it right. (We've also seen a lot of "how not to do it"—but that deserves its own book.)

All of these people and companies—the knowledge generators, the early adopters, and the leading market players—have paved the way for the rise of Healthy Building certification systems. The early adopters and players in leading markets now want a way to independently validate what they're doing for investors, tenants, and employees. This has given us the WELL Building Standard, Fitwel, RESET, and probably a few more coming soon. Some developers are working with us to use the 9 Foundations of a Healthy Building as a guide toward creating a Healthy Building.

All signs point to a growing Healthy Building market. There is unequivocally momentum in the system. Now the trillion-dollar question is, Are these just one-off flagship projects, or will this become the new business as usual?

Industry Composition: A Big Sector with a Long Tail

It's difficult to get a handle on the magnitude of the value of "built environment" assets in the world. On a planet with over 7 billion people, many families' primary assets are their homes. Commercial real estate alone as an investable, tradable asset class is worth trillions of dollars. Add to that schools, courthouses, hospitals, and factories and the industry is very large indeed: in excess of $260 trillion in US dollars, according to the global real estate advisory Savills.[14] Real estate of one form or another leads all other global stores of wealth.

How Is the Wealth Distributed?

In the commercial real estate space, the largest publicly traded property owner in the United States is Simon Property Group, with a market capitalization of about $50 billion. The 10th largest is Equity Residential with a market value of about $24 billion, and the 100th is Acadia Real Estate Trust with a market capitalization of just over $2.4 billion. The top 200 in aggregate have market capitalization well over a trillion dollars . . . but the biggest one represents just 5 percent of that total.[15] This means that there are a few large players and a very long tail down to mom-and-pop investors who might own a few apartments and a neighborhood shopping center with five stores in it.

At the same time, capital providers like banks and mortgage companies see a similar industry spread. From the largest to the top 100 to the next 1,000, the curve looks much the same. Caliber Home Loans, number 1, originated $43.9 billion in transactions in 2017. PrimeLending, number 10, did $14.5 billion. Move down to number 75, Homeowners Financial Group, and the volume drops to just over $1.4 billion. Again, a very large market with a few big players and very long tail of smaller ones.[16]

Why Is Understanding the Spread of Wealth Important?

The largest landlords, in the biggest cities, with the most high-profile tenants, with the largest balance sheets, looking at the longest leases—and courting the most sought-after knowledge workers—have the capability and the competitive interest to be at the absolute cutting edge and to let people know it. Those resources, those contracts, and those interests fall off quickly in markets that are not as robust, in labor markets that are not as competitive, and where rents don't justify large capital expenditures. Innovations do eventually propagate—office buildings in even the smallest out-of-the-way towns are now expected to have elevators and air-conditioning—but it will not be automatic. The "Class A" buildings in big cities with multinational corporations as tenants are the first to take up most new ideas in the real estate industry, and it can often take longer for the benefits to become apparent to smaller tenants in "B" or "C" space in smaller cities. Naturally, we hope that this book jump-starts and accelerates that idea dissemination since it's so important to people's health and well-being.

This means opportunity for many kinds of service firms, ranging from architects to contractors to Healthy Building specialists. Since only the largest firms have extensive in-house capability, almost all of the facilities thinking is outsourced. Sometimes this is to global behemoths like JLL, CBRE, and WeWork, and other times it is to local, smaller firms that have specialist knowledge, like Terrapin Bright Green, Environmental Health & Engineering, and KGS Buildings. These firms are differentiating themselves by focusing on energy, sustainability, . . . and health.

Clockspeed: Cycle Time for Adoption

Think of biology. Some small species of insects have a life span of days; small mammals like mice or moles have a life span of just months or years; people and elephants can live to 90 or 100; and some whales and tortoises may live well past the century mark. In a quickly propagating species like fruit flies, generations come and go in days or weeks and evolution can happen quickly. For people (or for whales), evolution is a lot slower.

The same phenomenon exists in industry. A new social networking app might have a life span of a few weeks or months before fading away or being subsumed. A new chip like the Intel Core i9 might have a selling life span of five years. In cars, brake calipers and brake shoes haven't changed in decades. When catalytic converters came on the scene, even though they were quickly mandated in the US fleet, it took almost 20 years for them to become 90 percent established. Why? Because cars have useful lives of 10 to 20 years. So it takes more than 20 years to change out the whole fleet.

In his seminal book *Clockspeed*, Charles Fine of MIT identifies this phenomenon and describes how businesses can work with their internal systems and, even more importantly, with their customers and their supply chains (in the world of our book, architects, contractors, and building product manufacturers), to accelerate a time cycle, adopt new technology faster, and compete better.[17]

Why do we care? Because buildings have an even longer life span than turtles. There is a good chance that as you read this you are in a home or at an office that's more than 50 years old. You probably wouldn't even think the age of the structure was worth mentioning unless it was around 100 years old. Consider Boston, where 85 percent of the building square footage expected to be in place by 2050 already exists.[18] The cycle time for the dissemination of advances in building technology can be very long indeed. In slow demographic growth economies like the United States, it will thus take a long time for the ideas in this book to fully propagate.

At the same time, most homes, offices, hospitals, and schools regularly undergo major renovations, sometimes taking things right down to the shell of the building. During major renovations, when the space is vacant and there is already disruption, is a good time to act on sustainability, on energy efficiency . . . and on making your building truly and measurably healthy. This window does not come around that often—and if this book is successful, we will ensure that decision makers don't miss that window.

On a global scale, the opportunities in new construction are enormous. In the United States alone, about $1.2 trillion of new construction is put in place each year (about 6 percent of the country's gross domestic product of $19 trillion).[19] Globally the amount of new construction is thought to be about $12.7 trillion annually, according to the Construction Intelligence Center.[20] Even though the existing stock is large, this massive level of new activity justifies building things right, starting now.

Like the real estate and finance industries, the construction industry is highly skewed. The largest firm in the Western world, Vinci from France, earned about $46 billion in revenue in 2017—less than 1 percent of the total.[21] There are few other industries in the world where the market leader has less than 1 percent share. This means that the opportunity to be an intellectual and operational leader in health is everywhere . . . and firms can take the leadership mantle.

What's Next: Sensors, Awareness, Communication, and Analytics

So far we have mostly considered technologies that are widely available today. We have argued for awareness and substantially increased investment in indoor air quality and other aspects of health you can measure in office settings. But the world is changing. What might be next for building owners, homeowners, workers, and investors?

Imagine this future scenario:

Nina and David were super excited about the arrival of their new baby, Sam. They were selecting a new apartment in the big city. The air in the big city was pretty bad, with almost daily warnings about outdoor air pollution, but they had read *The 9 Foundations of a Healthy Building* and were up on the science of how outdoor air pollution becomes indoor air pollution. Nina and David wanted to find a nice place for Sam, so they checked the online real-time indoor air quality trend data—now reported at a microscale level as a result of ubiquitous outdoor air monitoring in cities—and projection statistics compiled by the Fitbit, Alibaba, Dyson, Zillow, and Chase Consortium. They wanted to see which apartments in which complexes were rated the highest against key pathogens, as well as the pollutants that had led to so many of David's childhood allergies.

Armed with this info—much like shopping for a vehicle with Carfax in hand—the couple went to negotiate with apartment landlords. They cared about location and access to transit, although since neither worked in a traditional office those factors were not so important to them. They looked at two nice complexes in the city: the Starnight Building, a relatively modest design in a new building where the developers had made a big deal about so-called indoor air quality, touting its LEED, WELL, and Fitwel ratings; and the Warwick Building, which was older but very fancy, with lots of tall ceilings and plenty of woodwork from renewable sources.

In the end they paid a rent premium for an apartment in the Starnight Building, where, their analysis concluded, they would pay less for energy consumption in the long run because of the landlord's extensive capital investments in the building. More importantly, they calculated that they would sleep better and that Sam would breathe better. The air quality was objectively superior at the Starnight, based on data available from Morningstar's analysis of data from the consortium. Social media reports confirmed that others had had good experiences. A few years from now, they reasoned, Sam would score higher on his standardized college entrance examinations thanks to the advantage of clean air and water and its proven cumulative impact on brain development and human cognition. Nina and David were fortunate to have a choice; many other young parents couldn't afford a premium-air building like the Starnight.

The Future Is Already Here

Some may find this story far-fetched and alarmist. But consider what Google is already doing with its Sidewalk Labs project in Toronto. It is creating, digitizing, and democratizing data on city performance at an unprecedented local scale. Air pollution data is part of what they are monitoring, measuring, and reporting. Then look at what Google did in San Francisco, where they placed air pollution sensors on the top of Google Street View cars.[22] As the Street View cars did their normal routine, driving through every city street to update images and data for Google Maps, they were simultaneously collecting air pollution data. For the first time ever, residents could get a block-by-block look at air pollution in the city. Guess what? It varies significantly, even within a city. Now this hyperlocal monitoring approach is being exported to other cities. It's not hard to imagine a future in which air pollution monitors are on every streetlight (LED lights can already act as sensors for VOCs and other pollutants) or on every Google Street View car, or every Lyft car or UPS delivery truck. Nina and David will have this type of air pollution data at their fingertips.

As for *indoor* environmental quality data, consider what some companies like Awair, TSI, and Airthings are already offering today: the ability to install air-quality monitors on every desk in a large building or each room in a home within one day to stream real-time data about the indoor environment. Joe's team has deployed monitoring networks like these in homes and offices and universities as part of ongoing research on the links between indoor air quality and cognitive function. Many consumer products have air quality sensors built right into them and are already collecting environmental data indoors. Millions of homes already have environmental data being collected through these products, all of which can be freely shared and analyzed in open data cloud applications. This is just the beginning—seeing air pollution sensors in an office or apartment building will be as common as seeing a thermostat on the wall. (That's really just an air-quality sensor, too, when you stop to think about it.)

We are convinced that there will be ubiquitous sensing and air-quality data at consumers' fingertips in short order. But maybe you think what is farfetched about our Nina and David example is that, despite all of this data being readily available, consumers won't use it to make decisions. So let us move from a hypothetical to a real-world scenario, and move from homes to commercial real estate.

Talent and Tenancy

Recently we got a call from an executive at a *Fortune* 500 company (we can't disclose who). This executive oversees the global real estate portfolio for the company, as well as the development of a new corporate campus. He called us because something happened that had never happened to him before—he got a call from his executive counterpart in the Human Resources Department asking all sorts of questions about green and Healthy Buildings. Specifically, this HR executive wanted to know if their new headquarters was going to be a "Healthy Building." Why? She told him that the company was recruiting a top candidate for a job in the firm and this candidate was asking questions about the building she would be working in. The top prospect was interviewing the building! (A 2017 article titled "Are You Interviewing Your Building?" written by John Mandyck, then chief sustainability officer at United Technologies, seems prescient.[23])

This type of "bottom-up" demand for Healthy Buildings is likely to increase for three primary reasons. First is the expectation of transparency in all things, spurred on by social media. There is not much question that people share information, whether they are job seekers, home buyers, employers, credit rating agencies, or folks just looking for a good restaurant or a competent plumber. A recent example of this sharing related to work is the rise in popularity of the website Glassdoor, where people anonymously post about the company they work for, including their boss, workplace culture, salary, and, increasingly, the building. Here are a few examples of recent posts:

- **"Smells bad":** "Smells like garbage every day . . . better pay for the work and ventilation system for the summer."[24]
- **"Building smells like sewage":** "Yes, I would also hope this was a joke, but the building smells like sewage in between 7 and 9 A.M. in the morning. This just gives me even more the impression that they don't mind their employees."[25]
- **"Perks, but noisy open office":** "There is no noise insulation in the ceiling so you'll hear noise from the above floor. Sales and customer service teams are answering phones with no sound insulation in between desks. Years of complaining to management and facilities has barely gotten anywhere."[26]

- **"Unsafe and unprofessional workplace":** "The place is filthy and product is strewn everywhere. Fire exits and emergency equipment are blocked."[27]
- **"Great people but the office is way too cold":** "The office is too cold—so cold that it's sometimes hard to focus on the job."[28]
- **"Great mentors, bad lighting":** "The building we were in had very few windows, grey wall-to-wall carpeting, and dim lighting. Luckily they were talking about moving when I left!"[29]
- **"How is this much different than being on a virus-infected cruise ship":** "for 8+ hours every day, five days a week?"

You may not know it, but employees are already interviewing your building.

There are already huge catalogs of shared information about music, politics, travel, mutual funds, and more; why wouldn't there be crowdsourced data and a rating platform for air quality in apartments, homes, offices, schools, hospitals, and government buildings? The ability to contain information and control ratings has escaped into the world—and it's not coming back under corporate control.

Second, many companies are realizing that they are now in the health business, and they are marketing themselves as such. Consider that Apple's CEO, Tim Cook, said in 2019 that health-care disruption may ultimately be Apple's legacy, not the iPhone. Every company is a health-care company now—in some instances, literally.

Health and health care represent a third of the multitrillion-dollar US economy, so it's not surprising that these companies are aggressively moving into this space. Many forms of media are also raising awareness of health issues. It's possible to rely on mainstream media like the *New York Times,* social media like Facebook, YouTube, and Reddit, broadcast media like Oprah or CNN, and sifting and sorting algorithms like Google to look at websites like WebMD, Mayo Clinic, or the *New England Journal of Medicine* to learn more and more factual information about what goes into our bodies—whether ingested, inhaled, or injected. This barrage of information ensures that consumers are aware of what constitutes a healthy life, and it's only a matter of time before buildings join the health zeitgeist. To understand the scale of what we're talking about, think about it this way: health care represents a third of the US economy, and construction represents about another 10 percent, so between the two, we are looking at influencing almost half of the US economy in some manner in the Healthy Buildings movement.

Third, look at the rise of sensors, analytics, and big data, and think about what this means when it comes to providing objective and verifiable information on whether the building you are buying into is healthy. The Nina, David, and Sam scenario only makes sense if sensors are ubiquitous, and they are rapidly becoming so. Not long ago all a building could really tell you in real time was temperature and humidity—and you had to look at the gauge with your own eyes. A professional air-quality expert or Certified Industrial Hygienist taking samples to a lab had to wait days or weeks to measure things like lead paint, mold spores, asbestos particles, or formaldehyde. Today, your Nest or Ecobee or Carrier thermostat can tell you the history of the temperature and humidity in each room in your house, and your Airthings or Awair is starting to do the same for CO_2, CO, particulates, and much more. What's more, indoor air purifiers from Dyson or Honeywell don't just purify the air; they sense the environment and respond to out-of-boundary conditions, as well as displaying the data and sending it to your phone—or anywhere else you'd like. Imagine an apartment or office landlord aggregating all the readings in the building, anonymizing them, and tuning airflow and filtration for optimum levels with real-time feedback from the Internet of Things operating in the building. Big data and analytics could crunch this info for thousands or millions of indoor spaces. The big players in the building management system space are moving in this direction. Quickly.

Sensors aren't just in the inanimate space. Your Fitbit or Apple Watch can monitor heart rate and breathing, and some wearables measure blood sugar and more. (The promise of measuring personal health is what underpins Apple CEO Tim Cook's vision of Apple becoming known as a health-care disrupter.) Your device can share this information with your building to explore causal relationships between your space and your mood, but more importantly, it can then interact with the building systems to intervene autonomously. Do you think people won't be willing to share this kind of personal information? They already do on apps like Strava, where athletes exchange information about details like VO_2 max (maximum oxygen uptake during exercise), and connected exercise devices like Peloton that can track your RPMs and BPMs, allowing you to share your fitness and performance metrics.

Many third-party aggregators of this kind of information exist in other domains: if you have a 401(k) or IRA or other investment vehicle, mostly likely you rely on services like Morningstar or Lipper. Those financial analysis entities look at millions of data points for direction and trends of investments—and to measure the performance of the human (and machine) managers making decisions. Green building indexes already exist. For example, GRESB aggregates self-reported data on sustainability aspects of real estate portfolios and delivers this to investors. It added a health module to it sustainability reporting, showing where it thinks the market is headed. Then there are companies like GeoPhy, which we mentioned in Chapter 11, that aggregate publicly available information on real estate risk such as natural disasters exacerbated by climate change. This type of data is also fed into the investor market. A Morningstar rating or Carfax for your office or school is not farfetched; it's right around the corner.

The large pools of capital like pension funds, endowments, insurance companies, and sovereign funds look at two main criteria in their investments in debt and equities: What is the expected rate of return, and what is the risk or uncertainty around realizing that return? There is not much question that a building that repels renters or condo buyers is exposed to the uncertainty of lower rents and higher vacancies as better-informed tenants or buyers look at the data, realize the long-term impact of air and water on themselves and their loved ones, and gravitate to the objectively superior building. Investors will figure this out.

Will the ability to measure air quality—and to tie it incontrovertibly to health—become significant enough to people to actually move the needle over from other selection considerations like location, views, aesthetics, and cost? Today, no. Someday? Most definitely. A future of smart and connected curated indoor spaces is inevitable. The rise of the informed shopper—with choices enabled by sensors, open data, mobile platforms, apps, analytics, and social media—will be one of the key forces pushing us further up the Healthy Building adoption curve. Individuals, and the businesses that shelter or employ them, will drive best practice faster than government and regulation will be able to. This will amplify the positions of leaders—and laggards—among landlords, lenders, and vendors in the office, apartment, and institutional building industry.

The Future of Healthy Buildings

Our goal for this book was to present a vision for how to scale and accelerate a shift to healthier buildings for all. What happens next is . . . up to you. Faced with the collision of rapid population growth and rapid urbanization, nothing short of the health of people and the planet is at stake. Collectively we have the power—and responsibility—to influence the design and operations of billions of square feet of buildings around the world, thereby influencing the health of tens of billions of people globally.

The Healthy Building strategies in this book must not only benefit the 1 percent. Early adopters in major cities are essential for demonstrating that these strategies can be implemented and can yield business wins, without affecting budget or timeline. But are these first Healthy Buildings just vanity projects, or are the movement and awareness the new "business as usual"? The true measure of success will be determined based on how scalable these strategies are: how deeply and how quickly the core aspects of Healthy Buildings are picked up in suburbs, in smaller buildings, in museums and city halls, and in urban and peri-urban agglomerations all over the world. Getting Healthy Buildings right is an imperative. It can mean improving the lives of billions of people on the planet.

If you are reading this book, you are an influencer in the built environment and in the future of Healthy Buildings. You will guide the approach of using a human health lens to create better indoor spaces for people in schools, hospitals, theaters, restaurants, retail shops, places of worship, and commercial real estate of all sizes. If you are a landlord, building manager, architect, designer or contractor, business executive, sustainability professional, scientist, investor, or facility manager, or if you live and work indoors, you have a chance to maximize the potential for you and your colleagues or your family to live a healthy life.

You also are living at a time when advances in health science and building science are occurring rapidly—whether it's new empirical observations about human cognition under differing indoor conditions or the invention of personal air-quality sensors that can be placed anywhere and immediately make the air quality visible. That means you can act.

Throughout this book we have shown you how to harness the extraordinary power of indoor spaces to drive performance and productivity. You are now armed with everything you need to make a cogent argument for Healthy

Buildings in your organization. Hard science showing how buildings influence our health? Check. A financial argument for why Healthy Buildings are a sound business argument? Check. Tools for how to measure and track health performance? That, too. We have given you a sense of the global forces at play and the technological shifts that are creating the perfect conditions for an exciting future. This is an unprecedented moment in history—the convergence of health science, building science, and business science is giving us a chance to unlock the potential of our buildings to create economic value and advance health. It's a simple formula, really: *Healthy Building* strategies are *Healthy People* strategies and therefore *Healthy Business* strategies. It seems like a cliché, but these can lead us together to a *Healthy Planet.* How will you be part of this future?

Conclusion

Buildings, Business, Health, and Wealth

> We need a new generation of humanitarian design ideas
> underpinned by scientific research.
>
> —NORMAN FOSTER

MANY PEOPLE FEEL IT is no longer acceptable just to work in a building that makes them less sick; employees are starting to demand a space that makes them "more healthy." Getting there will require us to go from accepting "acceptable" indoor air quality (the current ventilation code) to demanding a space that is optimal for human health and performance. This is within reach.

Our goal in writing this book was to communicate, in simple language, the many ways in which our buildings shape our health and impact our businesses. If you remember nothing else in this book, we hope you will remember to ask yourself the question that we posed early on: "Why are we ignoring the 90 percent?"

We have become an indoor species, spending 90% of our time indoors. And while many countries have a comprehensive regulatory structure monitoring outdoor air pollution, there is nothing comparable for indoor environments. This is the case even though, as we have shown, the majority of your exposure to outdoor pollution occurs indoors. Further, indoor sources of pollution can be significantly higher than outdoor pollution, although we don't tend to think of indoor contaminants as "pollution" per se. We should. There are signs that this is beginning to change. A 2019 article in the *New Yorker* spoke of the problem of "indoor smog"—a label that makes a strong link between our traditional notions of outdoor pollution and our indoor world.[1]

We also wanted to make the point that Healthy Building strategies are good business strategies. For many twenty-first-century "knowledge worker" businesses, people costs are by far the largest single portion of their income statement. Office rent may be second, and the two of them together might account for 90 percent of the costs of those firms. We argue that a work environment that helps people to improve their health, productivity, and creativity provides more bottom-line benefit than does scrimping on ventilation, filtration, materials selection, and the incremental energy and operating costs.

There is also a bigger picture and ultimate motivating force for our work together in writing this book. We want you and your business to win, for sure . . . but we also want you to see Healthy Buildings in the larger context of the global mega-changes of population growth and urbanization that we mention. The global changes coming are so massive—almost 2 billion additional people by 2050, the vast majority of whom will live in cities—that buildings need to be a part of the solution to our sustainable development challenges. Buildings last a long time and they affect our lives for decades—even centuries. The decisions we make today regarding our buildings will determine the collective health of people and the planet now and for future generations. There isn't a lot of good news coming from scientists concerned with the environment, but buildings can be one of the rare cases where personal benefits and social benefits are not in conflict. We can have individual wins for our businesses while also having wins at a population-wide scale.

The way we see it, one of the most accessible ways to influence the health of people around the world is to influence the design, operation, and maintenance of the billions of square feet of enclosed space where we live, work, learn, play, pray, and heal. We think the key to making this theory of change operational is to show that it's a "win for all" scenario; that acting in your own self-interest can influence others to do the same, and that, building by building, we can begin to improve the health of all people, in all buildings, everywhere, every day.

Healthy Buildings as a Win for All

In the preface, we outlined four groups of people who might find our book useful: business owners; employees; building investors, owners, and developers; and all of us (society). The ultimate beauty of the Healthy Buildings movement is that there are wins for everyone involved once we consider how Healthy Buildings influence four performance factors: human performance, business performance, social performance, and market performance. These interests expand from individuals to businesses to regions to the economy. So let's revisit highlights from what we've covered and group them among these four performance factors to make clear that with Healthy Buildings, everyone wins.

Human Performance: A Chance to Do Your Best

Let's start with the unequivocal fact that a Healthy Building benefits the people who work and live inside it. We opened our book with a heavy focus on just a few factors where the science is irrefutable: bringing more fresh air into a building and filtering it more effectively are associated with better health outcomes. As a reminder, higher outdoor air ventilation rates have been linked with fewer sick building symptoms, lower disease transmission, and fewer missed days of work. More recently, rigorous double-blind method research in office environments shows that higher ventilation rates have a direct impact on our cognitive function. Specifically, better indoor air quality led to better performance in the decision-making of knowledge workers. This is not theoretical—we have shown you the empirical evidence.

We then extended this analysis by posing and answering the question, What else constitutes a "Healthy Building"? That brought us to the 9 Foundations of a Healthy Building, a synthesis of 40 years of science on all of the factors that drive human health indoors—ventilation, air quality, thermal health, water quality, moisture, dust and pests, lighting and views, noise, and safety and security. You are now armed with all the scientific evidence you need to create a healthier building.

Then, in Chapter 7, we ventured into the world of healthier building materials. Pretty building designs are sometimes mucked up by the junk we purchase and use inside them. (Recall our bodybuilder-on-steroids analogy.) Some products are laden with chemicals that act in a very subtle manner on our health; their slow workings on our minds and bodies are not easily sensed in the way that volatile organic compounds emitted from a scented surface cleaner immediately make your eyes water. These semivolatile chemicals slowly migrate out of products and into our bodies, quietly wreaking havoc on our hormone signaling system.

"In Chapter 8, we show how buildings can make us sick or keep us well when it comes to infectious diseases. These basic principles don't just apply when pandemics hit—they are everyday strategies that can help us limit the spread of infectious diseases all of the time, everywhere. A paradigm shift is underway when it comes to how we mitigate infectious disease transmission, and buildings with good ventilation and filtration are at the center of that shift."

Building on these foundations, in Chapters 9 and 10 we showed you not only that the science is clear but also that all of this is actually measurable and trackable using Health Performance Indicators (HPIs). We have given you the four-quadrant framework for measurement with HPIs, discussed certification systems that allow you to independently verify that performance (and offered our view on what every Healthy Building certification system should include), and talked about new sensor technologies that allow us to manage our buildings (and measure the health of our personal environments) in real time. This part of the book is the key link between the academic science and action in the real world. We can talk all day long about what should be done in the abstract based on the hard science, but unless there is a way to measure and track this, health performance of the building won't be part of the equation for most businesses.

You now have the tools to design, operate, maintain, and manage a Healthy Building. If you follow a Healthy Building strategy, you can create a building that not only is not assaulting your health or that of your employees but is in fact acting as a place of refuge and health promotion. So the first winners are the people inside buildings. That is enough of a motivator for some, but so far this has not been sufficient to spur all landlords, tenants, and investors to seek action and move us up the adoption curve. What's the next step?

Business Performance: Enlightened Self-Interest

While the basic health science on indoor environments has accumulated over decades, this alone has not really influenced practice. But newer techniques and new learning about how indoor environments affect human cognitive performance, concentration, and productivity have been a game changer. How so? They have brought in another winner in the Healthy Buildings movement: the business owner. We believe that these research findings flip the conversation. Instead of incremental decisions about additional costs, more rigorous health measures are now about profit. To wit: rather than tighten the budget on energy for ventilation, it's understood that spending a little more on better indoor air will allow you to reap dividends in the form of greater productivity, fewer sick days, better employee retention, and a net benefit to bottom-line profit. Until recently, the industry couldn't really measure how buildings were affecting the people who worked in them. Now we can.

Here, again, the evidence is empirical. Recall in Chapter 4 that we explored the costs of higher ventilation rates. We put this into a pro forma for our hypothetical consulting company, Health &Wealth, Inc. and saw that, indeed, there were costs for this company to increase ventilation rates. But that's a naïve analysis that doesn't factor in the benefits. Once you account for benefits from lower absenteeism and better human performance ("payroll effect" and "productivity boost" in our financial model), we showed that the costs for this one improvement are trivial compared with the significant benefits to the company—a 10.7 percent net gain to the bottom line. For one intervention. Where all the employees had to do was breathe! No training needed. No yearlong rollout of a new program. No change to workplace culture. Just breathe.

Even better, we showed in our model that there is room for the building owner to charge the tenant a rent premium for this better building. In our case, we factored in a substantial increase of 10 percent. This part is absolutely critical because it begins to address the issue of split incentives that have long hindered the adoption of Healthy Building strategies. Why would a building owner take on any additional costs if the benefits were to go to the tenant? Well, now we have the answer—they can take on the additional cost and justify a premium for that better building. The financial gains from adopting Healthy Building strategies are so massive that there is plenty to go around. The employees win, the business owner wins, and the building owner wins.

Therein lies the central tenet of our book: buildings impact people's health, and now we can objectively quantify how an investment in the building is an investment in the company. Healthy Buildings improve *human performance*. Better human performance improves *business performance*.

Social Performance: The 'S' in ESG for Buildings

We spent most of this book on the first two factors—human performance and business performance. Then, in Chapters 11 and 12, we introduced some new ideas regarding factors that will enable the nascent Healthy Buildings movement to scale faster and farther: *social performance* and *market performance*.

In Chapter 12 we looked at how buildings impact health and wealth beyond the four walls, leading to better social performance. This is big, because it moves the Healthy Buildings conversation from being one about individual gains to being one where the people *outside and around the neighborhood* also benefit. Healthy Buildings are central to the larger conversation about sustainability, environmental health, and public health.

Our climate is changing, and this is a direct result of climate-forcing gases that are being released into the atmosphere. A changing climate has brought on important questions about uncertainty, risk, financing, and resilience in the real estate sector. Consider our hypothetical building owner, Mary, and her counterpart from the bank, Nancy. A redrawn flood map moved Mary's property from a 1-in-100-year risk to a 1-in-20-year risk, putting her in violation of the loan agreement. This raised important challenges and questions that we are seeing all over the country—and world—today. Does Mary take steps to "harden" her building against extreme weather? Does the bank foreclose or refinance? If it refinances, under what terms? Beyond the local level, these types of questions are being asked at the institutional investor level as well. Sophisticated investors are using machine learning techniques and geographical information systems (GIS) to overlay real estate data with atmospheric data, climate predictions, and social demographics to estimate financial risk and support better decision-making.

With the building-energy-health-climate-resiliency nexus concept, we showed that buildings are part of the problem, yes, but also that Healthy Building strategies are part of the solution. Our energy system, dominated by fossil fuel combustion, is releasing greenhouse gases like carbon dioxide. With an all-out effort under way to address this situation, it's only natural that in addition to focusing on the generation side of the equation—moving to renewable energy sources—we also need to focus on the demand side. Here is where buildings enter the spotlight. As consumers of 40 percent of energy globally, buildings are responsible for a third of all greenhouse gas emissions (80 percent of global energy from fossil fuels $\times$ 40 percent used by buildings).

Healthy Building strategies that reduce energy use come with a health co-benefit in terms of reduced emissions of greenhouse gases. More immediate are the health benefits to the surrounding community from the reduction of air pollutants that are emitted from fossil fuel consumption. Air pollutants like $PM_{2.5}$ that have an acute effect on health will be reduced as buildings reduce their energy use. As with human performance and business performance, the social performance benefit can also be quantified. And these benefits are massive—for every $1 saved in energy in the United States, another $0.59 is gained in health and climate co-benefits, on average. In the developing world, it is closer to $10 saved in health and climate benefits for every $1 saved on energy.[2] As the energy grid gets cleaner through the adoption of renewable energy sources, buildings will not be off the hook. Over the past few years there is intense scrutiny of on-site fossil fuel consumption in buildings and the embodied carbon in materials like concrete and steel. The conversation on the social performance of buildings is just beginning.

Expanding the definition of Healthy Buildings to include energy conservation and other *quantifiable* outward-looking measures becomes a way to link the business interests of the property industry with the business interests of the public. Put another way, we can empirically demonstrate that Healthy Buildings provide benefits not only to the individuals in the building and the owners of the building but to everyone else as well—to society as a whole.

Why does this matter? It means that governments and municipalities have a reason to get in the Healthy Buildings game. Rest assured, the quantification of health co-benefits does not just matter to governments. It matters for real estate developers, owners, and investors, too. With the rise of environmental, social, and governance (ESG) investing, real estate developers, owners, and investors are now being asked about the S in ESG. What is the social performance of your real estate asset? This has been hard to quantify in the past—but that is no longer the case.

Market Performance: Consumers Get It

Rounding out the list of winners are the owners, developers, and investors who will win with the rise of informed shoppers and with the growing market demands for Healthy Buildings. For starters, let's look at how Healthy Building investors are poised to win, and how this will help propagate the Healthy Building movement. When David Levinson and L&L Holding show that they can command some of the highest rents in New York City for their "Tower for the People" at 425 Park Avenue, the value of that property increases, as does the value of the investment for their primary investor, Tokyu Land US Corporation. What do you think is likely to happen with Tokyu Land's next investment? It might choose to *only* invest in Healthy Building projects in the future, because it will have been demonstrated that this is a competitive advantage and a winning investment strategy.

What do you think Levinson's competitors will do when they see his building has commanded these high rents? New billion-dollar buildings and developments are going up in Manhattan every month. We can guarantee you that others will see what's happening and respond with their own designs. They recognize demand. When a player like Amazon hosts a nationwide competition for its new headquarters, developers, investors, and owners perk up—"How can I attract the Amazons of the world to my building?"

And then what do you think is happening in other markets beyond New York City? They are paying attention, too. From Seattle to Boston, from London to Hong Kong, from Shanghai to Bangkok, developers are planning new Healthy Buildings.

In the mind of an investor and developer, perhaps even more important than competing today is competing in the future. In Levinson's vision, pursuing elements of a Healthy Building at 425 Park Avenue is about future-proofing the building; if he doesn't aim for a Healthy Building now, the tenants who can pay the high rent premiums this year will just skip on over to the other side of town for a developer at Hudson Yards or around Wall Street who will offer a measurably better environment for the health and productivity of the tenant's knowledge workers. It's an arms race to better indoor air quality—and that's a good thing.

But more important than the top-down approach to Healthy Buildings is what's coming next—the rise of the informed shopper, whom we introduced in Chapter 12. The ubiquity of data and a barrierless approach to sharing personal information are creating bottom-up pressures for Healthy Buildings. Not only are we seeing buildings install sensors, but we are seeing workers bring their own sensors with them. Smaller, cheaper, better, and more connected. This is changing how the big commercial real estate players are thinking about their business. Bryan Koop, executive vice president for the Boston region of Boston Properties, a listed real estate trust with $2.5 billion in annual revenue, gave us this example. He has seen workers in some of the buildings his company manages bring in inexpensive real-time air-quality sensors and then bring that data to management. Not only did they bring the data to management, but they also brought the data to all of their coworkers in the same department. Real-time building environmental data is now being shared at the proverbial water cooler. The ensuing concern essentially shut down work in that department for over a week while the issue was addressed.

Koop sees this as all part of the shift from caveat emptor ("buyer beware") to caveat venditor ("seller beware") that's happening in every industry. Car buyers walk into a showroom these days and know more about the market price than the sellers do. Long gone are the days when the salesperson plays a game and walks to the back room to talk with the manager to "see if I can get you a better deal." Nowadays, while that salesperson leaves to talk with the manager in the back, the shopper is on his or her phone comparing car prices from every showroom in a 50-mile radius. By the time the salesperson comes back, the buyer knows more than the seller. Progressive Insurance jumped in front of this trend years ago with a set of advertisements telling customers that Progressive was posting all of its competitor's prices on its own web page; it knew customers were searching for the best deal across several websites anyway, bouncing around from site to site comparing prices, so they simplified the process for shoppers and put its prices next to their competitors on their own website.

This is coming to the real estate sector, and forward-thinking executives are preparing. Like Progressive, Koop at Boston Properties has a plan for how to leverage this shift in mind-set and put Boston Properties out in front. His strategy is to talk about air quality and other Healthy Buildings factors *first*, so that when a potential customer goes to another building and that building owner *doesn't* talk about air quality, Koop will win. "Who wouldn't want to be in a healthier building, and who wouldn't be willing to pay for it?" he asks.

The final piece of the bottom-up pressure is coming from the crowdsourced approach to evaluating companies and products popularized by websites like Yelp and Trip Advisor. With a few clicks a potential customer will know more about your restaurant or resort than you do by reviewing inside accounts about the service, experience, and impressions—complete with pictures. The days when a company controlled its brand with grandiose prose on its website next to Photoshopped images of its property or restaurant are over.

This approach has now reached commercial real estate with websites like Glassdoor. The vast majority of comments today on Glassdoor are about concerns like salaries, titles, and management styles. But we pulled a few examples of cases in which employees were starting to talk about their buildings and shared these with you in Chapter 12. This, we hope, is eye opening to our readers. As a forensic investigator, Joe has been called to the scene for investigations of cancer clusters and disease outbreaks in buildings, but in prior years these have largely remained under the radar, staying out of the news and the public realm. What happens when employees in a building where an alleged cancer cluster exists start posting on a site like Glassdoor? When the next talented recruit does her research on your business and sees that negative buzz, do you think she'll accept your job offer? When the owner goes to sell the building, will a potential buyer and investor see these issues and walk away, or will they demand a discounted price? In addition to potential health risks of a poorly performing building, there are very real brand risks. Healthy Buildings will become a risk-management tool for companies, helping them to protect their employees, brand, reputation, and investment.

Top firms are acting on these principles. When we spoke with Maureen Ehrenberg, former global head of facilities management at WeWork and JLL, she said that most employers today seek to have a happy, healthy, and engaged workforce and want to attract and retain top talent. She also agreed with the central concept we present throughout this book—that the *building* is key to making this happen. When she talks about a "smart" workplace, the goal is to leverage technology for the purpose of enabling better operations of a space from a comfort, ease, and access perspective *that drives employee productivity.*

It doesn't stop there. For Ehrenberg, it's also about "a commitment to the environment, health, and well-being, and an emphasis on helping people to 'do what they love' . . . founded upon the principles of a better tomorrow."[3]

In essence, she is saying indoor air quality is good business, yes, but creating healthy work environments is also a commitment to a better future for all. *Human performance* meets *business performance* meets *social performance* meets *market performance.*

So What Should I Do?

This book is aimed at the commercial real estate market in leading cities. But the lessons extend to other building decision makers, whether for a house purchase or a courthouse or a hospital or an airport, from New York to Singapore to Lagos. Individuals, vendors, lenders, and owners make choices. Here are a few of the key action steps:

- Ventilation is cheap and it matters. Run the fans, get fresh air, and filter it.
- There are 9 Foundations of a Healthy Building. Start with the basics and move up the menu.
- Measure healthy environments objectively and follow that with slight increments in capital spending that will bring large increments in the verifiable health of workers. Your most important key performance indicators (KPIs) are your health performance indicators (HPIs).
- The "Beyond the 4 Walls" impacts are important. Healthy Buildings will play a central role in the ESG conversation moving forward.
- Plan for a world where buyers and tenants know all about the performance of individual rooms and what to do with the information. Real-time sensors, aggregated data, benchmarking, social media connections, and predictive analytics will have force in the market as more and more people and firms "interview the building."
- Make sure that health and human performance are factored into the cost benefit analysis and decisions around your building. Otherwise, performance and productivity will be "value engineered" right out of your building, taking top talent and profits with it.

The Closing Handshake

With the analysis presented in this book, we think we've given evidence that overturns many of the arguments used as traditional barriers to adopting Healthy Building strategies—concerns about single winners, split incentives, first costs, certification costs, energy costs, and scientific evidence on health and performance. We've given you strong arguments to break these barriers down. Doing so will require, as many things do, smart leadership; leaders who can realize that the benefits far outweigh the costs. So much so that the decisions you make today about your buildings could very well determine whether you and your company are successful.

Just a few years ago, John wrote a Harvard Business School case study called "Design Creates Fortune: 2000 Tower Oaks Boulevard" that explored the economic benefits of better indoor environments and better employee health and performance through Vedic design.[4] The financial benefits were easy to model in a spreadsheet but hard to prove at that time. What wasn't clear, until now, is how the building performance and those benefits could be objectively quantified using health science.

Just a few years ago, Joe and his team conducted the COGFx Study, which explored the health benefits of better indoor environments and included some initial analysis of the economic benefits of this approach. The health benefits were clear, but what wasn't clear, until now, is how the financial performance of Healthy Building strategies could be objectively quantified using business science.

This is why we sought each other out to collaborate on this book. We were both tired of the hand-waving in our respective fields. For Joe, it was hand-waving around the financial performance of Healthy Buildings. For John, it was hand-waving around health performance in buildings. With this book we've turned the hand-waving into a handshake between the business and health worlds. We are happy to take your hands as well and walk together, using these new tools and techniques, into a future of healthier buildings and healthier people, more effective workers and stronger bottom lines, and more resilient cities and communities.

Notes

1. WHO ARE WE AND WHY SHOULD YOU CARE?

1. L. Iyer, J. D. Macomber, and N. Arora, "Dharavi: Developing Asia's Largest Slum (A)," Harvard Business School Case 710-004, July 2009, https://www.hbs.edu/faculty/Pages/item.aspx?num=37599.

2. The Twenty-Second Conference of the Parties to the UN Framework Convention on Climate Change.

3. S. Ro, "Here's What the $294 Trillion Market of Global Financial Assets Looks Like," Business Insider, February 11, 2015, https://www.businessinsider.com/global-financial-assets-2015-2; US Department of the Treasury, "Daily Treasury Yield Curve Rates," Resource Center, accessed October 2, 2019, https://www.treasury.gov/resource-center/data-chart-center/interest-rates/Pages/TextView.aspx?data=yield.

4. Centers for Disease Control and Prevention, "*Legionella* (Legionnaires' Disease and Pontiac Fever)," November 26, 2018, https://www.cdc.gov/legionella/about/history.html.

5. A. Mavridou et al., "Prevalence Study of *Legionella* spp Contamination in Greek Hospitals," *International Journal of Environmental Health Research* 18 (2008):

295–304; J. E. Stout et al., "Role of Environmental Surveillance in Determining the Risk of Hospital-Acquired Legionellosis: A National Surveillance Study with Clinical Correlations," *Infection Control and Hospital Epidemiology* 28 (2007): 818–824; J. L. Kool et al., "Hospital Characteristics Associated with Colonization of Water Systems by Legionella and Risk of Nosocomial Legionnaires' Disease: A Cohort Study of 15 hospitals," *Infection Control & Hospital Epidemiology* 20, no. 12 (1999): 798–805.

6. World Health Organization, "Legionellosis," February 16, 2018, http://www .who.int/news-room/fact-sheets/detail/legionellosis.

7. World Health Organization, *Health Effects of Particulate Matter* (Copenhagen, 2013), http://www.euro.who.int/__data/assets/pdf_file/0006/189051/Health -effects-of-particulate-matter-final-Eng.pdf.

8. Q. Di et al., "Air Pollution and Mortality in the Medicare Population," *New England Journal of Medicine* 376, no. 26 (2017): 2513–2522.

9. I. Kloog et al., "Acute and Chronic Effects of Particles on Hospital Admissions in New-England," *PLoS One* 7, no. 4 (2012): e34664.

10. V. Strauss, "Education Secretary Betsy DeVos Stumbles during Pointed '60 Minutes' Interview," *Washington Post,* March 12, 2018.

11. *Schools for Health: Foundations for Student Success* (Boston: Healthy Buildings Program, Harvard T. H. Chan School of Public Health, 2018), https://schools .forhealth.org.

12. David A. Coley, Rupert Greeves, and Brian K. Saxby, "The Effect of Low Ventilation Rates on the Cognitive Function of a Primary School Class," *International Journal of Ventilation* 6, no. 2 (2007): 107–112.

13. Oluyemi Toyinbo et al., "Modeling Associations between Principals' Reported Indoor Environmental Quality and Students' Self-Reported Respiratory Health Outcomes Using GLMM and ZIP Models," *International Journal of Environmental Research and Public Health* 13, no. 4 (2016): 385.

14. Ulla Haverinen-Shaughnessy and Richard J. Shaughnessy, "Effects of Classroom Ventilation Rate and Temperature on Students' Test Scores," *PloS One* 10, no. 8 (2015): e0136165.

15. Jisung Park, "Hot Temperature and High Stakes Exams: Evidence from New York City Public Schools" (working paper, Harvard University, 2018), https:// scholar.harvard.edu/files/jisungpark/files/paper_nyc_aejep.pdf.

16. Michael S. Mott et al., "Illuminating the Effects of Dynamic Lighting on Student Learning," *SAGE Open* 2, no. 2 (2012).

17. William J. Sheehan et al., "Association between Allergen Exposure in Inner-City Schools and Asthma Morbidity among Students," *Journal of American Medical Association Pediatrics* 171, no. 1 (2017): 31–38.

2. THE GLOBAL MEGA-CHANGES SHAPING OUR
WORLD, OUR BUILDINGS, AND US

1. United Nations Department of Economic and Social Affairs, Population Division, *World Population Prospects 2019: Highlights*, ST / ESA / SER.A / 423 (New York: United Nations, 2019).

2. United Nations Department of Economic and Social Affairs, "2018 Revision of World Urbanization Prospects," May 16, 2018, https://www.un.org/development /desa/publications/2018-revision-of-world-urbanization-prospects.html.

3. McKinsey Global Institute, *India's Urban Awakening: Building Inclusive Cities, Sustaining Economic Growth*, April 2010.

4. Rachel Carson, *Silent Spring* (Boston: Houghton Mifflin, 1962).

5. E. O. Wilson, *Half-Earth: Our Planet's Fight for Life* (New York: Liveright, 2016).

6. Joseph G. Allen et al., *Building for Health: The Nexus of Green Buildings, Global Health, and the U.N. Sustainable Development Goals* (Boston: Healthy Buildings Program, Harvard T. H. Chan School of Public Health, October 2017).

7. Environmental Protection Agency, *Advancing Sustainable Materials Management: 2015 Fact Sheet* (Washington, DC, July 2018), https://www.epa.gov/sites /production/files/2018-07/documents/2015_smm_msw_factsheet_07242018_fnl _508_002.pdf.

8. World Bank, "Fossil Fuel Energy Consumption (% of Total)," 2015, https://data.worldbank.org/indicator/ EG.USE.COMM.FO.ZS.

9. John Holdren, speech at Harvard University Center for the Environment, March 21, 2017.

10. World Health Organization, "Constitution of WHO: Principles," accessed December 2018, https://www.who.int/about/mission/en/.

11. Aaron Antonovsky, "The Salutogenic Model as a Theory to Guide Health Promotion," *Health Promotion International* 11, no. 1 (1996): 11–18.

12. I. Papnicolas, L. R. Woskie, and A. K. Jha, "Health Care Spending in the United States and Other High-Income Countries," *Journal of the American Medical Association* 319, no. 10 (2018): 1024–1039.

13. National Business Group on Health, "Large U.S. Employers Project Health Care Benefit Costs to Surpass $14,000 per Employee in 2018, National Business Group on Health Survey Finds," press release, August 8, 2017, https://www .businessgrouphealth.org/news/nbgh-news/press-releases/press-release-details/?ID =334; A. W. Mathews, "Employer-Provided Health Insurance Approaches $20,000 a Year," *Wall Street Journal*, October 4, 2018.

14. John A. Quelch and Emily C. Boudreau, *Building a Culture of Health: A New Imperative for Business* (Cham, Switzerland: Springer International, 2016).

272

NOTES TO PAGES 29–38

15. Eric Schmidt and Jonathan Rosenberg, *How Google Works* (New York: Grand Central, 2014).

16. Google, "Smelling the Carpet: Making Buildings Healthier, Along with the People in Them," accessed May 18, 2019, https://sustainability.google/projects/smelling-the-carpet/.

17. Correspondence with Kate Brandt, June 20, 2019.

18. H. Jung, "Modeling CO_2 Concentrations in Vehicle Cabin" (SAE Technical Paper 2013-01-1497, 2013), https://doi.org/10.4271/2013-01-1497.

19. *Merriam-Webster*, s.v. "sick building syndrome," accessed October 3, 2019, https://www.merriam-webster.com/dictionary/sick%20building%20syndrome.

20. Correspondence with Greg O'Brien, June 19, 2019.

21. Gianpiero Petriglieri, Susan J. Ashford, and Amy Wrzesniewski, "Thriving in the Gig Economy," *Harvard Business Review,* April 11, 2018, https://hbr.org/2018/03/thriving-in-the-gig-economy.

22. J. Manyika et al., "Independent Work: Choice, Necessity, and the Gig Economy," McKinsey and Company, October 2016, https://www.mckinsey.com/featured-insights/employment-and-growth/independent-work-choice-necessity-and-the-gig-economy.

23. US Occupational Safety and Health Administration, "Protecting Temporary Workers," accessed August 25, 2019, https://www.osha.gov/temp_workers/.

24. Ethan S. Bernstein and Stephen Turban, "The Impact of the 'Open' Workspace on Human Collaboration," *Philosophical Transactions of the Royal Society B* 373, no. 1753 (2018), https://royalsocietypublishing.org/doi/10.1098/rstb.2017.0239.

25. Correspondence with Greg O'Brien, June 19, 2019.

26. John D. Macomber and Griffin James, "Design Creates Fortune: 2000 Tower Oaks Boulevard," Harvard Business School Case 210-070, March 2010, 9.

27. Correspondence with Jim Whalen.

28. R. G. Eccles and S. Klimenko, "The Investor Revolution," *Harvard Business Review,* May–June 2019, https://hbr.org/2019/05/the-investor-revolution.

29. Larry Fink, "2018 Letter to CEOs: A Sense of Purpose," BlackRock, accessed October 3, 2019, https://www.blackrock.com/corporate/investor-relations/2018-larry-fink-ceo-letter.

30. David Gelles and David Yaffe-Bellany, "Shareholder Value Is No Longer Everything, Top C.E.O.s Say," *New York Times,* August 18, 2019.

31. Marc Benioff, "We Need a New Capitalism," *New York Times,* October 14, 2019.

3. WHY ARE WE IGNORING THE 90 PERCENT?

1. N. E. Klepeis et al., "The National Human Activity Pattern Survey (NHAPS): A Resource for Assessing Exposure to Environmental Pollutants," *Journal of Exposure Science and Environmental Epidemiology* 11, no. 3 (2001): 231.

2. Velux, "The Disturbing Facts about the Indoor Generation," accessed October 3, 2019, https://www.veluxusa.com/indoorgeneration.

3. Tweet from Richard Corsi, @CorsIAQ, January 24, 2014.

4. Environmental Protection Agency, "NAAQS Table," accessed October 3, 2019, https://www.epa.gov/criteria-air-pollutants/naaqs-table.

5. Chinese Ministry of Environmental Protection and General Administration of Quality Supervision, Inspection, and Quarantine of the People's Republic of China, *Ambient Air Quality Standards,* GB 3095-2012 (Beijing, 2012). Priemus and E. Schutte-Postma, "Notes on the Particulate Matter Standards in the European Union and the Netherlands," *International Journal of Environmental Research and Public Health* 6, no. 3 (2009): 1155–1173; Japanese Ministry of the Environment, "Environmental Quality Standards in Japan—Air Quality," accessed August 26, 2019, https://www.env.go.jp/en/air/aq/aq.html.

6. Occupational Safety and Health Administration, "Permissible Exposure Limits—Annotated Tables," accessed October 3, 2019, https://www.osha.gov/dsg/annotated-pels/index.html.

7. Jones Lang LaSalle Incorporated, "A Surprising Way to Cut Real Estate Costs," September 25, 2016, http://www.us.jll.com/united-states/en-us/services/corporates/consulting/reduce-real-estate-costs.

8. Building Owners and Managers Association International, "BOMA International's Office and Industrial Benchmarking Report Released," September 18, 2018, https://www.boma.org/BOMA/Research-Resources/3-BOMA-Spaces/Newsroom/PR91818.aspx.

9. US Bureau of Labor Statistics, "Occupational Employment Statistics: May 2018 State Occupational Employment and Wage Estimates—Massachusetts," last modified April 9, 2019, https://www.bls.gov/oes/current/oes_ma.htm.

10. R. W. Allen et al., "Modeling the Residential Infiltration of Outdoor PM2.5 in the Multi-ethnic Study of Atherosclerosis and Air Pollution (MESA Air)," *Environmental Health Perspectives* 120, no. 6 (2012): 824–830.

11. C. Chen and B. Zhao, "Review of Relationship between Indoor and Outdoor Particles: I / O Ratio, Infiltration Factor and Penetration Factor," *Atmospheric Environment* 45 (2011): 275–288.

12. Environmental Protection Agency, "*Exposure Factors Handbook* 2011 edition," *EPA / 600 / R-09 / 052F,* https://cfpub.epa.gov/ncea/efp/recordisplay.cfm?deid=236252.

13. Lance A. Wallace, *Project Summary: The Total Exposure Assessment Methodology (TEAM) Study,* EPA / 600 / S6-87 / 002 (Washington, DC: US Environmental Protection Agency, September 1987).

14. Rachel Weiner, "Lumber Liquidators to Pay $33 Million for Misleading Investors about Formaldehyde in Laminate Flooring," *Washington Post,* March 12, 2019.

15. R. E. Dodson et al., "Impact of Attached Garages on Indoor Residential BTEX Concentrations," in *HB 2006: Healthy Buildings: Creating a Healthy Indoor Environment for People, Proceedings,* vol. 1, *Indoor Air Quality (IAQ), Building Related Diseases and Human Response,* ed. E. de Oliveira Fernandes, M. Gameiro da Silva, and J. Rosado Pinto (Porto, Portugal: Universidade do Porto, 2006), 217.

16. US Environmental Protection Agency, "Idle-Free Schools Toolkit for a Healthy School Environment," accessed August 25, 2019, https://www.epa.gov/schools/idle-free-schools-toolkit-healthy-school-environment; P. H. Ryan et al., "The Impact of an Anti-idling Campaign on Outdoor Air Quality at Four Urban Schools," *Environmental Science: Processes and Impacts* 15, no. 11 (2013): 2030–2037.

17. N. Twilley, "Home Smog," *The New Yorker,* April 8, 2019.

18. A. W. Nørgaard et al., "Ozone-Initiated VOC and Particle Emissions from a Cleaning Agent and an Air Freshener: Risk Assessment of Acute Airway Effects," *Environment International* 68 (2014): 209–218.

19. D. K. Farmer et al., "Overview of HOMEChem: House Observations of Microbial and Environmental Chemistry," *Environmental Science: Processes and Impacts* 21, no. 8 (2019): 1280–1300.

20. C. J. Weschler et al., "Transdermal Uptake of Diethyl Phthalate and Di(n-butyl) Phthalate Directly from Air: Experimental Verification," *Environmental Health Perspectives* 123, no. 10 (2015): 928–934; G. Bekö et al., "Dermal Uptake of Nicotine from Air and Clothing: Experimental Verification," *Indoor Air* 28, no. 2 (2018): 247–257; G. C. Morrison et al., "Role of Clothing in Both Accelerating and Impeding Dermal Absorption of Airborne SVOCs," *Journal of Exposure Science and Environmental Epidemiology* 26, no. 1 (2016): 113.

21. Environmental Protection Agency, "*Exposure Factors Handbook* 2011 Edition," *EPA/600/R-09/052F,* https://cfpub.epa.gov/ncea/efp/recordisplay.cfm?deid=236252.

22. D. L. Bohac et al., "Secondhand Smoke Transfer and Reductions by Air Sealing and Ventilation in Multiunit Buildings: PFT and Nicotine Verification," *Indoor Air* 21, no. 1 (2011): 36–44.

23. K. Murphy, "What's Lurking in Your Countertop?," *New York Times,* July 24, 2008.

24. J. Allen et al., "Assessing Exposure to Granite Countertops," *Journal of Exposure Science and Environmental Epidemiology* 20 (2010): 263–280; J. Allen et al., "Predicted Indoor Radon Concentrations from a Monte Carlo Simulation of 1,000,000 Granite Countertop Purchases," *Journal of Radiological Protection* 33 (2013): 151–162.

25. John Mandyck and Joseph Allen, "The Nexus of Green Buildings, Global Health, and the U.N. Sustainable Development Goals," at the Distinguished Sustainability Lecture Series, Jaipur, India, October 4, 2017.

4. PUTTING THE BUILDING TO WORK FOR YOU

1. B. Franklin and W. T. Franklin, *Memoirs of the Life and Writings of Benjamin Franklin* (London: Colburn, 1809), 3.

2. J. Allen et al., "Associations of Cognitive Function Scores with Carbon Dioxide, Ventilation, and Volatile Organic Compound Exposures in Office Workers: A Controlled Exposure Study of Green and Conventional Office Environments," *Environmental Health Perspectives* 124, no. 6 (2016): 805–812.

3. J. Allen, "Research: Stale Office Air Is Making You Less Productive," *Harvard Business Review,* March 21, 2017, https://hbr.org/2017/03/research-stale -office-air-is-making-you-less-productive.

4. J. G. Cedeño Laurent, P. MacNaughton, E. Jones, et al., "Associations between Acute Exposures to PM2.5 and Carbon Dioxide Indoors and Cognitive Function in Office Workers: A Multicountry Longitudinal Prospective Observational Study," *Environmental Research Letters* 16, no. 9 (2021); J. F. Brundage et al., "Building-Associated Risk of Febrile Acute Respiratory Diseases in Army Trainees," *Journal of American Medical Association* 259, no. 14 (1988): 2108–2112; P. J. Drinka et al., "Report of an Outbreak: Nursing Home Architecture and Influenza-A Attack Rates," *Journal of the American Geriatrics Society* 44, no. 8 (1996): 910–913; C. W. Hoge et al., "An Epidemic of Pneumococcal Disease in an Overcrowded, Inadequately Ventilated Jail," *New England Journal of Medicine* 331, no. 10 (1994): 643–648; L. D. Knibbs et al., "Room Ventilation and the Risk of Airborne Infection Transmission in 3 Health Care Settings within a Large Teaching Hospital," *American Journal of Infection Control* 39, no. 10 (2011): 866–872; D. K. Milton, P. M. Glencross, and M. D. Walters, "Risk of Sick Leave Associated with Outdoor Air Supply Rate, Humidification, and Occupant Complaints," *Indoor Air* 10, no. 4 (2000): 212–221; O. A. Seppanen and W. J. Fisk, "Summary of Human Responses to Ventilation," *Indoor Air* 14, suppl. 7 (2004): 102–118; P. Wargocki and D. P. Wyon, "The Effects of Moderately Raised Classroom Temperatures and Classroom Ventilation Rate on the Performance of Schoolwork by Children (RP-1257)," *HVAC&R Research* 13, no. 2 (2007): 193–220.

5. ASHRAE, "The Standards for Ventilation and Indoor Air Quality," accessed October 4, 2019, https://www.ashrae.org/technical-resources/bookstore/standards -62-1-62-2.

6. S. E. Womble et al., "Developing Baseline Information on Buildings and Indoor Air Quality (BASE '94): Part I—Study Design, Building Selection, and Building Descriptions" (presentation, Healthy Buildings '95, September 11–14, 1995), https://www.researchgate.net/publication/237729515_Developing_Baseline _Information_on_Buildings_and_Indoor_Air_Quality_BASE_'94_Part_I_Study _Design_Building_Selection_and_Building_Descriptions.

7. W. J. Fisk, "The Ventilation Problem in Schools: Literature Review," *Indoor Air* 27, no. 6 (2017): 1039–1051.

8. M. J. Mendell et al., "Association of Classroom Ventilation with Reduced Illness Absence: A Prospective Study in California Elementary Schools," *Indoor Air* 23, no. 6 (2013): 515–528.

9. R. L. Corsi et al., "Carbon Dioxide Levels and Dynamics in Elementary Schools: Results of the TESIAS Study," *Proceedings of Indoor Air* 2 (2002): 74–79.

10. X. Cao et al., "The On-Board Carbon Dioxide Concentrations and Ventilation Performance in Passenger Cabins of US Domestic Flights," *Indoor and Built Environment* 28, no. 6 (2018).

11. J. G. Allen et al., "Airplane Pilot Flight Performance on 21 Maneuvers in a Flight Simulator under Varying Carbon Dioxide Concentrations," *Journal of Exposure Science and Environmental Epidemiology* 29, no. 4 (2019): 457–468.

12. D. K. Milton et al., "A Study of Indoor Carbon Dioxide Levels and Sick Leave among Office Workers," *Environmental Health* 1 (2002): article 3.

13. P. Wargocki et al., "The Effects of Outdoor Air Supply Rate in an Office on Perceived Air Quality, Sick Building Syndrome (SBS) Symptoms and Productivity," *Indoor Air* 10, no. 4 (2000): 222–236; B. W. Olesen, "Indoor Environment Health-Comfort and Productivity," 2005, http://perfectproblems.com/testashrae/Olesen-Health-comfort-productivity.pdf; W. J. Fisk, "Health and Productivity Gains from Better Indoor Environments and Their Relationship with Building Energy Efficiency," *Annual Review of Energy and the Environment* 25 (2000): 537–566.

14. P. MacNaughton et al., "Economic, Environmental and Health Implications of Enhanced Ventilation in Office Buildings," *International Journal of Environmental Research and Public Health* 12, no. 11 (2015): 14709–14722.

5. CREATING AND CAPTURING VALUE

1. Market Research Hub, "Global Construction Outlook 2021," April 30, 2017, https://www.marketresearchhub.com/report/global-construction-outlook-2021-report.html.

2. Federal Reserve Bank of St. Louis, "Average Sales Price of Houses Sold for the United States," August 23, 2018, https://fred.stlouisfed.org/series/ASPUS.

3. "Median Age of Maturing U.S. Housing Stock is 37," *Realtor Magazine,* August 13, 2018, https://magazine.realtor/daily-news/2018/08/13/median-age-of-maturing-us-housing-stock-is-37; N. Zhao, "Half of US Homes Built before 1980," Eye on Housing, National Association of Home Builders, August 1, 2018, http://eyeonhousing.org/2018/08/half-of-us-homes-built-before-1980/.

4. L. Zullo, "Tenant Energy Performance Optimization Case Study: Li & Fung USA, Empire State Building," NRDC, April 19, 2013, https://www.nrdc.org/resources/tenant-energy-performance-optimization-case-study-li-fung-usa-empire-state-building.

5. Harvard University, "Green Revolving Fund," accessed October 4, 2019, https://green.harvard.edu/programs/green-revolving-fund.

6. P. MacNaughton et al., "Economic, Environmental and Health Implications of Enhanced Ventilation in Office Buildings," *International Journal of Environmental Research and Public Health* 12, no. 11 (2015): 14709–14722.

7. M. Hamilton et al., "Perceptions in the U.S. Building Industry of the Benefits and Costs of Improving Indoor Air Quality," *Indoor Air* 26, no. 2 (2016): 318–330.

6. THE 9 FOUNDATIONS OF A HEALTHY BUILDING

1. Piers MacNaughton et al., "The Impact of Working in a Green Certified Building on Cognitive Function and Health," *Building and Environment* 114 (2017): 178–186.

2. P. MacNaughton et al., "Economic, Environmental and Health Implications of Enhanced Ventilation in Office Buildings," *International Journal of Environmental Research and Public Health* 12, no. 11 (2015): 14709–14722.

3. B. Stephens, T. Brennan, and L. Harriman, "Selecting Ventilation Air Filters to Reduce $PM_{2.5}$ of Outdoor Origin," *ASHRAE Journal,* September 2016, 12–20.

4. J. G. Laurent et al., "Reduced Cognitive Function during a Heat Wave among Residents of Non-air-conditioned Buildings: An Observational Study of Young Adults in the Summer of 2016," *PLOS Medicine* 15, no. 7 (2018): e1002605.

5. O. Seppänen, W. J. Fisk, and Q. H. Lei, "Effect of Temperature on Task Performance in Office Environment" (paper, Ernest Orlando Lawrence Berkeley National Laboratory, Berkeley, July 2006), http://eta-publications.lbl.gov/sites/default/files/lbnl-60946.pdf.

6. Tyler Hoyt et al., "CBE Thermal Comfort Tool," Center for the Built Environment, University of California, Berkeley, 2017, http://comfort.cbe.berkeley.edu/.

7. B. Kingma and W. van Marken Lichtenbelt, "Energy Consumption in Buildings and Female Thermal Demand," *Nature Climate Change* 5, no. 12 (2015): 1054.

8. A. Lydgate, "Is Your Thermostat Sexist?," *New Yorker,* August 3, 2015.

9. S. Karjalainen, "Thermal Comfort and Gender: A Literature Review," *Indoor Air* 22, no. 2 (2012): 96–109.

10. Y. Zhai et al., "Human Comfort and Perceived Air Quality in Warm and Humid Environments with Ceiling Fans," *Building and Environment* 90 (2015): 178–185.

11. Joseph Allen and Jose Guillermo Cedeno Laurent, "Want Air Conditioning and a Healthier Planet? Here's One Step We Can Take Today," *The Hill,* July 30, 2018, https://thehill.com/blogs/congress-blog/energy-environment/399549-want-air-conditioning-and-a-healthier-planet-heres-one.

12. Lawrence Berkeley National Laboratory, "Thermal Stress and Deaths during Heat Waves," accessed May 13, 2019, https://iaqscience.lbl.gov/cc-thermal.

13. Environmental Protection Agency, "National Primary Drinking Water Regulations," March 22, 2018, https://www.epa.gov/ground-water-and-drinking -water/national-primary-drinking-water-regulations.

14. ASHRAE, *Legionellosis: Risk Management for Building Water Systems,* ANSI/ASHRAE Standard 188-2018, 2018, https://www.ashrae.org/technical -resources/bookstore/ansi-ashrae-standard-188-2018-legionellosis-risk-management -for-building-water-systems.

15. D. L. Ryan, "High Lead Levels Found at Hundreds of Massachusetts Schools," *Boston Globe,* May 2, 2017.

16. Environmental Protection Agency, *Optimal Corrosion Control Treatment Evaluation Technical Recommendations for Primacy Agencies and Public Water Systems,* March 2016, https://www.epa.gov/sites/production/files/2019-07 /documents/occtmarch2016updated.pdf.

17. J. Allen et al., *The 9 Foundations of a Healthy Building* (Boston: Harvard T. H. Chan School of Public Health, 2017), 21, https://forhealth.org/9 _Foundations_of_a_Healthy_Building.February_2017.pdf.

18. D. Licina et al., "Clothing-Mediated Exposure to Chemicals and Particles," *Environmental Science and Technology* 53, no. 10 (2019): 5559–5575.

19. Environmental Protection Agency, "Update for Chapter 5 of the Exposure Factors Handbook: Soil and Dust Ingestion," September 2017, http://ofmpub.epa .gov/eims/eimscomm.getfile?p_download_id=532518.

20. P. J. Lioy, *Dust: The Inside Story of Its Role in the September 11th Aftermath,* foreword by T. H. Kean (Lanham, MD: Rowman and Littlefield, 2011).

21. Occupational Safety and Health Administration, "OSHA Factsheet: Laboratory Safety Noise," accessed October 7, 2019, https://www.osha.gov /Publications/laboratory/OSHAfactsheet-laboratory-safety-noise.pdf; "Chapter 39: Noise Hazard Assessment and Control," accessed October 7, 2019, http://www2.lbl .gov/ehs/pub3000/CH39.html.

22. D. Owen, "Is Noise Pollution the Next Public Health Crisis?," *New Yorker,* May 6, 2019.

23. S. Pujol et al., "Association between Ambient Noise Exposure and School Performance of Children Living in An Urban Area: A Cross-Sectional Population-Based Study," *Journal of Urban Health* 91, no. 2 (2013): 256–271.

24. A. W. Correia et al., "Residential Exposure to Aircraft Noise and Hospital Admissions for Cardiovascular Diseases: Multi-airport Retrospective Study," *British Medical Journal* 347 (2013): f5561.

25. S. Ganesan et al., "The Impact of Shift Work on Sleep, Alertness and Performance in Healthcare Workers," *Scientific Reports* 9, no. 1 (2019): 4635; S. M. James et al., "Shift Work: Disrupted Circadian Rhythms and Sleep—Implications

for Health and Well-Being," *Current Sleep Medicine Reports* 3, no. 2 (2017): 104–112.

26. IARC Working Group on the Evaluation of Carcinogenic Risk to Humans, *Painting, Firefighting, and Shiftwork,* IARC Monographs on the Evaluation of Carcinogenic Risks to Humans 98 (Lyon: International Agency for Research on Cancer Press, 2010).

27. O. Keis et al., "Influence of Blue-Enriched Classroom Lighting on Students' Cognitive Performance," *Trends in Neuroscience and Education* 3, nos. 3–4 (2014): 86–92; B. M. T. Shamsul et al., "Effects of Light's Colour Temperatures on Visual Comfort Level, Task Performances, and Alertness among Students," *American Journal of Public Health Research* 1, no. 7 (2013): 159–165.

28. L. M. James, "Blue-Enriched White Light in the Workplace Improves Self-Reported Alertness, Performance and Sleep Quality," *Scandinavian Journal of Work, Environment and Health* 34, no. 4 (2008): 297.

29. E. O. Wilson, *Biophilia* (Cambridge, MA: Harvard University Press, 1984).

30. R. Ulrich, "View through a Window May Influence Recovery from Surgery," *Science* 224, no. 4647 (1984): 420–421.

31. J. Yin et al., "Physiological and Cognitive Performance of Exposure to Biophilic Indoor Environment," *Building and Environment* 132 (2018): 255–262.

32. J. Yin et al., "Effects of Biophilic Interventions in Office on Stress Reaction and Cognitive Function: A Randomized Crossover Study in Virtual Reality," *Indoor Air,* published ahead of print, August 16, 2019, https://doi.org/10.1111/ina.12593.

33. J. Yin et al., "Restorative Effects of Biophilic Indoor Environment: A Between-Subjects Experiment in Virtual Reality," *Environment International* (2020).

34. J. Allen et al., *9 Foundations,* 23

35. Juliette Kayyem, conversation with authors, May 2019.

36. B. J. Allen and R. Loyear, *Enterprise Security Risk Management: Concepts and Applications* (Brooksfield, CT: Rothstein, 2017).

37. W. J. Fisk, D. Black, and G. Brunner, "Benefits and Costs of Improved IEQ in US Offices," *Indoor Air* 21, no. 5 (2011): 357–367.

7. OUR GLOBAL CHEMICAL EXPERIMENT

1. R. Ruiz, "Industrial Chemicals Lurking in Your Bloodstream," *Forbes,* July 11, 2012, https://www.forbes.com/2010/01/21/toxic-chemicals-bpa-lifestyle -health-endocrine-disruptors.html#7679e596bb91.

2. R. Harrington, "The EPA Has Only Banned These 9 Chemicals—Out of Thousands," *Business Insider,* February 10, 2016, https://www.businessinsider.com /epa-only-restricts-9-chemicals-2016-2.

3. ABC News, "Schwarzenegger Has No Regrets about Steroid Use," February 25, 2005, https://abcnews.go.com/ThisWeek/Health/story?id=532456&page=1.

4. C. Potera, "Reproductive Toxicology: Study Associates PFOS and PFOA with Impaired Fertility," *Environmental Health Perspectives* 117, no. 4 (2009): A148; C. C. Carignan et al., "Urinary Concentrations of Organophosphate Flame Retardant Metabolites and Pregnancy Outcomes among Women Undergoing *In Vitro* Fertilization," *Environmental Health Perspectives* 125, no 8. (2017): 087018.

5. Environmental Protection Agency, "Summary of the Toxic Substances Control Act," September 19, 2018, https://www.epa.gov/laws-regulations/summary-toxic-substances-control-act.

6. Rachel Carson, *Silent Spring* (Boston: Houghton Mifflin, 1962).

7. L. N. Vandenberg et al., "Low Dose Effects of Bisphenol A: An Integrated Review of In Vitro, Laboratory Animal, and Epidemiology Studies," *Endocrine Disruptors* 1, no. 1 (2013): e26490.

8. J. R. Rochester and A. L. Bolden, "Bisphenol S and F: A Systematic Review and Comparison of the Hormonal Activity of Bisphenol A Substitutes," *Environmental Health Perspectives* 123, no. 7 (2015): 648.

9. J. Allen, "Stop Playing Whack-a-Mole with Hazardous Chemicals," *Washington Post,* December 15, 2016.

10. Silent Spring Institute, "The Detox Me Action Kit by Silent Spring Institute," accessed October 7, 2019, https://silentspring.org/detoxmeactionkit/.

11. N. Kristof, "What Poisons Are in Your Body?," *New York Times,* February 23, 2018.

12. A. M. Calafat et al., "Polyfluoroalkyl Chemicals in the U.S. Population: Data from the National Health and Nutrition Examination Survey (NHANES) 2003–2004 and Comparisons with NHANES 1999–2000," *Environmental Health Perspectives* 115, no. 11 (2007): 1596–1602.

13. J. Allen, "These Toxic Chemicals Are Everywhere—Even in Your Body. And They Won't Ever Go Away," *Washington Post,* January 2, 2018.

14. V. Barry, A. Winquist, and K. Steenland, "Perfluorooctanoic Acid (PFOA) Exposures and Incident Cancers among Adults Living Near a Chemical Plant," *Environmental health Perspectives* 121, nos. 11–12 (2013): 1313–1318.

15. C8 Science Panel, "The Science Panel Website," accessed August 16, 2019, http://www.c8sciencepanel.org/.

16. P. Grandjean et al., "Serum Vaccine Antibody Concentrations in Children Exposed to Perfluorinated Compounds," *Journal of the American Medical Association* 307, no. 4 (2012): 391–397.

17. G. Liu et al., "Perfluoroalkyl Substances and Changes in Body Weight and Resting Metabolic Rate in Response to Weight-Loss Diets: A Prospective Study," *PLoS Medicine* 15, no. 2 (2018): e1002502.

18. Science Daily, "Unsafe Levels of Toxic Chemicals Found in Drinking Water for Six Million Americans," August 10, 2016, https://www.sciencedaily.com /releases/2016/08/160809121418.htm.

19. C. Lyons, *Stain-Resistant, Nonstick, Waterproof, and Lethal: The Hidden Dangers of C8* (Westport, CT: Praeger, 2007).

20. S. DeVane, "State Investigates Rising GenX Levels at Chemours Plant," *Fayetteville Observer,* January 18, 2019.

21. A. Blum et al., "Children Absorb Tris-BP Flame Retardant from Sleepwear: Urine Contains the Mutagenic Metabolite, 2, 3-Dibromopropanol," *Science* 201, no. 4360 (1978): 1020–1023.

22. Michigan Department of Public Health, "PBBs in Michigan—Frequently Asked Questions, 2011 Update," https://www.michigan.gov/documents/mdch _PBB_FAQ_92051_7.pdf.

23. Emory Rollins School of Public Health, Michigan PBB Registry, "Research," accessed August 24, 2019, http://pbbregistry.emory.edu/Research/index.html.

24. F. J. Di Carlo, J. Seifter, and V. J. DeCarlo, "Assessment of the Hazards of Polybrominated Biphenyls," *Environmental Health Perspectives* 23 (1978): 351.

25. K. Norén and D. Meironyté, "Certain Organochlorine and Organobromine Contaminants in Swedish Human Milk in Perspective of Past 20–30 Years," *Chemosphere* 40, nos. 9–11 (2000): 1111–1123.

26. Tom Webster, presentation at Boston University School of Public Health, 2006.

27. J. G. Allen et al., "Critical Factors in Assessing Exposure to PBDEs via House Dust: *Environment International* 34, no. 8 (2008): 1085–1091; J. G. Allen et al., "Exposure to Flame Retardant Chemicals on Commercial Airplanes," *Environmental Health* 12, no. 1 (2013): 17; S. Harrad and S. Hunter, "Concentrations of Polybrominated Diphenyl Ethers in Air and Soil on a Rural–Urban Transect across a Major UK Conurbation," *Environmental Science and Technology* 40, no. 15 (2006): 4548–4553; R. J. Letcher et al., "Bioaccumulation and Biotransformation of Brominated and Chlorinated Contaminants and Their Metabolites in Ringed Seals *(Pusa hispida)* and Polar Bears *(Ursus maritimus)* from East Greenland," *Environment International* 35, no. 8 (2009): 1118–1124; M. A. McKinney et al., "Flame Retardants and Legacy Contaminants in Polar Bears from Alaska, Canada, East Greenland and Svalbard, 2005–2008," *Environment International* 37, no. 2 (2011): 365–374; S. Hermanussen et al., "Flame Retardants (PBDEs) in Marine Turtles, Dugongs and Seafood from Queensland, Australia," *Marine Pollution Bulletin* 57, nos. 6–12 (2008): 409–418.

28. T. J. Woodruff, A. R. Zota, and J. M. Schwartz, "Environmental Chemicals in Pregnant Women in the United States: NHANES 2003–2004," *Environmental Health Perspectives* 119, no. 6 (2011): 878–885; K. Inoue et al., "Levels and Concentration Ratios of Polychlorinated Biphenyls and Polybrominated Diphenyl Ethers in Serum and Breast Milk in Japanese Mothers," *Environmental Health Perspectives* 114, no. 8 (2006): 1179–1185; S. Harrad and L. Porter, "Concentrations of Polybrominated Diphenyl Ethers in Blood Serum from New Zealand," *Chemosphere* 66, no. 10 (2007): 2019–2023; L. Zhu, B. Ma, and R. A. Hites, "Brominated Flame Retardants in Serum from the General Population in Northern China," *Environmental Science and Technology* 43, no. 18 (2009): 6963–6968.

29. H. Viberg, "Exposure to Polybrominated Diphenyl Ethers 203 and 206 during the Neonatal Brain Growth Spurt Affects Proteins Important for Normal Neurodevelopment in Mice," *Toxicological Sciences* 109, no. 2 (2009): 306–311; L. H. Tseng et al., "Developmental Exposure to Decabromodiphenyl Ether (PBDE 209): Effects on Thyroid Hormone and Hepatic Enzyme Activity in Male Mouse Offspring," *Chemosphere* 70, no. 4 (2008): 640–647; T. E. Stoker et al., "In Vivo and In Vitro Anti-androgenic Effects of DE-71, a Commercial Polybrominated Diphenyl Ether (PBDE) Mixture," *Toxicology and Applied Pharmacology* 207, no. 1 (2005): 78–88; L. H. Tseng et al., "Postnatal Exposure of the Male Mouse to 2, 2′, 3, 3′, 4, 4′, 5, 5′, 6, 6′-Decabrominated Diphenyl Ether: Decreased Epididymal Sperm Functions without Alterations in DNA Content and Histology in Testis," *Toxicology* 224, nos. 1–2 (2006): 33–43.

30. J. B. Herbstman et al., "Prenatal Exposure to PBDEs and Neurodevelopment," *Environmental Health Perspectives* 118, no. 5 (2010): 712–719; J. D. Meeker et al., "Polybrominated Diphenyl Ether (PBDE) Concentrations in House Dust Are Related to Hormone Levels in Men," *Science of the Total Environment* 407, no. 10 (2009): 3425–3429; K. M. Main et al., "Flame Retardants in Placenta and Breast Milk and Cryptorchidism in Newborn Boys," *Environmental health Perspectives* 115, no. 10 (2007): 1519–1526.

31. J. G. Allen et al., "PBDE Flame Retardants," 60.

32. T. Hamers et al., "Biotransformation of Brominated Flame Retardants into Potentially Endocrine-Disrupting Metabolites, with Special Attention to 2,2′,4,4′-Tetrabromodiphenyl Ether (BDE-47)," *Molecular Nutrition and Food Research* 52, no. 2 (2008): 284–498.

33. C. M. Butt and H. M. Stapleton, "Inhibition of Thyroid Hormone Sulfotransferase Activity by Brominated Flame Retardants and Halogenated Phenolics," *Chemical Research in Toxicology* 26, no. 11 (2013): 1692–1702.

34. H. M. Stapleton et al., "Identification of Flame Retardants in Polyurethane Foam Collected from Baby Products," *Environmental Science and Technology* 45, no. 12 (2011): 5323–5331.

35. California Environmental Protection Agency, "Evidence on the Carcinogenicity of Tris (1,3-Dichloro-2-Propyl Phosphate)," July 2011, https://oehha.ca.gov/media/downloads/proposition-65/chemicals/tdcpp070811.pdf.

36. Carignan et al., "Urinary Concentrations," 087018.

37. P. Callahan and S. Roe, "Playing with Fire," *Chicago Tribune,* May 2012, http://media.apps.chicagotribune.com/flames/index.html.

38. J. G. Allen et al., "Linking PBDEs in House Dust to Consumer Products Using X-Ray Fluorescence," *Environmental Science and Technology* 42, no. 11 (2008): 4222–4228.

39. D. Michaels, *Doubt Is Their Product: How Industry's Assault on Science Threatens Your Health* (Oxford: Oxford University Press, 2008); Naomi Oreskes and Erik M. Conway, *Merchants of Doubt: How a Handful of Scientists Obscured the Truth on Issues from Tobacco Smoke to Global Warming* (New York: Bloomsbury, 2011).

40. R. Hauser and A. M. Calafat, "Phthalates and Human Health," *Occupational and Environmental Medicine* 62, no. 11 (2005): 806–818.

41. I. Colón et al., "Identification of Phthalate Esters in the Serum of Young Puerto Rican Girls with Premature Breast Development," *Environmental Health Perspectives* 108, no. 9 (2000): 895–900.

42. C. G. Bornehag et al., "The Association between Asthma and Allergic Symptoms in Children and Phthalates in House Dust: A Nested Case–Control Study," *Environmental Health Perspectives* 112, no. 14 (2004): 1393–1397.

43. A. S. Young, T. Zoeller, R. Hauser, et al., "Assessing Indoor Dust Interference with Human Nuclear Hormone Receptors in Cell-Based Luciferase Reporter Assays," *Environmental Health Perspectives* 129, no. 4 (2021), https://ehp.niehs.nih.gov/doi/10.1289/EHP8054.

44. A. S. Nair, "DuPont Settles Lawsuits over Leak of Chemical Used to Make Teflon," Reuters, February 13, 2017.

45. T. Kary, "3M Settles Minnesota Lawsuit for $850 Million," Bloomberg, February 20, 2018, https://www.bloomberg.com/news/articles/2018-02-20/3m-is-said-to-settle-minnesota-lawsuit-for-up-to-1-billion.

46. *Literature Review of Remediation Methods for PCBs in Buildings* (Needham, MA: Environmental Health and Engineering, 2012).

47. HomeAdvisor, "How Much Does It Cost to Remove Asbestos?," accessed October 7, 2019, https://www.homeadvisor.com/cost/environmental-safety/remove-asbestos/; *Literature Review of Remediation Methods.*

48. C. Pellacani et al., "Synergistic Interactions between PBDEs and PCBs in Human Neuroblastoma Cells," *Environmental Toxicology* 29, no. 4 (2014): 418–427.

49. State of California, Environmental Protection Agency, "Chemicals Known to the State to Cause Cancer or Reproductive Toxicity," October 26, 2018, https://oehha.ca.gov/media/downloads/proposition-65/p65list102618.pdf.

50. A. S. Young, R. Hauser, T. M. James, et al., "Impact of 'Healthier' Materials Interventions on Dust Concentrations of Per- and Polyfluoroalkyl Substances,

Polybrominated Diphenyl Ethers, and Organophosphate Esters," *Environment International* 150 (2021), doi: 10.1016/j.envint.2020.106151.

51. Perkins + Will, "Transparency," accessed August 26, 2019, https:// transparency.perkinswill.com.

8. BUILDINGS AS A FIRST LINE OF DEFENSE AGAINST COVID AND OTHER AIRBORNE INFECTIOUS DISEASES

1. J.S. Mackenzie, P. Drury, A. Ellis, T. Grein, et al, "The WHO Response to SARS and Preparations for the Future," in *Learning from SARS: Preparing for the Next Disease Outbreak: Workshop Summary*, S. Knobler, A. Mahmoud, S. Lemon, et al., eds. (Washington, DC: National Academy Press, 2004).

2. Joseph Allen, "Employers Have Been Offering the Wrong Office Amenities," *Atlantic*, October 3, 2021, https://www.theatlantic.com/ideas/archive/2021/10/fresh -air-cool-new-office-amenity/620288/.

3. S. N. Rudnick and D. K. Milton, "Risk of Indoor Airborne Infection Transmission Estimated from Carbon Dioxide Concentration," *Indoor Air* 13, no. 3 (2003), doi: 10.1034/j.1600-0668.2003.00189.x.

4. Shelly L. Miller, William W Nazaroff, Jose L. Jimenez, et al., "Transmission of SARS-CoV-2 by Inhalation of Respiratory Aerosol in the Skagit Valley Chorale Superspreading Event," *Indoor Air* 31, no. 2 (2021), doi.org/10.1111/ina.12751.

5. Yuguo Li, Hua Qian, Jian Hang, and Xuguang Chen, "Probable Airborne Transmission of SARS-CoV-2 in a Poorly Ventilated Restaurant," *Building and Environment* 196 (2021), doi: 10.1016/j.buildenv.2021.107788.

6. Parham Azimi, Zahra Keshavarz, Jose Guillermo, Cedeno Laurent, and Joseph Allen, "Mechanistic Transmission Modeling of COVID-19 on the *Diamond Princess* Cruise Ship Demonstrates the Importance of Aerosol Transmission," *Proceedings of the National Academy of Sciences* 118, no. 8 (2021), doi.org/10.1073 /pnas.2015482118.

7. Reports and papers published to date can be accessed at the task force's web page: https://Covid19commission.org/safe-work-travel.

8. Joseph G. Allen and Andrew M. Ibrahim, "Indoor Air Changes and Potential Implications for SARS-CoV-2 Transmission," *Journal of American Medical Association* 325:20 (2021):2112–2113. doi:10.1001/jama.2021.5053.

9. National Academies of Sciences, Engineering, and Medicine, *Infectious Disease Mitigation in Airports and on Aircraft* (Washington, DC: National Academies Press, 2013), https://doi.org/10.17226/22512.

10. Nicole C. Deziel, Joseph G. Allen, Paul T. J. Scheepers, and Jonathan I. Levy, "The COVID-19 Pandemic: A Moment for Exposure Science," *Journal for*

Exposure Science and Environmental Epidemiology (2020), 1–3, doi: 10.1038/s41370-020-0225-3.

11. Joseph G. Allen and John D. Macomber, "What Makes an Office Building 'Healthy'?" *Harvard Business Review*, April 29, 2020.

12. Xiaodan Zhou, Kevin Josey, Leila Kamareddine, et al., "Excess of COVID-19 Cases and Deaths Due to Fine Particulate Matter Exposure during the 2020 Wildfires in the United States," *Science Advances* 7, no. 33 (2021), DOI: 10.1126/sciadv.abi8789.

13. Emily R. Jones, Jose Guillermo Cedeño Laurent, Anna S. Young, et al., "The Effects of Ventilation and Filtration on Indoor PM2.5 in Office Buildings in Four Countries," *Building and Environment* 200 (2021), https://doi.org/10.1016/j.buildenv.2021.107975.

14. Lidia Morawska, Joseph Allen, William Bahnfleth, et al., "A Paradigm Shift to Combat Indoor Respiratory Infection," *Science* 372, no. 6543 (2021), 689–691, DOI: 10.1126/science.abg2025.

9. HEALTHY BUILDING CERTIFICATION SYSTEMS

1. U.S. Green Building Council, "LEED v4," accessed October 8, 2019, https://new.usgbc.org/leed-v4.

2. GRESB Infrastructure, *2016 Report* (Amsterdam: GRESB, 2016), https://gresb.com/wp-content/uploads/2017/07/2016_Infrastructure_Report.pdf.

3. U.S. Green Building Council, personal communication, November 5, 2019.

4. P. MacNaughton et al., "Energy Savings, Emission Reductions, and Health Co-benefits of the Green Building Movement," *Journal of Exposure Science and Environmental Epidemiology* 28, no. 4 (2018): 307–318.

5. PR Newswire, "Tishman Speyer Launches Global Tenant Health and Wellness Initiative with Fitwel® Certification of Its Portfolio," October 23, 2017, https://www.prnewswire.com/news-releases/tishman-speyer-launches-global-tenant-health-and-wellness-initiative-with-fitwel-certification-of-its-portfolio-300541249.html.

6. Fitwel, "How Does the Fitwel Process Work?," accessed October 8, 2019, https://fitwel.org/certification.

7. RESET homepage, accessed October 8, 2019, https://www.reset.build/.

8. WELL, "WELL v2 Pricing," https://www.wellcertified.com/certification/v2/pricing.

9. Urban Land Institute, Center for Sustainability and Economic Performance, *The Business Case for Healthy Buildings: Insights from Early Adopters* (Washington, DC: Urban Land Institute, 2018), https://americas.uli.org/wp-content/uploads/sites/2/ULI-Documents/Business-Case-for-Healthy-Buildings-FINAL.pdf.

10. John Macomber, Emily Jones, and Joseph Allen, "A Tower for the People," Harvard Business School, 2020 (in press).

11. Interview of David Levinson, April 24, 2019.

12. Merlin Fulcher, "Foster Scoops Prize New York Tower," *Architects' Journal*, October 3, 2012, https://www.architectsjournal.co.uk/home/foster-scoops-prize-new-york-tower/8636694.article.

13. David Levinson, interview with Joe and John, April 23, 2018.

14. David Levinson, interview with Joe and John, April 3, 2019.

15. J. Carreyrou, *Bad Blood: Secrets and Lies in a Silicon Valley Startup* (New York: Alfred A. Knopf, 2018).

10. MOVING FROM KPIs TO HPIs

1. F. Barber and R. Strack, "The Surprising Economics of a 'People Business,'" *Harvard Business Review*, June 2005, https://hbr.org/2005/06/the-surprising-economics-of-a-people-business.

2. J. Doerr, *Measure What Matters: How Google, Bono, and the Gates Foundation Rock the World with OKRs* (New York: Penguin, 2018).

3. Tyler J. VanderWeele and Miguel A. Hernan, "Results on Differential and Dependent Measurement Error of the Exposure and the Outcome Using Signed Directed Acyclic Graphs," *American Journal of Epidemiology* 175, no. 12 (2012): 1303–1310.

4. J. G. Allen et al., "Green Buildings and Health," *Current Environmental Health Reports* 2, no. 3 (2015): 250–258.

5. J. G. Laurent et al., "Influence of the Residential Environment on Undergraduate Students' Health," *Journal of Exposure Science and Environmental Epidemiology* (2019), https://www.nature.com/articles/s41370-019-0196-4.

6. J. G. Allen et al., "Elevated Corrosion Rates and Hydrogen Sulfide in Homes with 'Chinese Drywall,'" *Science of the Total Environment* 426 (2012): 113–119; Environmental Health & Engineering, *Final Report on an Indoor Environmental Quality Assessment of Residences Containing Chinese Drywall*, January 28, 2010, https://www.CPSC.gov.

7. R. Maddalena et al., *Small-Chamber Measurements of Chemical-Specific Emission Factors for Drywall*, Report LBNL-3986E (Berkeley: Lawrence Berkeley National Laboratory, June 2010).

8. R. Maddalena, *Effect of Environmental Factors on Sulfur Gas Emissions from Problem Drywall*, Report LBNL-5026E (Berkeley: Lawrence Berkeley National Laboratory, August 2011).

9. US Department of Health and Human Services, Agency for Toxic Substances and Disease Registry, *Health Consultation—Possible Health Implications*

from Exposure to Sulfur Gases Emitted from Chinese-Manufactured Drywall (Atlanta: US Department of Health and Human Services, May 2, 2014).

10. Lawrence Berkeley National Lab, "Building Commissioning: A Golden Opportunity for Reducing Costs and Greenhouse Gas Emissions," 2009, http://cx .lbl.gov/2009-assessment.html.

11. L. M. Weatherly and J. A. Gosse, "Triclosan Exposure, Transformation, and Human Health Effects," *Journal of Toxicology and Environmental Health, Part B* 20, no. 8 (2017): 447–469.

12. Kaiser Permanente, "Banning Use of Antimicrobial Agents for Infection Control," December 11, 2015, https://about.kaiserpermanente.org/total-health /health-topics/kaiser-permanente-rejects-antimicrobials-for-infection-control.

13. J. P. Onnela, "Research Areas: Digital Phenotyping," Harvard T. H. Chan School of Public Health, July 26, 2017, https://www.hsph.harvard.edu/onnela-lab /research/.

11. BEYOND THE FOUR WALLS

1. Energy Information Administration, "How Much Energy Is Consumed in U.S. Residential and Commercial Buildings?," May 3, 2018, https://www.eia.gov /tools/faqs/faq.php?id=86&t=1.

2. World Bank, "Fossil Fuel Energy Consumption (% of Total)," accessed October 9, 2019, https://data.worldbank.org/indicator/EG.USE.COMM.FO.ZS.

3. D. W. Dockery et al., "An Association between Air Pollution and Mortality in Six US Cities," *New England Journal of Medicine* 329, no. 4 (1993): 1753–1759.

4. C. Liu et al., "Ambient Particulate Air Pollution and Daily Mortality in 652 Cities," *New England Journal of Medicine* 381, no. 8 (2019): 705–715.

5. Q. Di et al., "Air Pollution and Mortality in the Medicare Population," *New England Journal of Medicine* 376, no. 26 (2017): 2513–2522.

6. A. Zanobetti et al., "A National Case-Crossover Analysis of the Short-Term Effect of PM 2.5 on Hospitalizations and Mortality in Subjects with Diabetes and Neurological Disorders," *Environmental Health* 13, no. 1 (2014): 38.

7. R. Khalili et al., "Early-Life Exposure to PM 2.5 and Risk of Acute Asthma Clinical Encounters among Children in Massachusetts: A Case-Crossover Analysis," *Environmental Health* 17, no. 1 (2018): 20.

8. P. MacNaughton et al., "Impact of Particulate Matter Exposure and Surrounding 'Greenness' on Chronic Absenteeism in Massachusetts Public Schools," *International Journal of Environmental Research and Public Health* 14, no. 2 (2017): 207.

9. M. A. Kioumourtzoglou et al., "Long-Term PM2. 5 Exposure and Neurological Hospital Admissions in the Northeastern United States," *Environmental Health Perspectives* 124, no. 1 (2015): 23–29.

10. R. Raz et al., "Autism Spectrum Disorder and Particulate Matter Air Pollution before, during, and after Pregnancy: A Nested Case–Control Analysis within the Nurses' Health Study II Cohort," *Environmental Health Perspectives* 123, no. 3 (2014): 264–270.

11. J. J. Buonocore et al., "An Analysis of Costs and Health Co-Benefits for a US Power Plant Carbon Standard," *PloS One* 11, no. 6 (2016): p.e0156308.

12. Harvard Healthy Buildings Program, "CoBE: Co-benefits of the Built Environment," 2019, http://cobe.forhealth.org/.

13. Di et al., "Air Pollution and Mortality."

14. P. MacNaughton et al., "Energy Savings, Emission Reductions, and Health Co-benefits of the Green Building Movement," *Journal of Exposure Science and Environmental Epidemiology* 28, no. 4 (2018): 307–318.

15. For Health, "The CogFx Study—Indoor Environmental Quality," accessed October 9, 2019, https://research.forhealth.org/2016/12/17/cogfx/.

16. Evan Mills, *Building Commissioning: A Golden Opportunity for Reducing Energy Costs and Greenhouse Gas Emissions* (Berkeley: Lawrence Berkeley National Laboratory, July 21, 2009), http://cx.lbl.gov/documents/2009-assessment/lbnl-cx-cost-benefit.pdf.

17. Reuters, "Total of 79 Chinese Cities Trigger Air Pollution Alerts: Xinhua," December 1, 2018.

18. "Special Report: Global Warming of 1.5 Degrees C," The Intergovernmental Panel on Climate Change, https://www.ipcc.ch/sr15/.

19. Ali Ayoub and Nils Kok, "Who Cares about Climate Risk?," GeoPhy, May 8, 2018, https://medium.com/geophy-hq/who-cares-about-climate-risk-ca68236f2e62.

20. J. D. Macomber, "Climate Change Is Going to Transform Where and How We Build," *Harvard Business Review*, October 16, 2019, https://hbr.org/2019/10/climate-change-is-going-to-transform-where-and-how-we-build.

21. Emma Foehringer Merchant, "NY Governor Wants Zero-Carbon Electricity by 2040," GTM, December 18, 2018, https://www.greentechmedia.com/articles/read/new-york-names-100-carbon-neutral-electricity-as-priority#gs.HnsNTS06.

22. Environmental Protection Agency, *Inventory of U.S. Greenhouse Gas Emissions and Sinks: 1990–2017*, April 11, 2019.

23. J. J. Buonocore, P. Salimifard, D. R. Michanowicz, and J. G. Allen, "A Decade of the US Energy Mix Transitioning away from Coal: Historical Reconstruction of the Reductions in the Public Health Burden of Energy," *Environmental Research Letters* 16, no. 5 (2021), https://iopscience.iop.org/article/10.1088/1748-9326/abe74c.

24. Brian C. McDonald et al., "Volatile Chemical Products Emerging as Largest Petrochemical Source of Urban Organic Emissions," *Science* 359, no. 6377 (2018): 760–764.

25. E. O. Wilson, *Half-Earth: Our Planet's Fight for Life* (New York: Liveright, 2016).

12. WHAT'S NOW AND WHAT'S NEXT?

1. Everett Rogers, *Diffusion of Innovations* (New York: Free Press, 1962).

2. Clayton M. Christensen, *The Innovator's Dilemma: When New Technologies Cause Great Firms to Fail* (Boston: Harvard Business School Press, 1997).

3. Alice Hamilton, *Exploring the Dangerous Trades* (Boston: Little, Brown and Company, 1943).

4. D. K. Farmer et al., "Overview of HOMEChem: House Observations of Microbial and Environmental Chemistry," *Environmental Science: Processes and Impacts* 21, no. 8 (2019): 1280–1300; H. Zhao, E. T. Gall, and B. Stephens, "Measuring the Building Envelope Penetration Factor for Ambient Nitrogen Oxides," *Environmental Science and Technology* 53, no. 16 (2019): 9695–9704.

5. D. Singh et al., "Nanofiller Presence Enhances Polycyclic Aromatic Hydrocarbon (PAH) Profile on Nanoparticles Released during Thermal Decomposition of Nano-Enabled Thermoplastics: Potential Environmental Health Implications," *Environmental Science and Technology* 51, no. 9 (2017): 5222–5232.

6. A. Gandolfo et al., "Unexpectedly High Levels of Organic Compounds Released by Indoor Photocatalytic Paints," *Environmental Science and Technology* 52, no. 19 (2018): 11328–11337.

7. N. Vaze et al., "A Nano-Carrier Platform for the Targeted Delivery of Nature-Inspired Antimicrobials Using Engineered Water Nanostructures for Food Safety Applications," *Food Control* 96 (2019): 365–374.

8. James L. Heskett, W. Earl Sasser, and Leonard A. Schlesinger, *Service Profit Chain: How Leading Companies Link Profit and Growth to Loyalty, Satisfaction and Value* (New York: Free Press, 1997).

9. Tom Randall, "The Smartest Building in the World," Bloomberg, September 23, 2015, https://www.bloomberg.com/features/2015-the-edge-the-worlds-greenest-building/.

10. John Macomber, Emily Jones, and Joseph Allen, "A Tower for the People," Harvard Business School, 2020 (in press).

11. Alec Saltikoff, interview with Joe Allen, May 17, 2019.

12. Carrier, "Carrier Launches Healthy Buildings Program to Help Customers Reinvent Their Buildings for Occupant Health," press release, June 2, 2020.

13. Personal communication with Piers MacNaughton, July 17, 2019.

14. Yolanda Barnes, "8 Things to Know about Global Real Estate Value," Savills Impacts, https://www.savills.com/impacts/economic-trends/8-things-you-need-to-know-about-the-value-of-global-real-estate.html.

15. GFM Asset Management, "Top 200 US-Listed Real Estate Investment Trusts (REITs) by Market Cap as of 2017Q3," August 3, 2017, https://gfmasset.com/2017/08/top-200-us-listed-real-estate-investment-trusts-reits-by-market-cap-as-of-2017q3/.

16. Scotsman's Guide, "Top Overall Volume: Scotsman Guide's Top Mortgage Lenders 2017," accessed October 9, 2019, https://www.scotsmanguide.com/Rankings/Top-Lenders-2017/Results/Top-Overall-Volume-New/.

17. Charles Fine, *Clockspeed: Winning Industry Control in the Age of Temporary Advantage* (New York: Basic Books, 2008).

18. Boston Green Ribbon Commission, *Carbon Free Boston: Summary Report 2019,* https://www.greenribboncommission.org/document/executive-summary-carbon-free-boston/.

19. T. Wang, "U.S. Construction Industry—Statistics & Facts," Statista, July 17, 2019, https://www.statista.com/topics/974/construction/.

20. Reuters, "Global Construction Market 2018; Expected to Drive a Galloping Growth to US$12.7 Trillion by 2022," August 23, 2018, https://www.reuters.com/brandfeatures/venture-capital/article?id=48295.

21. T. Wang, "Leading Construction Contractors Worldwide in 2017, Based on Revenue (in Billion U.S. Dollars)," Statista, last edited August 9, 2019, https://www.statista.com/statistics/279942/the-largest-construction-contractors-worldwide-based-on-total-revenue/.

22. Stephen Edelstein, "Google Street View Cars with Built-In Air-Quality Sensors Are Going Global," The Drive, September 12, 2018, http://www.thedrive.com/tech/23529/google-street-view-cars-with-air-quality-sensors-are-going-globally.

23. John Mandyck, "Are You Interviewing Your Building?," Huffington Post, February 8, 2017, https://www.huffingtonpost.com/john-mandyck/are-you-interviewing-your_b_14642324.html.

24. "Smells Bad," Glassdoor, May 1, 2016, https://www.glassdoor.com/Reviews/Employee-Review-rePLANET-RVW10457626.htm.

25. "SLP Building Smells like Sewage," Glassdoor, May 15, 2018, https://www.glassdoor.com/Reviews/Employee-Review-Honeywell-RVW20588766.htm.

26. "Perks, but Noisy Open Office," Glassdoor, March 24, 2017, https://www.glassdoor.com/Reviews/Employee-Review-Square-RVW14337633.htm.

27. "Unsafe and Unprofessional Workplace," Glassdoor, October 1, 2017, https://www.glassdoor.com/Reviews/Wellco-Industries-Reviews-E1603538.htm.

28. "Great People but the Office Is Way Too Cold," Glassdoor, July 16, 2018, https://www.glassdoor.com/Reviews/Employee-Review-Local-Splash -RVW21504798.htm.

29. "Great Mentors, Bad Lighting," Glassdoor, August 5, 2015, https://www .glassdoor.com/Reviews/Employee-Review-INL-RVW7468192.htm.

CONCLUSION: BUILDINGS, BUSINESS, HEALTH, AND WEALTH

1. N. Twilley, "Home Smog," *New Yorker,* April 8, 2019.

2. P. MacNaughton et al., "Energy Savings, Emission Reductions, and Health Co-benefits of the Green Building Movement," *Journal of Exposure Science and Environmental Epidemiology* 28, no. 4 (2018): 307.

3. Interview with Maureen Ehrenberg, February 11, 2019.

4. John D. Macomber and Griffin H. James, "Design Creates Fortune: 2000 Tower Oaks Boulevard," Harvard Business Publishing Education, case study, March 21, 2010, https://hbsp.harvard.edu/product/210070-PDF-ENG.

Acknowledgments

JOE'S ACKNOWLEDGMENTS

I stumbled into the field of public health almost twenty years ago when my wife, Mary, pulled off the contact info tab on a help-wanted poster advertising a research assistant position at the Harvard School of Public Health. The rest is history. So my first thank-you is to Mary for grabbing that tab, and then to Angie Craddock, Steve Gortmaker, Maren Fragala, Robin Dodson, and Debbie Bennett for giving me my first job in public health.

Soon after I started graduate school at Boston University and met my doctoral adviser, Mike McClean, he asked if I had ever considered a doctoral degree, and the next thing I knew I was working with Mike as his first doctoral student. I learned from Mike how to mentor students, and I still find that I ask myself, "What would Mike have said to me in this situation?" A special thanks to my many great professors at BU, who reignited my scientific passion: Tom Webster, Wendy Heiger-Bernays, Tim Heeren, Roberta White, and Dick Clapp. Thank you.

My professional life was guided by two Jacks—Jack McCarthy and Jack Spengler. Under Jack McCarthy's leadership at Environmental Health & Engineering (EH&E), I took what I learned in the classroom and was mentored in how to make it practical. I received invaluable life lessons on how to be a good scientist and communicator, under pressure. As I was at EH&E for five years, I cannot name everyone who should be acknowledged, but special thanks to David MacIntosh, Jim Stewart, Taeko Minegishi, Matt Fragala, Kathleen Brown, Will Wade, Brian Baker, and the world's best engineer, Jerry Ludwig, for problem solving with me every day.

While at EH&E I had the unbelievable good fortune of also working with the inimitable Jack Spengler at Harvard. We started working on research together while I was at EH&E and formed a genuine friendship. He is a true visionary. Jack has been at the forefront of every great environmental health movement since the 1970s. So when he talks, I listen. Carefully. For 15 years he has been the invisible hand guiding me, never asking for credit. What I love most about Jack is his spirit—

generous with his ideas and always looking forward, with an unmatched passion. About everything. I'm forever indebted.

When I joined the Harvard faculty, I was warned by outsiders about the lack of collegiality I could expect in academia and told that, rather than collaboration, I would find only competition. I have found it to be the opposite. I'm grateful for Dean Michelle Williams and faculty colleagues for their support, guidance, and encouragement: Russ Hauser, David Christiani, Francine Laden, Elsie Sunderland, Francesca Dominici, Brent Coull, Diane Gold, Petros Koutrakis, Doug Dockery, Howard Koh, Aaron Bernstein, Ashish Jha, Juliette Kayyem, Alan Garber, Holly Samuelson, Ali Malkawi, Naomi Oreskes, and many more. To the corps of "junior" faculty, thank you for being wonderful colleagues: Tamarra James-Todd, Jin-Ah Park, Gary Adamkiewicz, Jamie Hart, Quan Lu, Kris Sarosiek, Zach Nagel, Shruthi Mahalingaiah, Carmen Messerlian, and Bernardo Lemos. To the administrative teams—thank you for the magic behind the scenes. Special thanks to Amanda Spickard and Sarah Branstrator for supporting our every move in the Healthy Buildings program, Jen Rice and Grant Zimmerman in the Office of Technology Development, and Heather Henriksen and the Office for Sustainability for collaborating on driving research into practice across Harvard.

I also want to thank my Healthy Buildings team, including past and present students Piers MacNaughton, Anna Young, Jose Guillermo Cedeno Laurent, Erika Eitland, Emily Jones, Sandra Dedesko, Parham Azimi, and CoBE collaborators Parichehr Salimifard and Jonathan Buonocore. This is a special team of postdocs, doctoral students, professional researchers, and administrators. On my first day at Harvard I was challenged with this question: "How will your research impact the world?" I wrote this question on the whiteboard in the Healthy Buildings program lab and we have used it as a way to reflect on the projects and research we are taking on. I'm fortunate to be surrounded by such a stellar group of scientists and people.

Thank you to my excellent colleagues at 9 Foundations, Inc., who work with me day in and day out to drive Healthy Building science into action. Special acknowledgment to long-time collaborators Jim McDevitt, Leslie Cadet, Emily Jones, and Ted Myatt, and rising stars Marissa Rainbolt, Linnea Champ, and Natalie Daranyi.

I want to thank a few of the pioneers of the Healthy Building movement individually, some of whom I have worked with directly, and others who have influenced me through their work. This includes Linsey Marr, Linda Birnbaum, Rich Corsi, Elaine Hubal, Frederica Perera, Tracey Woodruff, Charlie Wechsler, Bill Nazaroff, Carl Gustaf-Bornehag, and Bill Fisk. I have also been inspired and influenced by the next crop of superstar Healthy Building researchers—the likes of Shelly Miller, Marina Vance, Jon Levy, Brent Stephens, Pawel Wargocki, Michael Waring, Gabriel Bekö, Usha Satish, Christoph Reinhart, and Heather Stapleton, just to name a few. I'm also thankful for the first giant in the field of worker health, Harvard's first female faculty member, Alice Hamilton. To find myself in her lineage is, to say the least, humbling.

As we have said throughout this book, research in a vacuum doesn't do anyone any good. So I am particularly grateful for, and proud of, our collaborators in the business world: Mary Milmoe, John Mandyck, Kori Recalde, Ashley Barrie, Caren Kittredge, David Gitlin, Ajay Argawal, Greg Alcorn, Alec Saltikoff, David Arena, Mike Norton, Matthew Montanes, Geraldine Tan, Pasquale Eboli, Dino Fusco, Michele Schneider and the Salesforce team, Katie Hughes, Maureen Ehrenberg, Bryan Koop, the JLL team, Kelly Grier, Jay Persaud, Bob Fox, the Dursts, Samo, Janez, and Iza Login, David Levinson, Shami Waissman, Robin Bass, Ben Myers, Gerald Chan, and Norman Foster.

To my coauthor, John Macomber, who answered my cold-call email and agreed to that first lunch, thank you for engaging (and being engaging). Writing and reworking these chapters with you has helped strengthen and clarify my thinking in ways I could not foresee before we started talking. I'm glad we had that handshake.

Thank you to the terrific team at Harvard University Press, especially to our long-time and ferociously sharp editor, Joy de Menil, our first editor, Jeff Dean, and our publicist, Megan Posco.

In my personal life, I have been given the gift of a large, supportive, fun, and funny family. I am grateful for my parents for giving me street smarts, for my 5 siblings (10 counting their spouses), 16 nieces and nephews, 30-plus cousins and aunts and uncles, and my in-laws, Margaret, Bill and Ann. They have been a wonderful pillar of strength that has spanned my upbringing, education, and current career.

Last, and most importantly, to Mary and our three kids, Colby, Chelsea, and Landon. I love my work, but my first and most important job is as husband and dad. You bring purpose to my work and fill my life with happiness.

To Mary: thanks for pulling that tab in the halls of Harvard Medical School twenty years ago, and for a million other small nudges in the right direction ever since. You have patiently heard me talk enough about public health and my work that I now totally agree with you when you joke, "I have at least earned a master of public health degree by now, right?" Thanks for having fun with me and supporting me through all of this.

Feeling grateful . . .

Onward!

JOHN'S ACKNOWLEDGMENTS

Three phases of life led me to Joe and this book, and the concepts of modeling finance and environment to try to optimize outcomes for the system, writ large, and its occupants.

When I was a student at Dartmouth College and Harvard Business School, John Kemeny introduced me to probability theory and modeling with computing, Dana

Meadows to system dynamics and complex systems, and Bruce Greenwald to managerial economics. These concepts resonated then and they are still important to me now.

In my professional career in construction, there were many mentors, but the team that has been most consistent is that of my siblings and coinvestors, my brother George Macomber and sister Grace Bird. For 30 years I've also had a business partner in the real estate industry. Peter Nordblom and his late father, Rod, have modeled healthy buildings—and outside-the-box thinking about the wellness of those who occupy our buildings—at Northwest Park and more. Thank you all for showing me how a forward-thinking commercial landlord thinks and invests in practice.

Fred Moavenzadeh at MIT thought he saw a spark in 1988 and brought me to the front of the classroom. While the content and the venue have changed, I've never left the front of the room. Having a chance to help my own students become leaders who will make a positive difference in the world is a real blessing. Like Joe, coming to Harvard I worried about being accepted and welcomed. To my delight, I've been embraced and have found a particular affinity in the Harvard Business School Business and Environment Initiative and the Harvard University Center for the Environment. Arthur Segel, Rebecca Henderson, Forest Reinhardt, and Mike Toffel have been allies, colleagues, co-teachers, cheerleaders, and course correctors when needed. Our dean, Nitin Nohria, has illuminated a path for business to help solve the big problems of the world, and given all of us the resources to walk down that path.

My late father, George Macomber, would say, "How can we move the ball of humanity forward?" I hope this book will be useful to that end. My wife, Kristin, has been endlessly supportive of the startups, the turnarounds, the teaching, and everything in between. She's pleased when I'm away working on education projects, and she's happy when I'm home.

Mostly, though, I would like to acknowledge and thank my mother, Andy Macomber. She encouraged the life of the mind, gave me free range to chase my passions and ideas, instilled in me a sense of how to be respected and trustworthy, and reinforced the idea that for every one to whom much is given, of him will much be required. Thank you.

FROM JOE AND JOHN

We are grateful to the team at Harvard University Press for taking a chance on us as new authors. We were skillfully guided through the process and received smart edits from our outstanding editors Joy de Menil and Jeff Dean. To the three anonymous peer-reviewers, we very much appreciate your comments and insights on our first full draft. We also thank Harvard University student Sydney Robinson, whom we brought on to work on references, but who offered so much more with her careful reading and editing of the entire manuscript. Last, we thank the Harvard T. H. Chan School of Public Health's Dean's Innovation Fund, which contributed to the support of our efforts to foster greater collaboration between the business and health communities.

Index

air quality, indoor. *See* indoor air pollution; indoor air quality (IAQ)

air quality, outdoor. *See* outdoor air pollution; outdoor air quality

air quality sensors, viii

Allen, Joe, 18, 38; background of, 7–17

allergens: in dust, 108 (*See also* dust); dust mites, 107–108; mold, 106–107; mouse allergens, exposure to, 19

American Industrial Hygiene Association, 186

American Institute of Architects, 80

American Society of Heating, Refrigerating and Air-Conditioning Engineers (ASHRAE), 60, 80, 94; Covid-19 and, 154; design / construction and, 75; green building movement and, 165–166; indoor air quality standards, 60; Legionella risk management plan and, 102; thermal health and, 96, 98, 212; ventilation standards, 60–61, 79, 87

Anthropocene, 26

antimicrobials, 206–207

Antonovsky, Aaron, 27

Appalachian Mountain Club (AMC), 115

Apple, 242, 251, 252

asbestos, 139, 141

Ashford, Susan, 32

ASHRAE (American Society of Heating, Refrigerating and Air-Conditioning Engineers). *See* American Society of Heating, Refrigerating and Air-Conditioning Engineers (ASHRAE)

attack rate, 15

Ayoub, Ali, 227–228

Azimi, Parham, 153

Bad Blood (Carreyrou), 185

Barber, Felix, 191, 192, 199, 239

Bekö, Gabriel, 46

Bell's palsy, 202

Benioff, Marc, 36

benzene, 45

Bernstein, Ethan, 33

"Beyond the 4 Walls", 266

big data era, 34

Big Tobacco, 137

biodiversity, loss of, 25–26. *See also* climate change; resources

Biophilia (Wilson), 115, 116

biophilic design, 115–117

BIO program (Biophilic Interventions in Offices), 116–117

bisphenol A (BPA), 127–129, 138

bisphenol F (BPF), 127

bisphenol S (BPS), 127–129

BlackRock, 35–36, 216

bodybuilding, 124

Boston Properties, 264

bottom line, ix, 62–70. *See also* productivity

BPA (bisphenol A), 127–129, 138

BPF (bisphenol F), 127

BPS (bisphenol S), 127–129

Brandt, Kate, 30

Brenna, Terry, 91

Brin, Sergey, 29, 192

British Parliament, 22–23

BTEX chemicals, 45, 49–50

building codes, 75, 76, 77, 165

building engineers, importance of to health, 14

building materials, 240; Chinese Drywall, 204–205; selection of and reducing toxic load, 206–207; transparency about, 144–146

buildingomics, 85

Building Owners and Managers Association International, 41

buildings: centrality of, xi; changing, 20, 30–32 (*See also* mega-changes, global); contribution to air pollution, 17; cost of, 72; decision-making process around (*See* incentives; incumbents; inertia; information); defining health worthiness of, xi–xii; depletion of resources and, 25–26; Google and, 29–30; life span of,

CIHs (Certified Industrial Hygienists), 186–189, 202
circadian rhythms, 113, 115
cities, 5–6; changing, 20, 22, 24–26, 217, 257 (*See also* mega-changes, global); population in, 25; private investors and, 6
Clean Air Act, 39
clean air delivery rate (CADR), 156–157
clean energy future, 229–231
Clean Power Plan, 219
climate change, ix, 20, 26, 229, 257; buildings and, 217 (*See also* energy efficiency); effects of, 26; fossil fuels and, 218–219; Healthy Building strategies and, 261–263; impact on real estate, 226–227; Paris Agreement, 100; resiliency and, 227–228; thermal comfort and, 99–100. *See also* air pollution; energy efficiency; environmental, social, and governance (ESG) issues; fossil fuels; mega-changes, global
Climate Mobilization Act, 168
clockspeed, 246–247
Clockspeed (Fine), 246
CO (carbon monoxide), 40
CO_2 (carbon dioxide), 30, 57, 58, 61–62
CoBE (co-benefits of the built environment), 219–224
co-benefits of the built environment (CoBE), 219–224
COGfx Study, 56–59, 61, 62, 267. *See also* cognitive function
cognitive function, 56, 65; hydration and, 101; measuring, 207; ventilation and, 56–59, 65–66. *See also* COGfx Study; productivity
comfort, 96. *See also* thermal health
commissioning, 90–91, 205–206
competition, 162, 241–244
construction, new, 235, 247
construction industry, 3–4, 77; adoption of innovations in, 235; distribution of, 247; incumbents and, 73–76, 80; inertia in,

72–73, 76, 80; information and, 80; variation in, 233. *See also* real estate
Consumer Product Safety Commission, 204
consumers, demand for Healthy Buildings by, 262–266
contaminants: indoor levels of, 44–45. *See also* air pollution
Conway, Erik, 137
Cook, Tim, 251, 252
coronavirus. *See* Covid-19
corporations: broader purpose of, 35–36, 216, 262. *See also* business; values
Corsi, Rich, 39, 46
costs, perceived, 79–80
costs, real, 79
Covid-19, xi, 32, 147–148, 259; buildings and, 149; choir practice outbreak, 152; filtration and, 153; health-first mindset and, vii; Healthy Buildings and, viii; HVAC systems and, 152; indoor air quality and, 162; Lancet Covid-19 Commission, 154; lockdowns, 159; outdoor air and, 153, 154–157, 160–161; $PM_{2.5}$ and, 160; portable air cleaners and, 154; refusal to acknowledge airborne transmission of, 149; six-foot rule, 150; transmission of, vii, 148, 151–153; upgrading worker's home environments and, 203; vaccine, 159; ventilation and, 153; wildfires and, 160. *See also* disease, infectious; work-from-home
creative workers: responsibility for health of, 32–33. *See also* employees
Crossing the Chasm (Moore), 235
cruise ships, 148, 153
Cuomo, Andrew, 230

Danish Technical University, 46, 237
Declare Label project, 142
Delos, 170
demographic growth, 234–235
Demokritou, Philip, 238

and, 94; ventilation and, 56–59, 62–70.
See also bottom line; cognitive function
Progressive Insurance, 264
Prop 65, 142–143
psychrometry, 212–214
public good, outdoor air as, 235
public health, 9

radon, 51–52
Ramanujam, Mahesh, 168
real estate, 70, 72, 77; composition of
industry, 244–246; current state of
industry, 234–235; decision-making
process around (*See* incentives; incumbents; inertia; information); green
building certification and, 166–167; in
India, 4–5; social performance of, 36, 216
(*See also* environmental, social, and
governance (ESG) issues); 3-30-300™ rule
of, 40–41; variation in, 233; wealth
distribution in industry, 244–245. *See also*
buildings; Healthy Building movement;
investors; landlords; split incentives; work
environments
real estate investment trusts (REITs), 227
rebreathed fraction, 151
refrigerants, 100
remote work. *See* Covid-19;
work-from-home
renovations, 247
rental rates, 70
reproductive health, 125–126, 138, 140. *See
also* hormones
research: dissemination of, 169–170;
translating into action, 17–19, 86,
144–146. *See also* information
RESET certification, 174, 186
resilience, 217, 227–229
resources: changing, 20, 22, 24–26, 217 (*See
also* mega-changes, global); depletion of,
buildings and, 25–26. *See also* fossil fuels
respiratory viruses. *See* Covid-19; disease,
infectious; viruses

risk, 52, 76–77
risk management, 120. *See also* safety / security
risk management plans, 15
Rogers Adoption Curve, 235
Rosenberg, Jonathan, 29
Rudnick, Steven, 151

Safe Drinking Water Act, 105
safety / security, 117–121
Salesforce, 36, 74
Salimifard, Parichehr, 230
Saltikoff, Alec, 241
salutogenesis, 27
SARS-CoV-1, 148
SARS-CoV-2. *See* Covid-19
Sasser, Earl, 238
Satish, Usha, 57
Schlesinger, Leonard, 238
Schmidt, Eric, 29
Schneider Electric, 243
schools, 18–19, 39, 62
Schwarzenegger, Arnold, 124
Scialla, Paul, 170
Scialla, Pete, 170
scientific literature: lack of knowledge of,
17–19. *See also* research
security, 117–121
semivolatile organic compounds (SVOCs), 47
sensors, 252
service profit chain, 238–239
sex hormones, 138
shelter, 117. *See also* safety / security
shift workers, 113–114
shinrin-yoku (forest bathing), 115
shopper, informed, 264
sick buildings, 10–14. *See also* indoor air
quality; Sick Building Syndrome
Sick Building Syndrome, 31–32
sick days. *See* absenteeism
Sidewalk Labs project, 249
Silent Spring (Carson), 25, 126
Silent Spring Institute, 128
Singh, Dilpreet, 238